Go Your Own Way

women travel the world solo

Edited by Faith Conlon, Ingrid Emerick & Christina Henry de Tessan

SEAL PRESS

Go Your Own Way
Women Travel the World Solo

AVALON
publishing group incorporated

Published by
Seal Press
An Imprint of Avalon Publishing Group, Incorporated
1400 65th Street, Suite 250
Emeryville, CA 94608

9 8 7 6 5 4 3 2 1
Library of Congress Cataloging-in-Publication Data

Conlon, Faith
Go your own way : women travel the world solo / Faith Conlon, Ingrid Emerick, and Christina Henry de Tessan.
p. cm.
ISBN-13: 978-1-58005-199-6
ISBN-10: 1-58005-199-5
1. Women travelers-Anecdotes. 2. Voyages and travels-Anecdotes. I. Emerick, Ingrid. II. De Tessan, Christina Henry. III. Title.

G465.C6455 2007
910.4092'2-dc22
       2006038576

Book design by Domini Dragoone

Contents

Introduction

On a cool spring day, the three of us settled back into cushions in Ingrid's cozy living room, catching up after a long time. Five years earlier, we had worked together in the same Seattle publishing office. One of our final projects had been a literary anthology on solo travel, *A Woman Alone,* which we had coedited and published in 2001. Now we lived in different cities and our paths had diverged some, yet the idea to publish a companion volume had prompted us to schedule a long-overdue get-together. After we'd swapped stories and photos of our kids, the conversation turned from family to travel.

We discovered that the passage of time had brought changes to our lives and to our perspectives on travel. Christina shared that after the birth of her first child, she had started a new job that had given her the opportunity to do regular solo stints in major cities around the world. Once upon a time, she'd made this kind of travel her greatest goal, pinching pennies to get herself anywhere new and different. Ironically, it was only once she had a family and was more interested in nesting that it was suddenly thrust upon her on a regular basis. "Travel is so different now," Christina commented. "Where once I took such pleasure in preparing for every detail of a trip ahead of time, I am now so engulfed by anxiety in the anticipation of these trips that they almost do me in. My mind is a flurry of to-do lists running nonstop, day and night."

All of us are mothers and could relate to Christina's travel anxiety, as well as that blessed "point of no return," as we dubbed it—the moment when you are finally settled into your tiny plane seat, when there is nothing you can do for anyone anymore. How jarring and unsettling that longed-for moment can be. In a world full of people and demands, the sudden emptiness of being alone can be disquieting, yet also liberating, as we slowly remember again who we are as individuals.

As we discussed the strangeness of leaving the cluttered life and cluttered mind behind, we were struck once again by the fact that solo travel takes many forms at different times in our lives—and ultimately fulfills different needs. We discovered that we had once naively considered solo travel to be primarily about satisfying the soul-searching, confidence-building needs of our twenties. The focus was on proving ourselves, developing resourcefulness, getting lost, and finding our way back. But what we hadn't realized then was that the solo experience offers unique insight and perspective at any age, under any number of circumstances, both expected and unexpected. Even the confident, resourceful, and independent traveler has much to gain from the solitary journey—whether it's perspective on a life left behind, unexpected connections with locals, insights into how individual relationships are separate from the realm of global politics, or the simple and pure joy of a few anonymous days of not having to organize our hours around the needs of anyone else.

We also discussed the nature of foreign travel as Americans, and as solo women, in a world profoundly affected by the events of 9/11 and its aftermath. How it can feel like a political act, almost a patriotic duty, to go abroad. We had all traveled since 9/11, as had many of our friends and family members, and what we all found was a world different in many ways from the one portrayed by our fear-driven media. No doubt the world's hot spots are indeed hot spots, yet in our experience people the world over are eager to engage with Americans. We were reminded in these real-world exchanges that people are able to separate the actions of governments from those of individuals. What we found in our own experience—and what we read in the submissions we received and, ultimately, in many stories we selected—ran counter to what we had been hearing every day on our televisions and reading on the front page.

All of these considerations, personal and political, made us realize that the time was ripe to pursue a sequel to *A Woman Alone*. First and foremost, we wanted to inspire women to get out and travel. After all, the best way to quell fear, build bridges between cultures, and foster goodwill toward Americans again is to go out in the world and be an ambassador. As in the last book, we wanted to tap into the full range of women's solo experiences. We wanted to better understand the motivations of and consequences for women who go to the effort of visiting a place far from the familiarity of home. We also were curious about what others were discovering on their solo journeys.

Once we sent out the call for submissions and spread the word, it was immediately clear how sacred women's solo journeys are to them—how many forms they take, how many reasons they set off. Their experiences and what they gain from them vary widely, but they are ultimately no less intense at different ages and times in their lives. What they set out to escape or find may not be achieved exactly as planned, but they gain new insights into themselves and others—and return to their familiar lives with renewed energy. Judging from the number of women eager to tell their stories, it was clear that we were not the only ones struck by the power of the solitary journey.

We hope you enjoy the travels revealed in these pages, and we hope they inspire you to dream of your next trip, and go your own way.

Snake Eyes of Borneo

Holly Morris

I am a voodoo doll for a sadistic nurse who is probably suffering from seasonal affective disorder, an affliction endemic to the northwestern United States and certain Scandinavian countries. Forty degrees. A cold, relentless drizzle has fallen for two months straight; the gray ceiling of the Pacific Northwest is closing in with dreaded inevitability. I am in the travel inoculation ward of Group Health Cooperative, and it is a dark February day in Seattle. As the sixth silver needle plunges into my already-throbbing arm, I think, *Why am I doing this?*

Questions like this usually don't arise until I am two days from any-where, one Snickers bar left, trying to suction thick-as-syrup, muddy river water through a filter that falsely claims to remove all scents, tastes, protozoa, and bacteria. But this time, the reservations have hit me in the jab lab. I've become a junkie, weak in the face of my drug: adventure.

Peg, the nurse, tosses her modified Dorothy Hamill haircut slightly before saying, with a tinge of admonishment, "You've come in too late to be protected from dengue fever and Japanese encephalitis. Here are the malaria pills. They'll kill all your natural flora and fauna . . . "

"Um, *fauna?*" I gently interject, to no response.

" . . . so start taking acidophilus now. A small number of people get psychotic episodes from them, but I think you'll be fine.

"Most importantly," says Peg, unwrapping the final syringe, "if something goes very wrong and things *break* or *tear* or get *severely punctured,*" she pauses and looks me in the eye, "beg for an air-evac with an IV. *Don't* get a transfusion.

"Have fun," she concludes cheerfully, throwing the used needle into a bin that somehow hermetically seals itself, combining *Andromeda Strain* style with HIV reality.

I tell myself it is Peg's job to overreact. She is, after all, wearing incredibly sensible shoes.

Trips to the lab have become common since I left the deskbound world of book publishing for international documentary television. Lately, I've been an on-the-road correspondent for a series of outdoor adven-ture programs. On these shoots I've received vital lessons, such as how to lasso charging cattle, evade a posse of pregnant tiger sharks, rappel down cliffs, sweat through a sundance, run class-five rapids, and milk everything from emotional moments to smelly goats to interviews. I've been bit on, shit on, and hit on. I asked for adventure, and I got it.

Next stop: Borneo.

Eleven overpackaged meals, thirty-seven wet-naps, one flip-flopped magnetic field, and a day and a half after leaving Seattle, I've entered that jittery netherworld in which the body's hardwiring goes color-blind; the red wires are wrapped up with the green, and the black one just dangles. In fact, the brain is completely flummoxed about what that black one is for. Hunger is a vague, tinny presence that cannot be sated. I look around at my fellow passengers and feel like my entire person is an appendix: irrelevant, useless, taking up space amid much more worthy organs.

We are on the sixth and last leg of the journey and closing in on 115 degrees longitude, zero degrees latitude. Equatorial Borneo: red hot, and wet. Borneo is the third-largest island in the world (right behind Greenland and New Guinea), and is divvied up between Indonesia and Malaysia (with a chunk reserved as the sultanate Brunei). The split is just one result of a long history of vying—by white rajahs and the British Empire, among others—for this island's rich natural resources, primarily oil, timber, pepper, and rubber. Sarawak and Sabah, the states where a small film crew and I are headed, became part of the then-new country of Malaysia in 1963.

The jungle appears fast and definitively, like spilled ink from a well.

From up here it looks like a petri dish of mold. Dusty, dark green, bumpy, with tiny creases and valleys and shadows. A patternless pattern of crumpled anarchy. Definitely alive.

We are setting out for the interior jungle of Sarawak from the town of Limbang. Our guide, Martin, is in his early twenties and has chestnut skin and jet black hair. He is Dayak (the indigenous people of Borneo) and of the Iban tribe.

The network of chunky, easy-moving, tea-colored rivers is the closest thing to infrastructure in this part of Borneo. Our young, barefoot boatman is poised at the front of our hip-wide longboat, ready to pole when shallows, still water, or rapids threaten our progress. A beefy old outboard motor dangles from the back of the boat like a very important, yet untended to, participle.

On the river, the jaggy mold I saw from the sky has become a dark green, menacing mass that lines the river. The jungle seems aggressive, as if the vines and trees are taking back the water's edge, instead of cohabiting with it in pastoral bliss, as a forest might meet a babbling brook. I imagine the density beyond our sight as unreasonable and unforgiving. A vicious chaos. I notice Vanessa, our tall Dutch producer, noticing me recoil.

"Sorta feral looking," I say to her, explaining my discomfort.

Periodically the jungle breaks and gives way to waterside communities. Longhouses with roofs of corrugated steel (rather than the traditional wood and rattan) pepper the river highway. The longhouse is the traditional communal living structure, home to approximately fifteen families and up to a hundred people. People work together on the long porches and nod when we quietly chug by. "The Dayak do not like to be alone," says Martin.

Alone.

In my twenties, my travels and sojourns in the natural world were often alone. These days I travel with a camera crew and, in that odd television conceit, "pretend" to be alone—while speaking to a viewership of millions. The depth of irony here is obvious. That said, I've noticed on every shoot that I find myself—whether dangling off a cliff, temporarily lost in the Sahara, or in the bowels of a shipwreck—deeply, and often unexpectedly, alone. Like the Dayak, I never seek it out. But these exhilarating, often perilous, solo moments can be strangely transformative.

The dwellings appear fewer and farther between as hours drift by and we sink deeper into the anarchy I first identified from above, from outside. Urban Borneo thrives with the cultural and spiritual diversity of all of Southeast Asia. Malaysia's official religion is Islam, but zealous missionaries and North Borneo's status as a former British colony make Christianity widespread. Yet here in the interior of Sarawak, the rules of the West and the rules of the East are handily trumped by the rules of the Jungle—and animism is operative. Unlike Judaism, Hinduism, Islam, Christianity, and other doctrines of the world, Kaharinga (Iban animism) does not distinguish between this life and the hereafter, between the religious and the secular. Religion is everyday life. Animism, quite sensibly, is more interested in the here and now and the supremacy of nature. Natural phenomena, as well as things animate and inanimate, are all said to possess a soul.

To the upriver Iban's traditional eye, the steamy, humid atmosphere is thick with *antu* (spirits) and *petara* (gods). The spirits and the people work in concert. (A quid pro quo of sorts: We give you offerings, you help the rice crops grow.) The spirits hold the upper hand, to be sure, and their behavior can range from benevolent to capricious.

Martin grew up in a longhouse and, due partly to his excellent English, has landed a coveted job in the world of tourism. I am quizzing him as we make our way upriver.

"What are the biggest hazards?" I ask.

"Well. A few leeches, sometimes a snake. Only drink the bottled water," he responds casually, offering a whitewashed version of reality. In fact, I know there are tens of thousands of species in this national "park" (a misleading term that implies the jungle is somehow under the control of humans) and some of them, particularly the cold-blooded ones, could be a problem.

Put a frothing rabid dog in my path, and I respond with the calm of Atticus Finch. Bring on a mama grizzly, and I am as sharp as her claws slicing through the flesh of a wild king salmon. But show me a cold-blooded, slithering critter, and I turn into an irrational, mute, quivering . . . appendix.

Indulging a strange habit of dashing toward what I fear, I press Martin on the snake issue. Vanessa has told me there are twenty-five kinds of snakes in this part of Borneo, many of them poisonous.

"Yes," Martin admits, "there's the reticulated python, *Python reticulatus;* the Javanese reed snake, *Calamaria borneensis;* the red-headed krait, *Bungarus flaviceps;* the banded Malayan coral snake, *Maticora intestinalis;* the cobra, *Naja sputatrix;* and the . . ."

I hold up my hand to stop the recitation.

"You had me at python," I say.

My phobic (that's phobic, *not* phallic) response to snakes irks me. I can't stand having an irrational fear that plays right into the hands of Freudian pundits.

We continue to move through the hours at double the river's slow pace: outboard time. Our small procession of overloaded canoes sputters up toward the traditional Rumah Bala Lasong longhouse, where Vanessa and Martin have arranged for us to spend the night before journeying to see the Penan tribe tomorrow.

Twenty of us, our crew and other invited inhabitants of the longhouse, sit on mats on the floor in a large circle, and the women serve us a feast of steamed rice in bamboo cylinders, leafy green vegetables, and dried fish. The girls and women dress in heavily embroidered cloth with many bangles and wear skirts made of interwoven coins. The headman says a blessing and his lithe, tattooed arm swings a stunning black and orange rooster, with darting eyes and a poised-to-snap white beak, over the food. He deftly plucks two grand tail feathers from the bird's behind as an offering to the gods.

After the offering it is time to eat—and to continue to drink. I sip my fourth glass of fermented rice booze, which tastes like sake resin, and settle in. Destroying social harmony is a major transgression in a longhouse, and as *our* "host," I am expected to imbibe, drink for drink, with *the* hosts. *Tuak* is passed in bowls and jugs and swilled with exhortations of *"Ngirop, ngirop!"* For the first hour, I feel confident that I can go head to head, as long as nobody breaks out the

Jägermeister shots. The *tuak* is not terribly strong, though the copious amounts are troubling.

Events become fuzzy after hour two as my fatigue progresses from daze to death rattle. Interviews are derailed because I am unable to retain answers for more than six seconds, dashing any hope of a decent follow-up question. *"Ngirop!"* I hear, as another sloppy *tuak* is thrust under my nose, and I sway with fatigue as much as anything else. By hour three, after days of nonstop traveling, complete exhaustion taking hold, I am barely tracking conversations, including those in English. My last memory is an image of young Iban men in the middle of a circle, kicking high and wild, full of athleticism and punch.

I fall asleep sitting up and am half-carried, half-rolled through a doorway adorned with a carving of a crocodile swathed in a snake.

That night, dreams come fitfully. Snakes are slithering all over me and out of my hands, and I am unable to move. The auguries could be saying any number of things:

1. I am in touch with the ancient power of the serpent that embodies the female principle; I may be pregnant; I may be poised to transform or evolve; I am definitely in touch with my libido; I am dangerous to the foolishly unwary (this, according to the historical mythology of most ancient cultures).

2. Patriarchy has subsumed all matriarchal realms; thus, I am scared of the all-powerful penis and my own sexuality. I have issues (this, according to Freud et al.).

3. Animals and dreams are the vehicle for messages sent

17

from the parallel universe, which is with us at all times. The female god who rules that parallel universe is represented by the serpent dragon. The upshot: Someone important is trying to send me a message (this, according to Iban cosmology).

4. The holey mosquito net, which binds twelve of us (our crew and the host family) in a row like corpses, has pinned me in place, and I underwent a nocturnal panic attack that manifested itself in my sleep as snakes (this, according to my logic).

The *tuak* and jagged sleep leave a strange, not unpleasant pall on the next day as we set out for the deep interior and a visit with the Penan tribe, Borneo's last true nomads.

I've heard the locals say, "Upriver is a state of mind." Perhaps this is why the jungle seems different this time as we navigate its waterways. What seemed just a day ago to be a nefarious Rorschach test begins to reveal enchanting patterns and wildlife whimsy. Chains of orchids (of which there are some three thousand species in Borneo, which boasts 10 percent of the world's total orchid population) outline the trunks of sixty-foot-tall trees; chaotic assemblies of vines become launchpads for kingfishers and starlings.

Rhododendrons, their red blossoms bursting, push branches closer to the water. The regular crashing and crackling in the forest add dimension, rather than warning. Even the rapids are being welcomed as a good rollick and an opportunity to admire spectacular boatmanship, attuned to the uneven depths and eddies the river puts in our path.

The Penan hunter-gatherers inhabit the deep jungles of the central and northern parts of the state. An estimated three hundred Penan hunt, gather, run, roam, live, and die under the jungle canopy of the park; another seven thousand or so Penan have been jettisoned from their lands by the logging industry and put into "settlements" with promises of healthcare and education—promises that have gone largely unkept.

We travel by river out to one of these government-induced settlements, which is a line of clapboard dwellings accented with the odd bit of cloth swinging in the wet wind to dry. I sense depression. Unlike the upriver longhouse, which felt emboldened by tradition, pride, and humor—a place not at odds with modernity, but where the Dayak chose what they would incorporate—this settlement reeks of defeat. Forced settlement of nomadic people seems particularly cruel, as it cuts them off from their way of life, cultures, and traditions.

Moments after we arrive, a downpour begins. We run for one of the shelters and sit amidst some wet hay to drink tea and wait for the heavy rain to subside. "The Malaysian government backs the logging industry, and the Penan, to put it bluntly, have been in the way," Vanessa confirms.

When the rain stops, we gather near the water's edge. A middle-aged woman plays a nose flute that sounds to me full of sadness and hope and maybe epic tales. The men work on their hunting implements. The ancient and inspiring parts of the Penan culture begin to shine through the trappings of the settlement as the rain stops and daily activity resumes.

19

The Penan hunt and trap gibbons, macaws, civet cats, squirrels, and reptiles. I'm shown the poison-dart blowpipe, which has a 150-foot range and is used for killing small game, including monkeys. A Penan hunter blows a dart (whose tip has been dipped in poison) through the barrel of the blowpipe, using strong breath from the chest and stomach, rather than the mouth. The blowpipe is lighter than a gun, makes no sound, and can be shot with deadly precision. The poison, the blowpipe, and the darts, essential items of the Penan existence, are all handmade with materials found in the rainforest.

"Tomorrow is your hunt for wild bearded boar," Vanessa tells me. "So brush up on your blowpipe skills," she says with a mischievous smile.

Manners. Remember your manners, I think as I sit deep in the rainforest with a family of Penan hunter-gatherers, trying to swallow a third glop of wild sago. How I wish the glop were Jell-O salad, or matzoh ball soup, or anything but what it is. The mother twirls more gluey *na'oh* around a stick and hands it to me, and my gag muscle twitches as if contemplating a chunky (and not meant to be chunky) dairy product. Sago is wild palm, which the Penan depend upon for their housing, baskets, and food. It is 90 percent pure carbohydrate, and it used to be mixed with animal blood to form a mineral-rich source of nutrients. But Christian missionaries, reacting to the gore, convinced the Penan to stop eating blood. The nutritionally unbalanced staple that resulted keeps the Penan malnourished. To my Western palate, *na'oh* tastes like warmed Silly Putty. The plenitude of sago determines how long a nomadic Penan family stays in one place (it goes, they go).

At dawn this morning, we shoved off in our canoes and traveled several hours to arrive here, deep in a protected forest area in which a group of nomadic Penan is still able to practice its traditional way of life. To keep away from the incessant drizzle, we are huddled under a lean-to made of giant pandanus leaves and branches, built by the mother of the family. Berti, the father, dips the head of a just-sharpened dart into a dark liquid. The poison.

I down the third glop of sago, hyperaware that I have no choice, as the greatest transgression in Penan culture is *see hun,* or "failure to share." The prospect of another meal of sago is motivation enough to succeed in today's wild boar hunt. Give me the other white meat any day (even if it has a beard).

Having wheedled our way into this boar hunt, a rare "pure" remaining aspect of Penan life, I am feeling more than ever as if we are nefarious culture-skaters. We really should not be here. But my time to protest has long since passed. This is television, and we have set up "an experience," and—by god—it is my job to have it.

Only one gringa is allowed per hunt, so I am going out alone with the men of the tribe. Georgie, our Brit camerawoman, sets me up with the small Canon video camera and shoves a couple of extra tapes in my pocket. "Okay, mate, if you get one, make sure to get plenty of cutaways. And careful not to let the blood splatter on the lens" is Georgie's final advice.

Martin translates for the three men whom I will join for the hunt. The leader is Berti, the father of the family who shared their sago with me. As he issues instructions, Martin says, "Berti says to stay close, but never move in front of the group. When they catch one, beware of its teeth."

"Woouh, woouh, woouh," goes the high-pitched Penan chant as we trot along, and then quickly turn up the pace a notch to a steady run.

The men are wearing smallish skins that cover their loins. I am wearing thick cross-trainers, long, thin, wicking pants with eight pockets (four of which I have yet to find), and a microlight long-sleeve shirt with mesh ventilation under the armpits. I am Ex Officio. My shoes crunch clumsily on the forest floor; the men travel in near silence, as if they are human hovercrafts.

After about five minutes, I stop Berti and the guys and ask them to run around me in circles so I can get full frontal footage of them. I fear I will see only their backsides from here on out, given their increasing pace. No translator is on-site, so "asking them" means my running around in a circle, miming the hunt of a wild bearded boar (as if I have some idea what that entails). They laugh at the foolish tall white lady and gamely comply. Before we take off again, I get a close-up of Berti's feet. They are small and have an intriguing network of roundish muscle landscapes. Given the speed and gallantry with which they deliver him through a forest floor of logs, prickly sticks, and vines, it seems Berti's feet have a range of talents wholly incomprehensible to the average pampered First World foot.

"The Penan are so profoundly different," wrote Canadian linguist Ian

Mackenzie. "They have no writing, so their total vocabulary at any one time is the knowledge of the best storyteller. There is one word for 'he,' 'she,' and 'it,' but six for 'we.' There are at least eight words for 'sago,' because it is the plant that allows them to survive. Sharing is an obligation, so there are no words for 'thank you.' They can name hundreds of trees but there is no word for 'forest.' Their universe is divided between the land of shade, the land of abundance, and the land that has been destroyed."

The hunt begins in earnest. Berti and the two other men are ripping through the dense tangles of vines, trees, and kooky jungle growth at high speed with six-foot-long blowpipes and spears in their hands. The speed and agility with which they traverse the terrain is uncanny, and I wonder if they are doing *mal cun uk* ("follow our feelings"), a Penan way to navigate an unknown part of the jungle. I set the camera on autofocus, lock it on Record, and pull out every last one of my stops in order to keep up. *I will not fail, goddammit,* I think as I flail with gusto through the dense underbrush, willing my bad ankle not to snap.

Last year, CNN put me through their war-zone training for journalists in the swamps of Georgia, where I learned that camera operators have a misguided sense of security—that is, the irrational belief that you are invincible, that somehow looking through a lens protects your body as bullets fly by, grenades are lobbed, or, in the current case, you hurl yourself through a lethal jungle, full speed and sans peripheral vision, on the tail of Penan warriors who are wielding poison blowdarts in hopes of skewering a wild bearded boar. The adrenaline is pumping. *I am keeping up!* I can see the headlines now: "He blew the poison dart with the acumen of a thousand years of history and downed the squealing swine in a single shot."

Aha! The story is mine!

Just as I am about to delude myself that I am both a journalist and a hunter, I go ass over tit into a felled log, and a sticky, prongy vine becomes the new look in choker collars. My head is thrust back into a giant mossy divot in a hundred-million-year-old tree, another scratchy vine has bound my torso, and I am firmly lodged in some twisted B-movie, S&M jungle position. I look up at the thick canopy above, panting, thinking of Peg the nurse's final admonition and wondering if anything is *broken, torn,* or *severely punctured,* or if the term "air-evac" has ever even crossed the lips of a human being within a thousand-mile radius.

The Penan's hunting chants fade into the distance.

I am instantly miserable.

My head itches. I hurt. My wrists are sweating. In the back of my mind, anxiety simmers because I know this is the exact kind of moment I will be required to write about or describe to camera, and I think, *Can't I just have the fucking experience?* I enter a moment of schizophrenic self-pitying delirium: *What would others write?*

Ernest Hemingway: I am hot. I will just shoot the pig.

Anne Lamott: I'm feeling hot and my Birks were not the best choice but what I really want is to have a stiff drink but Sam wouldn't like it because he doesn't have a father.

Paul Theroux: I'm very hot. I feel as if I'm in the furnace of an old 1926 steam engine.

As I try to untangle myself, the punishing humidity fuels a steady stream of sweat into my eyes, which makes the wall of electric-green foliage that incarcerates me jitter like the preamble to an acid trip.

The spongy, fetid jungle floor is alive, a constant microorganismic frenzy. It is sending out an endless, deafening, gurgly hum that tells me that billions and billions of small creatures are surrounding me and are very hard at work and I am just lying there like a dead animal, soon to be decomposed.

Mosquitoes (malarial, I'm sure) swarm mercilessly. I become convinced that a slimy, overwhelming power is morphing me into something else and I will end up a moth—and not in that comforting reincarnation way.

I would just be a moth.

It's when I hear myself nearly whimper that I sober up and ask myself what a diva would do. *Take action.* I scramble to my feet and turn the camera on myself in a desperate *Blair Witch* moment. This is as good a time as any to deliver some "top tips" and "emotional diary entries," both of which were mandated by the series producer, who is currently sitting in a posh office back in London's Notting Hill.

"Whenever you're hunting for wild boar in the jungles of Borneo, wear a long-sleeve shirt," I say to camera and pan down my arm, which is dripping blood from the hostile vine. Of course, only one in a million viewers will ever hunt wild boar in this godforsaken hell.

Seems Berti and the others are long gone, and rightly so. My stealth-less presence made their chances of sticking a boar about as likely as my chances of finding my way out of this jungle unaided.

I just hope they'll come back for me.

I hang my sweaty overshirt (now ripped for additional ventilation) on a branch of a tree that I notice has been *molong*ed. The Penan tradition of *molong*ing trees consists of marking the trunk with a machete to signify it as a fruiting tree, rather than a lumber tree. If a tree has been *molong*ed, other Penan will not cut it down, but will only pick fruit from it.

I wander about twenty yards and position myself in what passes for a clearing. Like any good Chicagoan, I try to face the virtual door so that when a threatening mobster character comes in to take me out, I will be prepared. Unfortunately, the jungle is all doors. Pity the editor who has to go through the footage I burn during the next ten minutes as I deliver my "diary moments," which rumble closer to a pitch of pure panic with each minute that the Penan hunters do not come back for me.

"Excuse me, but I do *not* think Julia Roberts was put through this when she did a show in Borneo. Please, they just wheeled her out of the trailer, stuck baby orangutans on her ample breast, and rolled film." And finally . . .

"My brother gets my record collection; my sister, the dog. . . ." I turn off the camera and watch the blood weep down my leg from the latest leech incursion. I sop the ooze from another ulcer, an older bite. Leeches have three jaws, each of which contains a hundred teeth. They use one end of their body for attaching to their host while the other end feeds. Their saliva contains an anticoagulating agent and a mild anesthetic so they can suck you dry unnoticed. In a half hour a leech can consume up to five times its body weight—that is, half a shot glass of blood. They can balloon from two centimeters to two inches fat, depending how much blood they suck. I flick off a small leech that is beginning to dig in at my ankle.

And then it becomes painfully clear that one tampon was not enough for today's excursion.

The army of jungle bugs turns up the volume a notch in unison. At this moment, in the belly of the beast, Borneo's tropical rainforest seems endless and all-consuming. Hard to conceive that it could all be destroyed. Yet if all systems remain go—that is, the logging continues 24/7 under floodlights, and the Penan who are staging protests do not prevail—it will be gone in five to ten years. Forever. Poof. But my compassion for the rainforest atrophies with each moment the environment keeps me trapped and fearful. No Stockholm Syndrome for this panicking pig hunter.

I slide into what my friend Kate calls the "secret happy place." That is, the place in your mind where you go when your heaving face has been planted over the toilet in a third-class Indian train for six hours straight; that place you go when your sister has had one too many cocktails at Christmas dinner and you can see her wind up to chuck a hardball at the dysfunctional house of mirrors that tenuously holds the gathering together; that place you go when you have intestinal parasites and shit your pants on a Guatemalan Bluebird bus (and that place you go after you clean yourself up and it happens again five minutes later); and finally, that place you go when you've been abandoned by Penan tribesmen in the jungles of Borneo and find yourself seeping from five different holes— some natural, some not.

My secret happy place is under a piece of heavy oak furniture where I mouth to myself, "You're all alone in this world and the sooner you realize that the better; you're all alone in this world and the sooner you realize that the better." My decades-old ritual response to pain (secret but, come to think of it, not very happy) has been adapted, in

27

this case, to: "You're all alone in this world—*except for the goddamn crew, who'd better come find me*—and the sooner you realize that—*one dumb gringa life is nothing compared to the genocide*—the better. You're all alone in this world—*calm down calm down . . . oh god. Jesus. I'm not cut out for this nomad life*—and the sooner you realize it . . . "

To calm myself, I try to buy into the Penan belief in the interconnectedness of all things material and spiritual, a belief that puts a more palatable spin on death. After all, when you're in the tropics with very limited access to medical facilities, death can strike at any moment and, in the cosmos of the local people, fate can never be avoided. Without a conceptual distinction between this life and the hereafter, one cultivates an easy acceptance of death. This, in turn, it is said, leads people to live joyously.

I am so *not* there.

Another ten minutes pass, and I begin to wonder if this is all one of those malaria pill–induced psychotic moments Peg mentioned.

And then it happens. Eight feet to my right, at about two o'clock on the cosmic clock, a five-foot-long black and green snake with orange stripes slithers into a patch of sun that has managed to defy the thick jungle canopy and beam onto the forest floor.

The snake stops.

I stop.

The world stops.

The snake does not recoil to strike, nor does it coil to sunbathe. The snake simply lifts its head three inches off the ground and stares. At me.

Oddly, instead of heightened panic, I feel utter calm. No itching. No fear. A strange union.

It sticks its tongue out at me.

I stick my tongue out at it.

Everything has disappeared—the jungle cacophony, the weeping leech sores, television. This staring contest lasts a full two minutes. It's said that looking into the eyes of an adult orangutan is like looking at a hundred million years of history—calming and frightening at the same time. I avert my eyes in submission. The snake slithers away and I am left to interpret its message.

A half hour later Berti finds me sitting on a log. I don't tell Berti or anybody about the snake. The visit was like a strange gift from Boo Radley, hidden in the trunk of a tree. Nobody's business, really. Especially not the cable-viewing public's. There was no kill today, but somehow I think I got the story.

"Tell us what it was like," Georgie asks, sticking a hulking camera in my face.

"I already did, to camera, in there," I say, pointing into the arboreal abyss and handing her the Canon. "Let's be done for the day," I say.

On the way back I think about Berti's feet and the snake's eyes, and the twirling sago and the disappearing magic. All the secrets that are being felled.

Wolf
Pleasures

Julianne Balmain

You wake up in New York City and you are hungry. After a red-eye flight, a day of meetings, and a night of business cocktails, you open your eyes to the bland surroundings of a corporate-account hotel with a view of the rooftop air-conditioning unit. Downstairs, the suits are out. You perceive there is a brief wait for a table in the hotel restaurant, where you can get the same cartoned orange juice and foam-core pastries you ate at the breakfast meeting the day before, all for around the price of dinner at your favorite restaurant back home. Remarkably, you are tempted. But only for an instant. Then you have an idea. No, it's less than that. It is only a flicker of an impulse, but it is enough to get you out of there. The same subconscious, animal voice that tells the wolf to seek the tastier mouse on the next hillock over tells you to head for the subway.

You exit the revolving doors and join the rush-hour crush, observing the locals in their push to get to work without making eye contact with strangers. Then the moist grime of the subway, the shriek of brakes. Doors close, faces fly by on the platform. Another train oddly keeps pace for a few seconds and you stare at those across from you, hurtling indifferently along at whatever speed, in a lit box next to your hurtling lit box. Their train brakes and vanishes. You consult your map and choose a station. A few minutes later, you emerge into the brighter, friendlier light of SoHo, far from the frown of skyscrapers. It's a sunlight somehow suffused with possibility and humanity in a way big-city business districts around the world, with their hard reflective glass and granite cliffs, rarely are. (This may be why Central Park, decked out at the moment with cherry blossoms, green hillocks, and scampering children, is so delicious and startling. What is it *doing* there? Like that sweet stretch of little shops and juice stands on Madison around 70th, a walk I can never resist.) SoHo, Little Italy, NoLita, TriBeCa light in midmorning invites leisure, contemplation, mental recreation. It's full of life. In the shadow of skyscrapers, the only options are weak coffee and meeting rooms. Good people in bad places.

You pause just outside the subway exit. Where now? You chose your destination based on the dimmest recollection of a neighborhood. Ask a stranger? Choose a direction at random? You linger, waiting for a sign. Beside you, a man dressed in business-casual trousers and a linen shirt the color of dust talks on his cell phone. You hear the magic words so clearly that you know, no matter whom he's talking to, the message is for you.

"Right. I'm going to have breakfast, then I'll be in the office. We can talk then."

Bingo. He closes the phone. You follow. Half a block down, he opens the door to a place with marble-chip floors, ceiling fans, and comfortable old wooden tables. You choose one. There is a tiny bowl of sea salt and a small pepper mill on the table. There is a collection of free newspapers. From your grateful perspective, the clientele, as well as the servers, appear beautiful, kind, and intelligent. You open the menu. They offer organic eggs and freshly squeezed orange juice, pancakes and fresh fruit, waffles, omelets, and home fries, all to be had for the price of the tip at the hotel joint. *This is the pleasure of life,* you think, settling back with your *New York Times,* local edition. This is the pleasure of taking small chances, the greatest and perhaps singular joy of traveling alone.

Because we all know the hard truth: All but the very best and rarest of travel partners would—accidentally, unwittingly, inadvertently, unconsciously, innocently—have interfered with this delicate breakfast-hunting process. That moment of hesitation at the hotel, for example. Might not the two of you have decided to stay and shell out $25 each for the continental treatment? Knowing you were seriously hungry and other options were uncertain and might not materialize, that it might be hard to get a cab, that there could be traffic, that he or she, as lovely a person as he or she is, can't handle the noise and the crowds and the stairs and the soot on the subway and thus gets grouchy at the mere suggestion of a subway ride before coffee. Knowing, let us be honest, that it would be worth sixty or seventy bucks and plasticized pastries to not have to deal with your fond companion when he or she is getting a "little grumpy" and doesn't realize it. Knowing that if another, better breakfast experience did not swiftly manifest itself and a long and perhaps frustrating or ultimately unsuccessful hunt ensued, hunger increasing and blood sugar falling with each passing moment, you yourself might become irritable and a quarrel or bad feelings could arise, bringing with them lasting if minor consequences. And in fact that someone—you, him, her—might be saddled, perhaps for years, with the blame for a failed outing stemming from such a minuscule infraction as hoping for a better breakfast. Marriages have ended over less, not to mention business relationships and friendships.

Or the two of you might have distracted one another with pleasant chatter and observations and not overheard the man on the cell phone. You might thus have walked far in the wrong direction and been brought down by bad vibes in an area with negative urban feng shui. Alone, your intuition is acute. Your senses are heightened and responses swift. Alone, you are the wary wolf on the trail of tender, succulent prey. Together, you are cows munching with heads down, each assuming the other has a plan.

And that's all taking for granted your companion woke up around the time you did, got ready in a reasonable period of time, and didn't have any tedious errands to run or phone calls to make. The wolf despises dawdlers.

Life being what it is, your companion might even be a fool with defective instincts causing him or her to reject the perfect spot once found. The peril! Your tiny joys depend upon such nuances of character. They hang from a thread, the menace of a travel companion standing over them with scissors in hand. Not so when you roam the city alone. You are astute and aware, master of your destiny. With each independent stride, you come a little more back to life after the numbing toll even the most enjoyable business pursuits exact. These moments of solitude and independence are a potent sweetness that can sugar many a sour day ahead, should you encounter them, and you certainly must. They are money in the bank. Mice in the wolf's hungry belly. Sourdough toast, marmalade, organic eggs, and crisp bacon on the plate in front of you.

And so you read your paper, eat your breakfast, and eavesdrop on your neighbors. You exchange a few chuckles with them as appropriate. When breakfast is over, the real challenge begins. It is easy to have breakfast alone. But what of the rest of the day? A wolf would head back to the den to roughhouse with the pups and nuzzle the dear ones. Maybe curl up in a pile and nap, nose to toes. You, on the other hand, are on your own with a whole day ahead of you. In my case, I had one meeting to go to and two hours to get there. After that, I was on my own. I decided to wander.

The Bowery between Prince and Houston is wide and gritty. It's lined with restaurant-supply dealers whose dirty windows are stacked with used appliances and bulk-order plates, glasses, and mugs. The curb fills up with trucks unloading the stainless-steel flotsam of the industrial kitchen. I walked vaguely in the direction of my appointment. I had plenty of time. Even this ugly stretch of the Bowery looked fresh in the morning light. I was swimming in it, drifting along. Up ahead, a scruffy transient sat against a brick wall with his knees up, canoe style. An old broom with the straw rubbed down to the cross-stitching was across his lap and he was paddling with it, dipping it in gingerly on either side, easy with the current. His expression was that of Thoreau looking out on Walden Pond on a particularly fine morning.

Few places offer so many precocious, tiny pleasures in so few paces as Manhattan. On a narrow street, next to a sushi restaurant in which a powerful, stern-looking chef was preparing for the day, a tiny door stood open five steep steps below street level. Into it were crammed three more cooks in crisp whites, these younger and less certain, their gestures quick and nervous. Outside, two wooden crates of purple sea urchins sat on the back of a truck, waiting to be shoved into the tiny space. Farther on, an unmistakably French woman tidied the colorful leather bags in the front window of her store. Another unlocked the door, and I heard them exchange their "bonjours" as I walked past. Yep, French. I went over a block and back the other direction, inspecting the environs. The smell of sugar and lemon wafted out of a tiny nail salon decorated with joint grass and Thai sculpture. An equally tiny space next door doubled as art gallery and bar. The anchor of my appointment kept me from drifting too far out to sea. Over the years I have discovered that the difference between a great trip and a miserable one is whether or not I have taken the time to mark the route with small, well-spaced obligations, like cairns in the wilderness.

I once landed in Paris on a dreary January morning. I had no business in Paris; the ticket was irresistibly cheap. Who wants to go to Paris in January? I thought I did. As soon as I arrived, a creeping sense of dread began to inch its way up from my toes, headed for the hollow spot in my stomach. *Courage! Keep the faith!* I rallied the spirits and headed out into an icy rain, peacoat buttoned snugly, wool scarf wrapped 'round, hat on, gloves secure. Paris can be very cold and gloomy in January. I knew this. *Why did I come?* I thought glumly. *Why?* At home I had friends, family, love. Here I had nothing.

The battle lost, I entered a tiny, cheerful-looking café on one of the oldest and most charming streets on the Ile de la Cité and ordered hot chocolate. The young waitress, with the face of a timeless beauty and a perfectly disheveled updo, looked at me warily. I reeked of fear and loneliness. I don't know if it's been proven, but I believe the body emits a special pheromone at such moments, warning others away. In an act of masochistic betrayal, it broadcasts the presence of fear, loneliness, and desperation. Pheromone #9, I call it, the scent that says, "Hi, I'm needy." Or perhaps it is only the wild, jittery look in the eye that puts others off. In any case, the restaurant was empty. It was the wrong hour for drinking chocolate or anything else. The hollow rasp of cup striking saucer shook the room like Quasimodo's bell. I swallowed the syrupy chocolate and went walking again. I met no one, spoke to no one, saw nothing of interest. I was just at the point of going back to the hotel to mope in bed and consider changing my return ticket when I remembered the cardinal rule of solo travel: When in doubt, turn to the sacred. In my case, that meant the Rodin Museum, which happened to be a short *métro* ride away.

I passed into the museum and entered the world of kindred solitude, or so I imagined. I know nothing scholarly about Rodin. Nothing of his life, other than that he was mentor to the poet Rilke at one point. But his work emits the richness and pain of long solitude, the kind that echoes the ultimate solitude of existence itself.

The structure was all grandeur and marble, surrounded by a magnificent garden. The garden reminded me that nature does not hate winter; it is only a work in a different palette. Leaves in every shade of yellow, ochre, brown, gray, and black carpeted the ground, while bare trees stood like minimalist statues, defiant forms reaching to a soft white sky.

Restored, I left the grounds and exited onto the sidewalk that ran along the high stone wall around the estate. Looking at the wall, no one would guess what pale golden light and marvels of sculpture and story lay just on the other side. I would have to move swiftly. Too much traffic, wet concrete, and closed doors would bring the demons out from their hiding places once again.

I spotted a bistro. Not as sweet looking as the café where I had the chocolate, and certainly less hip, but inviting. She who hesitates is lost, especially when battling the demon loneliness. I plunged in. Heat and the buzz of conversation vanquished my anxiety. The fat man at the door greeted me with enthusiasm and took me to my seat. I ordered the chicken potpie, salad, and red wine. They brought the wine first. By the time I finished my glass, the place was full. I ordered another. The owner came over followed by a man in a suit with a newspaper folded under his arm. He explained there were no more tables, and besides, Monsieur would not bite the nice *Américaine*. Monsieur joined me and did not bite, but he did abandon his newspaper to offer a lively conversation on the subjects of Rodin, Rilke, Balzac, Napoléon, and the Parisian love affair with Corsica. And so the curse was lifted. Paris opened its winter cloak and drew me into the warmth, revealing each day of my week of solitude some new beauty or tiny revelation. I returned home exultant, the well filled to overflowing.

On the flight home from New York to San Francisco, I considered the plight of the lone wolf. She may be part of a pack, or may have friends, a he-wolf companion, pups, parents, and relatives back at home. But as every really accomplished and agreeable wolf knows, you have to get away from the pack, travel far to the distant hilltop, and howl with lonely stoicism now and then in order to maintain your sanity, not to mention a fluffy, glossy coat. The lone wolf lives in us all, waiting for the opportunity to stretch her legs and see what's out there.

But was I really alone in Paris or New York? Hardly. I had the cities themselves as companions. Place seldom disappoints. Places deliver their charms and gifts, their pocket treasures and grand celebrations, their sunsets and smells and characters, regardless of your mental or emotional state. Places surprise you at the most unexpected moments with outpourings of generosity, and with unabashed freedom of spirit. Places give and give, asking nothing in return. A place grows and changes and has a life. To know a city is to make a marvelous friend to revisit for years and share with others. That must be why it is restorative, healing, and transformative to commune deeply with a worthy place. Great places offer a form of love, kindness, and generosity that is godly and extrahuman—outside the self, outside human relationships. Maybe that is why pilgrimage is such a universal phenomenon. The creator gave us the ten thousand, ten million places in which to explore and discover ourselves and, perhaps more important, those things outside ourselves.

The sea. Mountains. Wild places, ancient ruins, old cities. They open themselves to travelers who need them and who are ready to pay attention. Even the best and most respectful travel partners can interfere with this quiet, delicate rapport. To hear the tender song of place, go alone and listen.

Abandoned in Uzbekistan

Stephanie Elizondo Griest

I wouldn't have admitted it, but I was lonely.

I had just put Lareina, my confidante of the past year, in a taxi and watched her disappear into the deserted streets of Tashkent. This had become a ritual over the past few days: waving from the curb and trying not to cry as yet another member of my tight-knit group departed for their next adventure. Lareina was bound for Hong Kong, where a new apartment, high-powered job, and boyfriend awaited.

Not for me. My Luce Scholarship had just ended and I had no clue what to do now. Join a potential love interest in Colombia? Hustle for rent in New York City? Return to my family in South Texas and get a "real job"? Or continue traveling, *sola?* I had opted to stall for time in Moscow, where couch-surfing opportunities abounded, but had just learned that my best friend there had been denied permission to send me a visa. I could be stranded in Uzbekistan for days—even weeks—while the Russian embassy scrutinized my papers.

After Lareina's cab pulled away all I felt like doing was sulking in my motel room, but I knew that indecision would drive me crazy if I did. Absolute freedom can be as paralyzing as confinement when you don't know what you want. So I took to the street instead, hoping for a distraction.

Strolling through the old neighborhoods of Tashkent is like thumbing through the pages of Scheherazade's *One Thousand and One Nights.* The high wooden doors of mud-plastered compounds lead to inner courtyards that serve as dining nooks, with low-to-the-ground tables set atop Persian-style rugs and brocade pillows used as seats. I peered inside one and saw a family of five breakfasting on unleavened discs of *lepeshka* and fresh honeydew, sipping their tea out of bowls. Within these medieval corridors, you can almost feel the presence of Tamerlane, the fourteenth-century conqueror who left so many majolica-tiled mosques and terra cotta minarets in his wake.

Continuing on to the farmer's market that morning, I arrived in time to see the vendors unloading crates of meats and cheeses and burlap bags of grain from their trucks. Old ladies in kerchiefs were selling bottles of homemade yogurt; butchers in blood-soaked aprons hacked at carcasses. Eggplants, squashes, cherry tomatoes, and yellow melons glistened in the sun. I considered buying a tiny gourd filled with cloves for the day I actually owned a cabinet—and, moreover, a kitchen—but panicked when I realized what that symbolized. Stability. Responsibility. A job with benefits. A husband and 1.5 kids. I tossed the gourd back in the bin and hurried out of the market.

A neon sign soon caught my eye: *Mir Burger* (WORLD BURGER). My heart pounded. Would they sell french fries there? I usually avoid food I can buy at home, but my body had ingested little but yaks and sheep that past month. Slipping inside the burger joint, I ordered a jumbo pack of fries and a vanilla shake and slid into a yellow booth. Mir Burger was no misnomer: Mongolians, Iranians, Turks, Russians, Koreans, and turbaned Sikhs ate side by side while Celine Dion belted out the theme song to *Titanic*. I watched a pair of sixteen-year-old Uzbeks smoke cigarettes with one hand and dip fries into ketchup with the other. Their generation had grown up in the communist era and was now coming of age with the dawn of capitalism. They looked so hip in their stretch pants, halter tops, and hoop earrings, it was hard to believe they were only a generation or two removed from the skullcapped, bearded vendors preparing Kebabs and vats of *plov* over an open coal fire outside the storefront window.

The french fries left me feeling nostalgic and even more lonely, like I should be rushing off somewhere fun with friends. How was I going to travel sola if I couldn't handle being alone?

Needing some company, I decided to return to the Indian restaurant where our group had held our final meal together. The co-owner—a bubbly Uzbek named Sveta—had urged us back. Hoping she'd remember me, I descended into the dimly lit tavern that emanated cumin and cardamom.

"Where have you been? I have been waiting all week! Sit down, you must be starving," Sveta sang out in Russian, pointing at a table for two. She disappeared behind a tapestry featuring Ganesh that was pinned over a doorway, resurfacing a few moments later. She had changed into a silky blouse with spaghetti straps, a slitted black skirt, and five-inch heels, her bleach-blond hair streaming down her shoulders. After shouting out to someone in the kitchen, she joined me at the table and fired off questions about every member of my group, whom she had met only briefly but recalled with remarkable detail.

A teenager in a black miniskirt and frilly white apron soon emerged from the kitchen carrying a tray full of food. To my amazement, she plunked down everything I had ordered on my first visit: basmati rice, vegetable curry, and a cup of hot chai. Sveta introduced her as Albina, an architecture student at the local university.

"Is that what people wear in America?" Albina asked, staring down at my mud-caked hiking boots.

"It's what we wear when we leave it," I offered.

"And those?" She pointed at my well-worn corduroys.

"When we want to be comfortable," I replied.

"I thought Americans wore Calvin Klein and Polo," she pouted.

I could relate to Albina's disappointment: My own discovery that communists didn't wear star-crested berets had been equally disillusioning. Since we were on the topic of fashion, I inquired about the women I'd seen in the countryside who connected their eyebrows with

43

charcoal pencils and had mouths full of gold teeth. Did their head scarves indicate they were Muslim?

"Nyet," Sveta laughed. "They just do that to keep their hair out of their faces, like *babushki* (old women). Muslims don't have to wear scarves here. We can dress any way that we like."

They can thank the Soviets for that. In 1927, the Soviet Union launched a *hujum* against customs it deemed oppressive to women, including dowries, child brides, and veiling. Unfortunately, these measures were insensitively implemented with tragic results in many cases. Rather than educate Central Asian men about the emancipation of women, the Soviets simply mandated that veils be burned at public ceremonies. Women received no protection against the wrath of their families for following these orders, and thousands were reportedly killed or maimed by husbands, fathers, and brothers.

Women throughout central Asia started veiling again after the collapse of the Soviet Union, but the Uzbek government took a firm stance against the practice, passing a "Law on Religion" in 1998 that forbade religious dress in public. At that time, men could wear skull caps but any woman caught veiled in public was subject to arrest. When I asked Sveta and Albina if they knew any women who wore the veil, Albina tossed her auburn-dyed hair and scoffed, *"Nyet,* this is Tashkent. We're very cosmopolitan here."

"You're Muslim?" I asked, eyeing her miniskirt.

"Of course," she said, pulling out a necklace tucked inside her cleavage and holding it up for me to see. The tiny gold charm said "Allah" in Arabic script.

Post-Soviet Muslims! I'd never met any before. I eagerly started

44

quizzing them. Did they pray five times a day? *(Nyet.)* Eat pork? *(Nyet*—too fattening.) Attend services at the mosque? *(Nyet*—women were forbidden there.) Make a pilgrimage to Mecca? (A what? To where?) Read the Koran? *(Nyet*—they couldn't read Arabic. Nor Uzbek, for that matter.)

Now I was disappointed. "And you're still Muslim?"

"Da," they replied, sounding bored.

Sveta changed the subject: "Let's go shopping!" Albina clasped her hands in excitement. "I'll go change!" she exclaimed, bounding toward the kitchen. She returned seconds later in an off-the-shoulder silk dress and matching silver shoes.

I was feeling rather butch in my hiking boots and corduroys as I hoisted my backpack onto my shoulders and watched Sveta and Albina touch up their makeup and grab their dainty handbags. As we headed into the street, they reached for my hands in the innocent, school-girl fashion of Slavic women. We skipped over to the nearest shopping mall and beelined to the cosmetics department, where the sales attendants had the same snooty smugness as their American counterparts (only instead of Chanel and Estée Lauder, they sold Ivory soap and Vaseline). Sveta sampled every brand of hand lotion before settling on a bottle of Yves Rocher.

Our next stop was a black-and-white checkered ice cream parlor. Having downed two meals already, I insisted I wasn't hungry, but they ordered me an enormous hot fudge sundae anyway (and two glasses of water for themselves). While I force-fed myself the whole-milk cream, Sveta and Albina filled me in on the restaurant's scandalous clientele. One gentleman had been bringing in his wife and mistress on alternating

45

evenings for years. His wife had recently caught on, however, and retaliated with an affair of her own with one of the cooks. The night before, the mistress and the husband had dined on lamb chops in the front of the restaurant while the wife and the cook shared dessert in the back.

Albina had to return to her shift at the restaurant, but Sveta had an appointment at the sauna and invited me to join her. We hailed a cab, which took us to an upscale part of town and dropped us off beneath a sign portraying a seductive woman winking from beneath a broad-brimmed hat. The front door opened into a café where half a dozen well-to-do women nibbled on caviar. They all turned to stare at my hiking boots and corduroys as we walked through the doorway. A receptionist handed Sveta a key and she led me down the hall.

Having frequented the Russian version of a sauna in Moscow, I had an idea of what the afternoon would entail—namely, stripping down to nothing and roasting on a communal set of bleachers with a dozen other women—but Sveta's key opened to a faux marble room with its own whirlpool Jacuzzi and connecting private sauna. Plastic conch shells and starfish lined the pea green–tiled Jacuzzi; two lounge chairs were propped up against the vanity. Russian pop music blasted through hidden speakers. Sveta kicked off her heels, slipped off her clothing and hopped into the Jacuzzi before I had even removed my boots. *"Tak khorosho!"* she sighed, her cheeks flushed from the heat. "Aren't you coming in?"

Having also disrobed in front of Russian women before, I knew what was coming. I peeled off my clothing quickly, hoping to hide under the suds before Sveta could notice—and inevitably comment upon—my body's imperfections.

"Your breasts are too small!" Sveta chirped as I removed my bra. "And you've got pimples on your back. Don't you get enough sex?"

Dear god—did it show? I peered down at my neglected body.

"My gynecologist says you should have sex with your husband or boyfriend at least twice a week and a lover once a week to clean out your system and keep everything balanced and in order," Sveta said as I slid into the warm water.

I tried to imagine my seventh-grade sex education teacher breaking this news to us. "Now your dermatologists may recommend Oxy pads, girls, but there's only one way to really get a good complexion . . ."

"What's so funny?" Sveta demanded. "You don't see any pimples on my back, do you?" She turned around to show off her flawless skin, then briskly changed the subject. "Time for the sauna!"

I climbed out of the pool and followed Sveta through a narrow doorway into a tiny, smoldering chamber. As the woody heat penetrated my pores, sweat trickled out like a saltwater spring. I eased myself onto the scorching wooden platform and started to sizzle. In Russia, trips to the *banya* generally conclude in a tribal dance where women beat each other with birch leaves to "bring the blood to the surface." Yet here, there was nothing but a sack of salt. When I asked about it, Sveta scooped out a handful, grabbed my arm and started scrubbing.

"It helps you sweat out your oils," she explained.

This seemed logical: I had been doing the same to eggplant for years. So I closed my eyes and tried to relax as Sveta worked her way from fingertip to fingertip. Then she lowered me flat on the platform, scrubbed a path from my ankles to my neck, and flipped me over to tackle my back

47

and butt. Satisfied, she handed me the gunny sack, stretched out onto the platform, and motioned for me to begin. Trying to imagine Sveta as a giant purple vegetable, I set about scrubbing.

"*Tak khorosho.*" She grinned like a cat in the sun.

Coated with salt and slick with oil, we returned to the first room and hopped into the Jacuzzi to rinse off. As I dried myself off with a terry cloth towel, I felt the loneliness of the past twenty-four hours seep clean out of my pores.

To my considerable surprise, the Russian embassy approved my request for an emergency visa the following day. I booked the next day's flight to Moscow.

I rose with the sun my last morning in Uzbekistan. My bags were already packed; I sat beside them for a long time as uncertainty churned in my belly. This was it: I was about to begin life post-college and post-fellowship. From here on out, there was no prescribed path—a prospect that both exhilarated and terrified me. I wanted someone to mark this moment with me—to chase my taxi halfway down the street blowing kisses, as I had done for every other member of my group. But I had only my yak-smelling backpack for company.

I walked along the creaky floorboards toward the front desk, handed in my key and headed out the door. To my astonishment, Albina and Sveta were huddled together on the front steps. I'd only told them that I would be leaving "early" in the morning. There was no telling how long they'd been waiting. They slipped their hands into mine and led me down the steps to the curb, where a taxi waited. As the driver loaded my potbellied backpack into the trunk, I hugged them fiercely.

"You have your passport, *da?* And your ticket, Stesha! Do you have your ticket?" Sveta asked anxiously.

"When you get to the airport, don't forget to check in!" Albina instructed. "And keep your backpack with you! *Bozha mou,* don't leave it on the plane!"

As my taxi rolled away from the curb, Sveta and Albina began to trot alongside, waving and blowing kisses. I blew kisses and waved back until they blended in with the mosaics on the misty horizon.

Resisting Florence

Lucy McCauley

There's something about entering a city for the first time through the pages of a book. The experience somehow becomes magnified—each vista, every winding street, each sound and scent overlaid with an extra mantle of significance. From reading E. M. Forster's *A Room with a View*, I'd begun to know Florence long before I ever set foot in Italy. So it was with that heightened sense of place that I stepped out of my pension onto the Florentine streets for the first time.

It was December, and the winter light fell white and misty gray, like the light in a dream. I'd intentionally planned the trip alone, leaving myself free from having to compromise about itineraries. I also decided to heed the admonition of Eleanor Lavish, Forster's freethinking romance novelist, to leave the Baedeker guide shut and the map behind and let the city take me where it would. As I moved through those cobbled, serpentine streets, trying not to find my way out of the labyrinth but rather to follow its subtle design, I began to understand what Camus meant when he called Florence "one of the only places in Europe where I understood that underneath my revolt, a consent was lying dormant." My only agenda: to find the Piazza della Signoria, where Forster's young heroine, Lucy Honeychurch, fainted into the arms of George Emerson, that odd and unconventional young man destined to become her husband.

The thirteenth-century piazza, the setting for public speeches and executions, contains the Loggia dei Lanzi, beneath which sculptures clamor together, with names as violent as their appearance: *Rape of the Sabine Women; Abduction of Polixena.* And then there's Perseus, holding Medusa's severed head. A cluster of symbols that any self-respecting feminist would find telling—classic depictions of patriarchal attempts to control feminine power. The sight of these statues was the final sensory assault that would topple Lucy Honeychurch's delicate constitution after she'd witnessed a stabbing in the piazza. She swooned, and when she awoke, with George Emerson hovering above her, her life had changed forever, though for a while she would deny it.

I couldn't have articulated it at the time, but I too wished to be changed forever by Florence. Not by meeting my George Emerson; rather,

I sought to merge with another kind of lover, every bit as compelling: the city I'd read about, with all of its sensual delights and offenses. The taste and essence of Florence. Something that I imagined the Piazza della Signoria and the loggia of statues possessed.

But after a long first day wandering the streets of the city, I instead found myself pausing along the banks of the Arno River for a rest. I gazed at the jumbled perfection of the Ponte Vecchio, its nestled buildings in myriad sizes, shapes, and hues of gold that somehow created a harmonious medley. After a while, I pulled out a sketchpad and began to draw.

The old man was at my elbow before I realized he was near.

"Come, come," he said in heavily accented English. Faded eyes peered at me from beneath a black cap. Absorbed in my sketch, I smiled politely and turned back to my drawing. It was then that I felt his hand on my shoulder, giving it an insistent shake.

"No, no, you must come! *Perseo, Perseo,*" he persisted urgently. "Now is an important moment."

I looked at him. A snowy mustache, perfectly trimmed. White hair curling at each temple. A man who'd been handsome once, probably flirtatious in the way Italian men are famous for. Perhaps even now he was testing the powers of his charm.

"*Perseo,*" he said again, his eyebrows raised in a plea. He pointed to the crowd that I hadn't noticed across the street—clustered outside what I now realized must be the Uffizi Gallery (based on a quick glance at the guidebook back in my pension). Just beyond that Uffizi, I knew, stood the Piazza della Signoria and the loggia with its dra-

52

matic statues. My mapless wanderings had somehow brought me to my destination after all.

I am not proud of what I did next, or, rather, didn't do. I wish I could say that I responded immediately to the way the old man's urgent tone had moved me. But I hesitated, kept sketching, while silently deciding what to do. I didn't want to appear naive, like some too-eager tourist. What kind of fool goes dashing off across the street with a strange man? And what did he mean by *"Perseo"*?

At time time, I didn't recognize the Italian name for Perseus—that mythic archetype of a young man on a quest. The King of Seriphos, so the myth goes, sent Perseus to retrieve the head of Medusa, the only mortal of the three Gorgon sisters. Perseus knew that anyone who gazed on the Gorgons' nightmarish aspects—dragon-scale skin, hissing serpent hair— would be literally petrified. So when he found the sisters asleep, he used their reflection in his shield to single out Medusa and cut her head. His gruesome task complete, Perseus flew away on his winged shoes.

The old man who'd approached me along the banks of the Arno wandered off, shaking his head, leaving me to ponder my behavior.

The paradox of traveling alone is that, though you do so in order to remain spontaneous, the fact that you're solo can also make you neces- sarily self-protective, a little wary, even. Particularly if you're a single woman. A good and life-preserving instinct. Yet . . .

As I continued sketching, looking up periodically to study the Ponte Vecchio, the man's words echoed in my ears. In his gravelly voice

I heard a lifetime of someone who'd laughed often and loudly, wept freely, whiled away nights with friends, smoking black tobacco on front-door stoops. Exactly the kind of Italian, fused with life force, that Forster describes.

Suddenly, the drawing I'd been so busy with looked banal. I was curious about what had gotten the old guy so worked up. And given his surely (I realized now) well-meant gesture, I felt foolish, regretting my wariness—my hypertuned feminine radar, the subtle barriers I'd learned to place between myself and the world. I was no better off than Lucy Honeychurch, prim in her buttoned-up coat, observing the sights of Florence while rigidly resisting its sumptuous embrace.

I dropped the sketch unfinished into my bag and ran to where the crowd had gathered. In that moment, I knew that, rather than Forster's Lucy, I wished to be more like Medusa: sensual, primal, and (her demise at the hand of Perseus aside) fearless. Willing to drop my armor—even without an arsenal of hissing snakes.

In the crowd, I looked for the man's black cap but couldn't pick it out in that sea of covered heads. The people all stood with necks craned, looking up, and I did too. It was then that I saw the green-bronze statue of Perseus, his winged shoes lifting him heavenward. An enormous crane suspended the Renaissance sculpture in the air, inching it slowly toward a doorway in the Uffizi Gallery.

A woman beside me said that Perseus was going in for restoration and would be out of public view for perhaps a decade. No longer would Benvenuto Cellini's masterpiece stand among the other dramatic statues under the loggia of the Piazza della Signoria, where it had stood for centuries, inducing fainting spells in characters like Lucy Honeychurch. If the old man hadn't alerted me, I realized, I might have finished my sketch, moved on to the Ponte Vecchio—and missed seeing Perseus altogether.

With each movement of the crane, the crowd alternately gasped at the threat of the sculpture crashing down or applauded at the sight of Perseus suspended in midair, both elegant and gruesome: his graceful torso, the curve of his thigh. A jagged sword in his right hand, his left holding high Medusa's severed head, haloed with snakes. For an hour I stood with the crowd, mesmerized by the sculpture's slow, pendulum-like swing. I thought how only Italians would do this, turn out by the hundreds to watch this transition in the life of an artwork. And suddenly I felt a kind of kinship with those around me—teenagers and mothers with babies and old men in black caps—all manner of Florentines bearing witness to the spectacle of Cellini's sculpture going in for rehab. All of us sharing a perspective on Perseus few had ever seen, perhaps not even his maker, from the bottom looking up.

At the same time, I was reminded of a more encompassing view of life that I'd almost forgotten—as something to take part in, rather than to stand apart from. That was what had drawn me to Florence in the first place: Forster's portrait of the Italian spirit in all its exuberance. I had been willing to leave the guidebook behind, yet I'd almost let my reserved and cautious internal guide keep me from attending a ripe, glorious moment.

Today when I come upon my half-finished sketch of the Ponte Vec-chio, I think of that Italian man who approached me like a winged-shoed messenger. And I stop my perpetual motion and wonder if I'm not being reminded of something that even Forster's Lucy at last understood by the end of the novel: that happiness comes in moments. Only by allowing yourself to enter those moments and be present for them will you know their transformative power.

Armed and Dangerous

Michele Peterson

I must have a weakness for men in skirts. There was really no other explanation for why I should have been standing at the edge of a forest, buying a bow and arrow from a long-haired man in a tunic.

"Use this one for *puerco* (pig)," he explained, carefully drawing a yellow-feathered arrow out of the quiver, "and this one for *venado* (deer)."

Although it was unlikely that I'd ever need to shoot my own dinner, I listened carefully to his instructions. It was hard not to like him. He was

Lacandón, a member of one of North America's last surviving tribes of forest-dwellers. Residing deep in the jungle bordering Mexico and Guatemala, they have been retreating farther and farther into their diminishing rainforest preserve in the face of increasing urbanization. Of course, it's hard to be militant when there are only six hundred of you left.

Most people don't have an opportunity to meet a Lacandón unless they take a bone-jarring two-day trip down a dirt highway, canoe across a parasite-infested lagoon, and then hike a half day into Sierra del Lacandón National Park to one of their communities. Otherwise, the Lacandón are most often seen when they come to town to trade.

Palenque, a dusty town best known for its Mayan ruins, was one of those trading centers. I'd arrived at its ruins early, before the tourist buses. The Lacandón looked desperate for business and had only one product for sale: the handcrafted bow and arrow. Since it was the first sale of the day, I got the equipment—plus full instructions on stalking and capturing wild game—all for the bargain price of twenty-five pesos (about $3).

"Ready to go?" he asked, dismantling the arrows, feathers, quivers, and bow. Wrapping it up in brown paper as capably as a butcher at a Piggly Wiggly store, he handed it over and pointed to a path in the jungle.

Armed with my bundle, but feeling more Friar Tuck than Robin Hood, I headed off alone into the rainforest—on a quest to learn more about the Red Queen of Palenque.

I was actually an inadvertent solo traveler. My original plan had been to spend a week in Chiapas, taking cooking lessons and exploring its colonial towns before meeting up with my partner in Guatemala for a few weeks of visiting his family. On the map, it had looked like just a short hop across the border. In reality, it was a fourteen-hour bus ride across the highlands. And to make matters worse, heavy rains had washed away many of the roads, and armed gangs were blocking the main highway, robbing and assaulting travelers.

So, while waiting for the situation to calm down, I'd spent some extra time in San Cristóbal de las Casas, visiting shrines to the Virgin of Guadelupe by day and lying in my bed, suffering through the hotel mariachi band's endless renditions of "Hotel California," by night. I'd even had a bout of food poisoning to occupy my time.

By the end of two weeks, I was ready to move on. The highway situation hadn't improved but I craved anonymity. A solo woman in a Latino town stands out at the best of times, and I'd worsened the situation by amassing a following of scrawny stray dogs, who followed me up and down the cobblestone streets while I fed them from a large bag of kibble that I refilled each morning from the bulk bin at the *tienda*. Evenings, the pooches got real food, thanks to food scraps that I stashed in a large, smelly baggie. Recently the locals had begun pointing out even more needy hounds, and I was feeling a bit like a canine version of the Pied Piper.

Worse, I suspected I was being spied on. The hotel clerks, whom I'd originally considered very solicitous, seemed to have become vigilante chaperones. Privy to the conversations I had on the hotel's one phone in the lobby, they were intent upon preserving my honor for whenever my *esposo* (husband) and I would be reunited. Each evening they took turns grilling me on where I was going. One night, they caught me sneaking past the front desk after midnight to go to a movie and took particular glee in advising that he'd called. My partner didn't offer much sympathy and just laughed, saying I was causing a scandal.

We'd been together for fifteen years and had long ago worked out a happy truce in our relationship that accommodated my long absences for travel. But I knew that his family still thought it was all very puzzling. His mother, a feisty woman in her own right who lived on the family's *finca*, a farm in Guatemala's isolated lowlands, worried about my propensity to travel around the world to what seemed like obscure places.

"Watch out for *el barbudo* (the bearded one)," she once warned, referring to Osama bin Laden, when I headed alone to Vietnam. If a plane crashed anywhere in the world, she was convinced I'd surely been on the flight and would fret until I called her.

So while I understood the hotel staff's noble intentions, they were making me crazy. Finally, when I was nabbed having coffee with an Italian male backpacker and jumped like a high school teenager caught making out on her parents' basement couch, I knew it was time to move on.

Turning down repeated offers from my partner's three brothers, who wanted to form a posse and come rescue me, I had scanned the map for a place to hang out until my flight home. Inspiration arrived at Na Balom, a museum and guesthouse at the edge of town. Built in the nineteenth century, the museum was the home of Danish archaeologist Franz Blom and his Swiss photographer wife, Trudy, in the 1950s. Now dedicated to preserving the Lacandón culture and advocating preservation of the rainforest, it is full of anthropological relics, faded photos, and lush gardens. Among those exhibits, I discovered that the Lacandón

were a matriarchal society. My previous impression of early Mesoameri-
can society had been that it was a predominantly male-oriented culture,
with females confined to being sacrificial maidens or crones. But here
among the archives, I learned of female deities, powerful warriors who
played important roles on battlefields, in the underworld, and during
childbirth. An entry in an archaeologist's diary even reported fantastical
tales of women nursing dogs. More recent accounts told of the tomb of a
warrior queen—known as the Red Queen, due to the red cinnabar covering her sarcophagus—discovered in 1994. Considered one of the richest
tombs ever found, it captured my imagination and inspired me to travel
the six-hour bus ride east into the jungle to learn more.

That was how I found myself alone in the rainforest, armed with a bow
and arrow. Craving some solitude, I had begun my hike at a seldom-used
pathway away from the main entrance to the park. Within just a few
moments, I found myself alone on the trail. The morning mist had lifted,
but the rainforest was still dark with shadows. The trail was soft as felt
underfoot, thanks to a blanket of decomposed vegetation and fallen
leaves. My photocopied map indicated that the Red Queen's tomb was
near the Great Plaza—which was where I believed I was headed.

Although the ruins of Palenque are well known on the archaeological-
group-tour circuit, the entire site stretches across sixty-five square kilometers. Rising out of a fertile plateau in eastern Chiapas, its lush rainforest borders the Maya Biosphere Reserve, a vast tropical jungle that
stretches into northern Guatemala, Belize, and the southern Yucatán.

Home to an impressive diversity of plant, bird, and mammal species, vast sections of it are still undiscovered. In the 1990s, it sheltered members of the Zapatista Army of National Liberation, who seized control of San Cristóbal de las Casas in a 1994 uprising. In recent years, although the Zapatistas had reached an uneasy peacetime truce, the jungle's remoteness still presented dangers of its own. Farther south, the El Petén region had even been the location for the reality series *Survivor: The Mayan Empire.*

Hiking along, oblivious to the vastness of the jungle surrounding me, I heard what sounded like a freight train derailing. It burst from the trees with a roar, shook the skies, and then subsided. The forest that had seemed so peaceful now seemed ominous. The trail that had been well trodden when I started out now looked overgrown and unused. I realized that I hadn't seen anyone for well over an hour. Picking up my pace and walking at a speed just short of a run, I remembered that during Guatemala's civil war decades earlier, my partner's father had been kidnapped by guerillas in El Petén.

Although the risk was low that I myself would be snatched by guerillas, there was definitely potential to be robbed by thugs. Plus, it was getting hotter and the humidity was building. Realizing my map was not drawn to scale, I began to think that my tomb-hunting plan had been more foolhardy than adventurous. I had no idea how much farther it would be.

Despite my growing fear, I was also annoyed. I seemed to have a propensity for poor judgment. This wasn't the first time I had found myself in a predicament. Previously, I'd waded alone down a jungle stream, looking for ruins of Vietnam's ancient Champa Kingdom, and relied on a small child to lead me back to town. In Guatemala's remote Sierra de las Minas mountains, I'd decided to hunt down the source of a rare blue jade—in the middle of the rainy season. Although I'd never had a serious mishap, I realized that, far from being a warrior queen/explorer, I was just an idiot with an overactive imagination. I had no water, no compass, or any other supplies. Plus, the bundle of arrows I was lugging under my sweaty armpit had become a liability—I was more apt to fall on an arrow than shoot any dinner or attacker with it.

Suddenly, the roaring sound increased and the trees started rustling around me. It was now almost directly overhead.

That did it. I turned tail and started going back the way I had come. Not quite a run—but almost. Vines entangled in the undergrowth seemed intent on tripping me. The noise of my hasty retreat drowned out any sounds shadowing me.

Out of breath, I reached a fork in the path and, unable to remember my original route, chose the trail on the left. Within minutes, I could see glimmers of sunlight through the foliage. Soon a wide expanse of grass, punctuated by large ceiba trees, materialized. An armed security guard sat resting on a rock at the end of the jungle path, smoking.

"Howler monkeys," he said, pointing back at the woods and distant noise. "Lots of them. They don't like visitors."

Behind him rose the ruins of Palenque. First occupied in 100 BC, it flourished as a center for Mayan religion and commerce between 620 AD and 740 AD. In total there were more than 1,500 buildings, only a third of which had been excavated. The tallest, the Temple of the Inscriptions, emerged out of the foothills of the jungle cliffs like an eight-layer wedding cake. Nearby would be Temple 13, the tomb of the Red Queen. Taking a deep breath and cooling off with a splash of water from a water fountain at a nearby restroom, I headed across the expansive clearing to begin exploring.

Archaeological accounts of the discovery of the Red Queen's tomb report that a badly preserved skeleton belonging to a thirteen-year-old boy was found at the extreme western end of the sarcophagus. One of its main features was cranial deformation—deliberately flattened heads were considered a sign of beauty in Mayan times. A second skeleton, that of a woman who had died at the age of thirty, was also discovered. Both individuals had been sacrificed to accompany the Red Queen on her journey to the underworld.

Inside the vaulted burial chamber itself, the Red Queen was discovered lying on her back with her face covered in a jade mask. She wore a belt of three small limestone axes and carried an obsidian blade in her hand. Her age at the time of her death was between forty and forty-five years old. Her body was covered heavily with a red dust that was identified as cinnabar. Today, the sarcophagus is a simple rectangular limestone box that is tucked behind a vaulted Mayan arch and protected from present-day looters by a frame of iron bars. Although its interior is still stained by the blood-red dust, the tomb's treasures have been removed for safekeeping. Some temples at Palenque have snakelike ventilation ducts to assist the soul in its passage to the underworld, but the walls of this tomb seemed oppressive, and I could stay only a few moments in the fetid, moist air before I had to hurry back out into the sun.

Outside, I took a seat on a crumbling piece of temple wall that emerged from an unexcavated mound behind the ruins. Moisture rose from the vegetation that enveloped the gray stones deep in the shade, and the sunlight revealed walls splattered with bat guano. When night fell, bats would leave their dens in large, swooping flocks.

I tried to imagine life here over one thousand years ago. Who was the boy who was sacrificed? Was he related to the Red Queen? What did she die of? Perhaps more of her story would be unraveled in future excavations. Although my quest for the Red Queen had resulted in more questions than answers, I'd at least had a glimpse into her life. I'd also gained an appreciation of Palenque's splendor and its role in Mayan culture, whose influence has endured to modern times. I'd also learned that perhaps each of us is a warrior in our own way. Despite shortcomings in planning, my solo expedition had been a worthwhile foray. I'd plunged into the unknown and emerged intact.

Later, as I returned to the trading post to catch a bus back to town, I spotted my Lacandón friend in the white tunic. He was encouraging a German backpacker to take a trek into the Lacandón forest. The backpacker was tempted but still concerned about safety.

"Should you decide to go," I offered, "I do have a bow and arrow you can use."

In Gudrid's Footsteps

Susan Richardson

In my guesthouse room here in Hellnar, on Iceland's Snaefellsnes Peninsula, I toss and turn, flip my pillow over, kick off the duvet, and toss and turn again. I'm at the start of a three-month solo journey in the footsteps of a tenth-century Viking called Gudrid, whom I consider the most intrepid woman in world history. It's a journey that I've been planning for two years—it will take me from Iceland to Greenland to the northernmost tip of Newfoundland—and excited though I now am at being in the area that shaped the early years of Gudrid's life, I'm also more than a little anxious about the challenge I've set for myself.

Eventually, at around 5 AM, I give up trying to sleep and wander out of my room into the guests' lounge to search the bookshelves for some distraction. My eyes immediately fall on Viking cards, by Gudrun Bergmann—a set of tarot cards created by the woman who owns and runs this guesthouse.

I carry the pack of cards and the accompanying book to a table in front of the glass doors leading onto the sundeck, though "sundeck" seems something of an exaggeration this morning, as both sky and sea are titanium gray. Gudrun's introduction to her Viking cards is infinitely more colorful. She ignores the popular image of the plundering pirate and writes instead of how the Vikings celebrated the cycles of the sun, had a deep respect for nature, and knew how to use medicinal plants for healing. In designing the cards, she chose symbols from the everyday life of the Vikings, as featured in the Icelandic sagas, and then gave them a contemporary interpretation. Finally, she urges us all to "go Viking," using our own shamanic powers "in the inner realms of our reality."

Feeling rather more sham than shamanic, I go on to read the cards' instructions for use. I can either shuffle and pull out just one of the thirty-two cards or else make a spread of several cards, which is designed to answer more specific questions. Since it's hard to be specific on so little sleep, I opt for the former, shuffle, cut—and pull out the Helmet. According to Gudrun's contemporary interpretation, this could mean that I'm currently battling through life well, or, alternately, that I've entered into life's battles but forgotten to put my protective helmet on.

For curiosity's sake, I replace the card, shuffle, extract another from the deck—and get the Helmet again. Not fair. I want the Viking Ship, which would represent the explorer in me, or, at the very least, the Drinking Horn, which fueled the creativity of Viking poets and is the card that carries a message of joy.

When I shuffle, cut, choose a card, and get the Helmet for the third time, I begin to think there's something deeply weird going on. Is it a whole deck of Helmets? No, the top card, when I turn it over, is the Spear, signifying goal setting and asking, "Are you purposefully heading somewhere in your life, or have you no idea where you are going?"

Actually, I do. I'm carrying the cards over to the bookshelves, going out of the lounge, along the corridor—and back to bed.

"Do you have a map of the area that I can borrow?" I ask Gudrun after breakfast. She's a slim, white-haired woman, with dimples deep as craters when she smiles.

"Yes, of course. What do you plan to do today?"

"Walk from here to Arnarstapi, where Gudrid was fostered, then try to locate her place of birth."

Gudrun nods. "Good. It's a beautiful walk through the Hellnahraun lava field. And a very important leyline intersects with the path you'll be taking."

"Meaning what, exactly?"

"The leylines of the planet are a sort of energy grid. The one you will meet comes all the way from the pyramids in Egypt," she explains in faultless English. "A few years ago, I measured the energy of this leyline with a special dowsing rod, so I know it's open and activated up to a very high level." Perhaps the skepticism shows on my face, for she adds, "Other people have mapped the leylines around here, too. They all consider the Snaefellsjökull glacier to be the heart chakra of the world."

I'm spared from getting an explanation of this, as she goes off to fetch the map for me, along with a few photocopied sheets of paper. "You can either read a lot more about the location of the leyline or just feel your way through," she informs me with a smile as she hands them over. "Now, is there anything else you would like to ask before you go?"

"No, I don't think so." Pause. "Actually, yes, there is."

She raises her eyebrows.

"I kept getting the Helmet," I say. "I used your Viking cards three times this morning, and the Helmet kept coming up."

The smile fades from Gudrun's face. "You have already charged into battle, but you may not be completely ready for it," she says. "Be prepared."

I prepare for my walk by filling my rucksack with a rain jacket, energy bars, and water, which originated from a nearby spring and is referred to by Gudrun as "glacier champagne," from the jug on the table at breakfast. Then I head out of the guesthouse into the settlement of Hellnar, which consists of no more than twenty buildings, most of them perched at the top of a grassy slope plunging down to a small harbor. A quay and sea wall reach out from the beach, one side of which is formed of black sand with occasional larger lumps of lava. Huge mounds of seaweed, all black but for a few bright-pink strands like a girl singer's hair, have accumulated at the water's edge, while on the unsheltered side beyond the quay is a ridged cliff face that looks as if it's buckling, like one of Salvador Dalí's clocks. This part of the beach terminates in a cave, filled by the cries of the hundreds of gulls roosting inside.

The most notable feature of the landscape, however, is the backdrop to the whole settlement—Snaefellsjökull, a glacial cap of ice topping a dormant volcano. Plaits of lava trail down its lower slopes, and as I look at its twin rounded icy peaks with a dip in the middle, I can't help thinking it's shaped exactly like the female genitals. By contrast, the much lower mountain, Stapafell, to the right, is all male, with a sharply pointed summit and what look to be near-vertical slopes of brown scree.

Armed with my borrowed map, I head toward the cave full of gulls. The path to Arnarstapi starts just to the left of it and immediately dives into the lava field, with its waves of gray moss—covered rocks, reminding me of spilt porridge. There's obviously been no rain or dew here lately; since moss lacks roots, it absorbs water whenever any falls and is then transformed from this dormant gray state into a vivid green.

Soon the path moves farther inland and the bird cries become more distant. Several tributary paths lead to lookout points on the cliff tops, though—from one of these, I spot a solitary pair of black and white birds nesting in the midst of hundreds of clamoring gulls. Having been prepared enough to bring my bird-watching book with me, I'm able to identify them as Brünnich's guillemots.

I begin to wish I'd brought a botany book with me, too. There are so many more flowers growing among the chunks of lava than I expected, most of them hugging the ground and only one plucky plant, with clusters of yellow flowers, daring to venture a little higher.

I, meanwhile, have to venture a little lower. I've reached Draugalág, Ghost's Hollow, where the leyline is believed to cross the path on its way to the glacier. According to an old folktale, the ghost of a young woman, who brought misfortune to the people of Hellnar by killing their livestock, was exorcised at Draugalág and never caused trouble again. Gudrun's photocopied info tells me that in former times, as a result of this exorcism, the energy here was murky and negative, but it has since been cleansed, and there's no better place to meditate in the whole of Iceland.

Me and meditation have never gone too well together, but it seems like a good opportunity to pause for a while and reflect anew on what I know of Gudrid's extraordinary life. I scramble down some mossy rocks into the hollow but am not really sure exactly where I should position myself—is the whole hollow vibrating with cosmic energy, or just a certain part of it? I eventually plump for the flattest rock I can find, so I can at least sit in relative comfort while I consider Gudrid's many achievements.

As I know from my reading of Icelandic sagas, she grew up here in the west of Iceland in the late tenth century, moving between her foster home in Arnarstapi and her birth father's home nearby. As a young woman, she survived a perilous sea journey to Greenland and established a thriving farm there. Her thirst for adventure propelled her west again, this time to Vinland—believed to be present-day Newfoundland—where, along with her second husband and a small group of fellow Vikings, she traded with its indigenous inhabitants and built up a valuable cargo of wild grapes and timber. She also gave birth to the first European in North America, some five hundred years before the voyage of Columbus. After moving back to Iceland, she gave birth to another son and settled on a farm in the north-central region of the country. Upon the death of her husband, her days as a wife came to an end, but her days as a traveler certainly did not, as she embarked on a pilgrimage, by boat and on foot, to Rome. She ended her days as a nun back here in Iceland, a quiet finale to her deliciously unconventional life.

"Hi there!" A woman's voice slices through my thoughts. "Is there some kinda bird down there you're looking at?"

"No." I haul myself to my feet and shake out my stiff legs. "I was just taking a rest."

"Oh. I thought it might have been a bird. There are so many birds along this trail, it's unbelievable."

I clamber up out of the hollow and back onto the path. There are in fact two women, both in pink shell suits and bright white sneakers, and neither makes any move to start walking again.

"One thing I just gotta ask," says Shell Suit Number One. "Do you know if birds copulate through the body or through the beak?"

I'd love to be able to say, "Through the beak," but I am actually too flabbergasted to say anything.

"I've learned so much on this vacation—Iceland's the best country. And do you know, I haven't seen one dirty restroom!"

I'm beginning to wish it were possible to do another spot of exorcism down in the hollow. Instead, though, I have to settle for heading on toward Arnarstapi—and am mightily relieved when the Shell Suits start moving in the Hellnar direction.

I emerge from the lava field through a gate onto a grassy cliff with expansive sea views and arctic terns in constant motion, flying from cliff-top colony to sea, and back again with food. It's good to have grass, rather than sharp lumps of lava, under my feet again. Even though I'm wearing stout walking boots, my soles are feeling a little sore. For Gudrid, of course, the terrain would have been even more challenging, dressed as she was in thin leather shoes and with a long woolen skirt constantly snagging on the jags of lava.

After crossing a stream, I amble along toward a series of eccentric cliff formations, including a massive freestanding arch and a blowhole, with sea surging in the bottom and the stench of guano rising from the top. Striking though these are, it's the basalt pillars I find most fascinating, basalt being a volcanic rock that, after its molten origins, cools, contracts, and solidifies into either vertical or horizontal columns, depending on the way the lava is flowing. I try to search for an appropriate image for the horizontal columns. Cigars? Logs piled up in readiness for winter? Or how about those cylindrical chocolate-lined biscuits that are sometimes served with cappuccino?

The path ends in Arnarstapi's harbor, larger than Hellnar's, with lots of fishing boats moored and a quay heaped high with crates, ropes, nets, and buoys. From here, there are views of yet more cliffs and sea stacks, populated by yet more nesting birds. Fulmars, with their distinctive tubular beaks, nuzzle on the most minuscule of ledges, while in the distance, the arctic terns are a blizzard against the brown backdrop of Stapafell. Gudrid and her foster parents would certainly never have lacked for eggs and birds to eat here.

I linger in the harbor area for quite some time, enjoying the fact that the sun has found its way through the clouds, turning the sea from arctic gray to tropical turquoise. In the distance is another small settlement, Búdir, above which I can just about make out some waterfalls, glinting like silver snails' trails down the sides of the mountains. It's been suggested that Búdir was the departure point for Gudrid's storm-thrashed voyage to Greenland, and I imagine her now, huddled night after cold cramped night beneath one of the half-decks, short of both food and fresh water, her skin raw with sores from wearing perpetually wet clothing. Once again, I'm conscious of how easy I've got it in comparison, protected whenever I need to be in my three-layer, windproof, waterproof Gore-Tex.

I turn away from the harbor and join the only road through the settlement. Since there's no exact record of where Gudrid's foster home was located, I have to content myself with exploring the Arnarstapi of today. I discover that it's a small, though stretched-out, village, with single-story blue- or red-roofed dwellings and an extensive area for camping. There's a café, too, with a faded information board outside, on which there are details about the walking trail from Hellnar. It informs me that I've seen beach peas, marsh marigolds, and sea campions, while the plant with clusters of yellow flowers that rose above the rest was alpine lady's mantle.

From the café, I cut across the grass to Arnarstapi's most prominent landmark—a giant, man-shaped artwork, made from lots of flat stones piled on top of each other. Beard, prominent nose, and pointed hat have all been crafted using the same technique. According to a plaque resting against one of his mammoth shins, it's a representation of Bárdur Snaefellsás, a character from one of the Icelandic sagas and the beneficent spirit of the glacier. He's believed to act as a guardian not only of the west coast of Iceland and its ocean surrounds, but also of all the air traffic between Europe and North America.

Forget about the flight path of transatlantic aircraft; right now, it's the flight path of arctic terns that I'm more concerned about. Bárdur happens to be located slap-bang in the middle of their colony, and they're not happy that I've encroached on it, too. I'm aware of an angry squawk and the red flash of a beak as one of the birds swoops down, aiming for my head. No sooner have I recovered from the shock than it's turned and is on its way back again. I take shelter under the arch of Bárdur's legs, but as soon as I venture out, the Hitchcockian squawk/swoop/whoosh-of-air routine resumes. When five others get in on the act and a beak makes contact with my skull for the first time, I have to resort to holding my rucksack on top of my head as protection.

As I do so, I'm struck by something seriously spooky.

Be prepared. The Helmet.

A few hours later, with skull thankfully still intact and only my earlier skepticism about Gudrun's Viking cards rather dented, I'm striking out along a mud track toward the spot where Gudrid's birthplace is said to be located. The sun's appearance was short lived; the mountains to the east are now brooding black silhouettes, and a chill wind has started gusting. I'm feeling the cold, even though I'm walking at a brisk pace and the track is in a dip and fairly sheltered. A redshank lands on a fence post on its spaghetti-thin legs and manages, against all odds, not to be blown off. Tiny white flowers cower close to the ground, while tall pink ones on slender stems try to sway out of the way of the wind's bullying.

The track peters out into tussocky, hummocky grass, the sort where you can twist your ankle, even in sturdy walking boots, especially if you're keeping an eye out for ancient Viking ruins rather than overgrown ditches. To the soundtrack of dozens of bees busying themselves among the flowers, I scan the surrounding land and gradually begin to pick out a series of rectangular grassy ridges. Excitement surges through me as I realize that these must have been the lower parts of the walls of the farm where Gudrid was born. Having been fascinated by this Viking woman's life for the past five years, and having planned my pilgrimage in her footsteps for the past two, I'm now finally stumbling over the same uneven ground on which she was raised ten centuries ago.

After wandering round the ruins for a while and wondering how the walls could ever have been thick enough to give Gudrid sufficient shelter from this wind, I rejoin the path. I'm about to turn back toward Hellnar when I notice a ladder stile over a fence and a much more obvious gravel track on the other side. Curious, I decide to follow it, heading uphill to a plateau backed by the Snaefellsjökull glacier. There's a picnic table and a brightly colored information board, on which I expect to read facts about the flora and bird life in the area, like on the one at Arnarstapi. To my surprise and delight, though, the information it offers is all about Gudrid. As well as a summary of her life in both Icelandic and English, there's a map depicting all her different sea journeys, with a different color for each route. She's shown cradling a baby in Vinland, hand in hand with both husbands in Greenland, and being blessed by the Pope in Rome. Here on the Snaefellsnes Peninsula, however, she's alone and looking out to sea.

Alone, I look out to sea now too, and notice, as I turn, a small statue on top of a plinth of lava. This time, my surprise and delight reach the peak of the glacier, for I discover it to be a memorial statue to Gudrid by Ásmundur Sveinsson, Iceland's most significant twentieth-century sculptor. In spite of being so small—just a couple of feet high—this version of Gudrid comes across as dynamic and strong: She bestrides a Viking ship, one hand on the prow and the other curved over her head to grip the right hand of her naked baby. He's perched on her left shoulder, and his own raised left hand is the highest point of the sculpture. Though she wears a close-fitting gown that shows the outline of her breasts and the rest of her body, she's surprisingly unsexualized—her face is square with a wide nose, her arms solid. A few unfortunate splodges of bird shit adorn her torso too, courtesy, perhaps, of the arctic tern above us—a nonaggressive one that is merely struggling to assert itself over the wind.

As I shift my gaze from the statue and look west, to where yet more lava has pooled down from Snaefellsjökull, a man in orange Puma track pants and two women appear, via a path that can be accessed from the road around the peninsula. They are busy talking about where it is in Florida they buy their clothes, and they head straight for the statue without noticing the information board.

"How come it isn't life-size?" says the man. "It ought to be life-size."

"Why?" says one of the women. "She's, like, so ugly. Fat, too."

"Yeah." The second woman wrinkles her nose. "Who is she, anyway?"

I'm in bed back at the Hellnar guesthouse. Summer at this high latitude means twenty-four hours of daylight and out-of-sync body rhythms, but in contrast to last night, I'm relaxed and ready to sleep. After one day of my journey in Gudrid's footsteps, I feel that I'm learning to connect with the landscape that both formed and fortified her on quite a profound level. I'm glad to be traveling solo, I decide, unlike the various people I came across today on my walk.

I realize, too, that it's hard to believe a whole millennium separates me from Gudrid. As I drop off to sleep, I ponder leylines and cosmic energy and wonder if I've been too quick to dismiss them. Perhaps the time has come for me to "go Viking." After all, I may be alone on this journey, but I already feel that Gudrid is a powerful presence.

French Laundry

Alexia Brue

We were two college girls in search of foreign adventure with an income. In the summertime, every self-respecting town in the South of France throws itself a festival. Our hunch was that festival season equaled abundant jobs. Marisa, my freshman-year roommate, and I envisioned six weeks of making crepes and meeting fun-loving French people who would show us the sights and invite us into their homes for doses of home-cooked hospitality. *A Year in Provence* had only recently glamorized the region, so it hadn't been Mayled by coach tours and reduced to a cliché of laconic artisans and truffle hunts. This section of southern France still felt charmingly secluded, as if a local bon vivant could be waiting in any bistro to badger you, with that unique Gallic cocktail of affection and patronization, about the merits of his favorite côtes du rhône.

When we arrived in Avignon in the summer of 1992, it was an enticing mixture of raffish and refined. Grungy Kurt Cobain wannabes strummed guitars, surrounded by mangy dogs and women accessorized with melodious anklets and Sanskrit tattoos. This bohemian scene coexisted peacefully with fashionable European families—the kind who live in Paris but have homes in St.-Tropez or St.-Rémy—shuttling in between art galleries, concerts, plays, and expensive restaurants.

We found an apartment on our second day: a cramped but well-located studio in which the shower stall and kitchen sink were practically one—in fact, the kitchen faucet on a hose doubled as the showerhead. A single twin bed on a shaky wooden frame and a small desk next to the window were the only furniture. I wouldn't call it minimalism, because that would imply restraint, as if there were space to add other elements. We alternated nights sleeping on the bed and in a sleeping bag on the floor.

Given France's chronic job shortage, it seems fitting that our first experience in the French workforce was unemployment. We scanned storefronts for HELP WANTED signs (RECHERCHÉ VENDEUSE or RECHERCHÉ SERVEUSE), but saw none. Never mind, maybe the patisserie and café owners needed to meet us—well-scrubbed, relentlessly cheerful American girls with work permits, no less—to know they needed help. Our first realization was that our resumes were useless. Anyone hiring summer help doesn't care whether you know Excel, or that you're president of the college debating union. Our second, altogether more damning, realization was that our so-called "proficient French" was in actuality "insufficient French." The professor of our upper-level French class had, it turns out, been speaking misleadingly slowly. We were far from ready to face the French public. Forget taking crepe orders and ringing them up in French—it was time to look toward the back of the house.

We optimistically persevered in delivering our thirty-second elevator pitch to any business owner willing to listen. We'd take turns, cautious of overwhelming them with two unemployed Americans, and were usually met with a brusque, falsely apologetic *"Tant pis! Mais nous n'avons pas besoin d'autre."* The hotel owners, we noticed, seemed to deliver the least stinging *"nons,"* and that, frankly, was encouraging.

The daily rejection was affecting Marisa and me in different ways. While yes, the employment situation was more hostile than I had imagined, I remembered my grandfather's recipe for resilience: "If someone spits on you, pretend it's rain." Marisa, on the other hand, was taking each rejection personally. In all our dorm-room fantasies about the summer, the job search had just been a formality. In our minds it was a done deal—one of us would work in food service, the other in retail, which translated into free food and discount clothes. We guessed that by week three we'd be speaking only French to each other, and around that same time we would meet French boyfriends who would conveniently be best friends. We pitied our classmates who were doing the whole Eurail, "If it's Tuesday, it must be Belgium" thing. We were going to live local.

By day three of our job search, Marisa was barely able to pull it together to walk into a hotel and ask for a position. Once, she came out looking particularly weary. "What's wrong?" I asked.

"The manager recognized me. I applied there two days ago."

"At least you made an impression on him," I said. "Here, this next one is all you," I said as we walked from the enormous cobblestoned square that houses the Pope's Palace, through a narrow passageway that opened onto a quiet square anchored by an imposing facade. The block-long frontage of the building was pale yellow sandstone, the color of hay baking under the sun. On each side of the formal wooden doors was a glass case containing menus printed in elegant black cursive. A uniformed doorman opened the door, and a swish-looking couple sashayed out, leaving a fragrant trail of his-and-hers Hermès cologne. Of course, there was so much separating me from this chic couple—fifteen years, couture clothing, the ability to communicate in French—but I fell in love with what I imagined to be the world inside this hotel. La Mirande exuded a quiet, moneyed confidence that was overwhelmingly attractive, given my near franc-less existence. I wanted to work here, but I'd just transferred application rights to Marisa, who might as well have been wearing a KICK MOI sign.

"I'm not up for it, I'm really not," she said, as she played with one of the topiaries that marked both sides of the doorway. I couldn't tell whether this was an invitation to give her a pep talk and convince her to apply.

"Yeah, take a break, good idea. Get your head back in the game," I said. It was not my finest hour as a friend. The tall, uniformed doorman opened the door and smiled at me, as if I were a guest just milling outside. Inside, the floors were white, black, and gray marble mosaic arranged in a dizzying, Escher-like pattern. The vast first floor was scented with lilies. It was, without a doubt, the most luxurious, inviting hotel lobby I had ever seen.

I stepped up to the reception desk, modulating an expression of delicate beseechment and dignified poverty. In careful French, I explained that I had a work permit and was looking for a job. Did they need additional help during the festival season? The receptionist was tall and wore a crisp navy jacket and a scarf tied around her neck like a glamorous Air France flight attendant. I looked at her expectantly. When looking for a job, you must give the impression of expecting to hear a yes. My face felt red and shiny compared to her white, powdered complexion, and despite my efforts to appear confident, I feared she might ask the doorman to take me out with the trash. But instead, she gave me a tight smile and asked me to wait *pour un moment* while she picked up the phone and said something quickly, followed by two staccato *"ouis."* "Wait over there, please," she said, and pointed toward a few cushioned wicker chairs inside a grand two-story indoor patio.

It felt good to be alone, speaking for myself, reacting in the moment, and not worrying about someone else, and then I noticed that a man was walking toward me. Noticeably tall, he wore a tan linen suit and white shirt that hung off him almost scarecrowlike. Everything about his presence indicated restraint—this was not a man who gorged himself on food or who glad-handed people. He introduced himself as Martin Stein—he was German but a longtime resident of France—and invited me to sit with him and the head of housekeeping in one of the pillowed chairs. It was my first interview in a foreign language. I understood next to nothing and tried to follow the rhythm of the conversation, nodding at the appropriate intervals. One phrase was continually repeated: *"faire la lessive."* I was torn between not wanting to give away my lack of French and not wanting to sign up for something horrible like garbage collecting and sorting.

"Excusez-moi, qu'est-ce que c'est ça—faire la lessive? Je ne comprends pas," I said. Martin's enormous brown eyes fell on me. "It means doing the laundry," he said with a shy, slightly apologetic smile.

"Ah, oui, bien sûr, j'adore la lessive."

He gave me an amused smile and asked me if I could start the next day.

I met Marisa out on the street. "So?" she asked.

"I start tomorrow . . . doing the laundry."

"Was it beautiful in there?" she asked, trying to be happy for me.

"Yes, it looks like it was decorated by some libertine monks who won the lottery. The boss is really cute. I think we had a moment, but I don't think I'll see him much in the laundry room."

That was the last time I walked through the front door at La Mirande. I worked ten hours a day loading the industrial-size washing machines with sheets and towels, and then Et, my Laotian taskmistress, and I would feed all the sheets through the hot mangle and they'd emerge as crisp as new money. When I got home at 6 PM, Marisa was usually in our cubbyhole apartment, snoozing on the twin bed. I snapped out of my cheerful French world of gossiping chambermaids and Et's constant *tut-tut*ing, and back into an English world of dwindling traveler's checks and unemployment woes. I reminded myself—I was the lucky one. I was working. I was making money, however unpleasantly, however much I had to sweat for every *sou*. I was out in the world, speaking French all day. But each night it felt like I had a second job: cheering up Marisa.

We would wander out for drinks or dinner, up to the Palais des Papes, where we would sit at one of the outdoor cafés and watch chic couples and families with teenage children stream into the palace for the evening's play. I was now making enough money to afford to attend the cheaper festival shows, but Marisa was broke and I couldn't afford two tickets. We sipped our drinks slowly, golden floodlights illuminating the stone palace, both aware of the irony that in this fantasy setting we were bored. So much for speaking French together—we could barely keep a conversation going in English.

One night a British college student we'd met at a free concert invited us to an outdoor party with his crowd of fabulous-seeming French friends. Marisa's shyness when faced with ten cool, sexy twenty-two-year-olds speaking motormouth French was excruciating. I wanted to mingle with these people, and if they had no interest in suffering through my halting French, at least I'd try to soak up some of their linguistic magnificence. Several people asked me about working at La Mirande, what it was like beyond the glorious facade, and I tried to answer them but couldn't help but notice Marisa studying her cuticles. I felt responsible for her and stayed by her side, even when a cute guy named Jean-Claude wanted to read my palm. I realized that Marisa and I weren't as independent as I had thought. Although I had believed there was safety in numbers and imagined that a travel companion would propel me to be more daring and meet more people, I found that it was having the opposite effect. Traveling with someone requires hourly decisions and a compatibility that most marriages don't have. And our expectations for companionship were different: I wanted a dinner buddy to share the day's adventures with, and she wanted a sorority sister.

A week later I came home to find Marisa singing softly as she cleaned and packed. Our friend Jason from college was traveling through Avignon, and she had decided to join him on the road. Her parents had wired money. Was I all right with her leaving me on my own? she wondered. Was she being a terrible friend to abandon me?

"Go and make the best of your summer," I said. "I'll be fine. Really, it's okay."

When she and Jason left on the morning train to Marseille, I waved them off with a single, undiluted emotion: relief. That night when I got home from work, I looked around the apartment. Everything in it belonged to me. The mess was mine alone. I looked out the window, down onto the narrow, winding street three stories below. I lit a cigarette and poured myself a glass of lousy côtes du rhône and wondered what I'd do with my weekend. I was alone and I couldn't have been happier.

Part II

Marisa's departure coincided with Martin's asking if I were interested in a side project. *His own laundry?* I wondered drolly.

"Would you be willing to translate the history of the hotel from French into English?" he asked. I looked at him disbelievingly. He might as well have asked me to stand in for the head chef at La Mirande's Michelin-starred restaurant. "I'll make sure Et lets you off work early, and you can join me upstairs in my office and translate for an hour." Surely Martin could have found a more qualified person for this, or even done it himself. His English was in every way superior to my French. It was as if he knew that I needed a daily reminder that I was a college student and not a laundress.

At five o'clock, I would roll my last soggy sheet through the steaming mangle, Et looking bitter and annoyed that she could not get bitter and annoyed at me—after all, these were Martin's orders—and I would practically skip up the back stairs (after splashing cold water on my face) and into Martin's spare white office smelling of five-hundred-year-old stone and freshly cut lilies from the hotel's garden. I would sit at a small desk that looked directly out onto the Place de la Mirande and concentrate on translating the hotel's precisely written French history, studded with lots of arcane words and frequent use of the pluperfect.

In the fourteenth century, La Mirande was built as a cardinal's palace, the home of Pope Clement V's nephew during the seventy-year period when Avignon replaced Rome as the seat of the Holy See. La Mirande's history told of lavish banquets in honor of various popes with "castles of food, fountains of wine," and all the pageantry and excess associated with the ancient Roman decadence that early Christendom sought to curb. I worked slowly (it was only an eight-page document and I was in no rush to finish), pausing often to look over at Martin; his eyes would meet mine through his shaggy brown hair, and then we'd both shyly smile and return to our work.

Now that I no longer had an attention-starved friend to rush home to, I lingered in his office past six. "Let me just finish this paragraph," I'd say. "You're very diligent," Martin remarked softly.

On my third translation evening, Martin asked me, "Have you ever been to the opera?" I had been dragged to many operas; I'd even seen *Turandot* outdoors in Rome's Baths of Diocletian when I was twelve. But I sensed that Martin wanted to take me to my first opera, and I decided to let him play Henry Higgins. "Um, no, I've seen musicals but never operas."

"Would you like to come to an opera with me this weekend in Aix-en-Provence?" I'd been in Avignon for nearly four weeks. I'd had exactly four days off so far. My roommate had been depressed and disheartened. Overnight, everything had turned around. Sure, I still had the same sweaty job, but it had a patina of glamour and intrigue, given Martin's attentions.

That Saturday, Martin and I met at 10 AM and set off in his small silver Fiat for Aix-en-Provence, about an hour southeast of Avignon. We inched our way through the city streets and left the confines of the city ramparts for the first time since I'd arrived by train a month ago. Martin pointed out the narrow footbridge that inspired the children's song "Sur le Pont d'Avignon." I experienced the weird childhood sensation of being on an amusement park ride. Although driving in a car is one of the more quotidian experiences in familiar surroundings, when you're traveling, relying only on public transportation and your own two feet, there is something thrilling about watching a foreign world whiz by from the comfort of a car.

As we drove toward Aix, we exchanged all the autobiographical details that establish intimacy. Martin told me about medical school in Italy. "I left medical school to study architecture," he told me, "because an old building always has a better prognosis than an old person." We drove through the tunnels of plane trees, so distinctly French that you glance around for the old man on a bike with a baguette strapped across his back, and I imitated for Martin the Québécois French accent that I'd heard growing up in Vermont. There were long pauses in the conversation as we glimpsed fields yellow and purple with mustard seed and lavender. As we passed the signs for small villages—St.-Rémy, Ménerbes, Bonnieux—Martin described the restaurants of each to me.

In comparison with Avignon, Aix was a more elegant and sleepy city, perhaps owing to its historic role as a spa town. We visited two museums that sounded uniquely snooze-inspiring: the Tapestry Museum and the Museum of Old Aix. Left to my own attention span, I could have explored both museums in thirty minutes. I usually took a quick-step approach to museums, staying just long enough to soak up the general feeling. But we lingered in the seventeenth-century Bishop's Palace, Martin explaining how each tapestry illustrated a chapter of history. And we admired an entire series on the life of Don Quixote. At the Musée du Vieil Aix, I adjusted to Martin's pace and spent over an hour among the marionettes.

We ate an early dinner on rickety wooden chairs at an outdoor café. I tried to sip my glass of white burgundy as slowly as Martin and almost succeeded. But I couldn't possibly eat as slowly as he did. The monkfish cooked in anise-flavored butter and served with ratatouille was so perfectly cooked, seasoned, and salted that it begged to be devoured. It was hard to understand that you could be as passionate about food as Martin was and still eat as slowly as he did.

Walking over to the theater, the warm, still air smelled of hyacinth and lavender. Medieval arches led into the open-air Théâtre de l'Archevêché, and we found our seats and stared up at the stars, our arms brushing against each other. Martin had this way of blushing with his eyes; he blinked for an extra two beats whenever he felt embarrassed. Then Don Giovanni appeared and, over the course of two hours, proceeded to seduce every woman on stage.

We had several other innocent dates—lingering over dinners in Avignon and picking through flea markets in neighboring towns. On one excursion Martin bought a seventeenth-century copper bathtub to refinish for his apartment. We spoke only French, which gave our conversations a slow, romantic pace, with glances and hand gestures conveying more than words. Although I often wondered what a kiss might feel like, and, I imagine, so did he, it never happened. It was a sweet friendship of mutual admiration, uncomplicated by physical affection. When we said goodbye at the end of the summer, Martin gave me a long kiss on each cheek. It's funny—in retrospect, all the details I remember sound so intimate: the soapy smell of his skin, how he didn't wear strong-smelling cologne like the French men, how soft the hairs were on his arms, the length of his blinks. And yet I never even saw the inside of his apartment.

"Thank you for showing me Provence," I said the night before I left.

"Keep working on your French, and next summer you can work upstairs at the hotel."

Almost fifteen summers have passed since then. I have no idea where Marisa is or what she's been doing since graduation. Although I didn't take Martin up on his offer to go back the following summer, our paths have crisscrossed through the years. We have met in New York and Avignon and shared long blinks and furtive glances.

Unwelcome Hospitality

Katie Krueger

A pile of phone numbers is wedged between the pages of my journal, a visual testament to the *teranga,* or hospitality, of which the Senegalese are so fiercely proud.

Welcome a stranger into your life and share what you have, they say, and someday God will reward you. As a traveler, living in this land of hospitality is paradise; as a woman, it is exhausting.

I am unpacking in my new apartment in Dakar, having left my host family's house the day before. I sit down and flip through the pile, finding numbers for teenagers, men my father's age, married men, widowers, professors, street vendors, lawyers, waiters, bus passengers, beggars, bankers, and taxi drivers. They were men who approached me everywhere: on the street, in cyber cafés, at the corner boutique, at bus stops. A woman traveling unaccompanied in Senegal, I quickly learned, is a magnet for men wishing to accompany her. Our exchanges would begin in a friendly way, but in a matter of minutes I would find myself dodging personal questions: *Are you married? Do you have a Senegalese boyfriend? Would you like one? Why don't you marry me and take me to the United States?* Before long, my guard was up nearly all the time. It was difficult to believe that the invitations to dinner, the beach, day trips, or downtown tours were simply hospitable.

There is only one number that I actually want: Amse's. I pluck a folded slip of paper from the stack and open it to see his neatly printed name and number. At the memory of his cheerful face, I smile ruefully.

Amse. I met him in Marché Sandaga, my least favorite place in Senegal. There, in the heart of downtown Dakar, already-narrow streets are lined with fabric boutiques, electronic equipment stands, wandering fruit sellers, and vendors hovering over three square feet of carefully aligned merchandise. In front of each store, there is an exterior wall of West African men: the vendors and the touts. Walking past them as a *toubab,* or foreigner, a woman often feels like she is walking the gauntlet. You look straight ahead, avoid eye contact with all people, and try to make it safely to the other end while being bombarded by men who come up to you and assail you with personal questions meant to win your loyalty and, eventually, either your business or your hand in marriage.

Amse popped out from a fabric store and started off like all the hawkers do. *"Bonjour!* Welcome to Senegal. *Ça va? Nga def?"*

I had found that the best way to make a quick break from the mass of overly aggressive salesmen who volunteer themselves as marriage potential is to tell them that I am going to meet my husband, who works in the city. After lunch near his office, we will go to our friend's shop on the other end of the market. My imaginary afternoon lets the hawkers know that I have lived in Dakar too long to be tricked into a *toubab* price, and that my husband negates any relationship possibilities.

I gave this spiel to Amse and expected him to politely leave, but instead he burst out laughing. Because of my rusty French, I had actually said that I worked in the market, and that I was on my way to the shop of my husband, on the other end.

"I have heard a lot of stories before," he said, "but I have never had a *toubab* tell me that we share a job!" I was embarrassed and wanted to be angry, but his good looks got even better when he laughed. I could not help but smile, and then suddenly we were sharing a moment of genuine laughter. Before leaving that day, I visited his friend's fabric shop, and on my way out he accompanied me to the bus stop, where I happily stuffed his phone number into my pocket.

A month went by and I did not hear from Amse. I grew skeptical of ever developing a real friendship with any of the men I met in Dakar. They seemed to want one of two things: sex or money. *Amse was probably after the same thing,* I thought. *I was just too naive to see it.*

A week before I was to move into my apartment, I returned to Marché Sandaga. Although I dreaded having to put on my invisible armor just to buy dish towels and clothespins, I knew it was the only place for affordable one-stop shopping. I took a taxi to the Place de L'Indépendance and stopped at the ATM. I scolded myself for wearing a sundress with no pockets and forgetting my money belt. Plenty of nightmare tales of pickpockets and purse snatchers at the market normally had me distributing my money strategically—some in my money belt, bra, purse lining, and wallet—but today's outfit left me with no choice. All my money would be in my purse. Leaving the ATM, I walked quickly and braced myself for Marché Sandaga. Sure enough, nearly four blocks before I got there, I was spotted.

"*Bonjour!* Welcome to Senegal. *Ça va? Nga def?* My name is Pop." I ignored him, but he continued the one-sided conversation by asking me about my country, my life here in Senegal, and, of course, my marital status. First I tried to gently blow him off by giving him disinterested one-word answers, but that did not work. Then I asked him, in no uncertain terms, to leave me alone. He ignored this, too. His personal questions and offers continued and I became uncomfortable. Did he really expect me to tell him whether I had experienced *all* of Senegal's *teranga* yet, or accept his invitation to do so? Finally, I lost my patience. "Go away!" I snapped.

He changed from French to broken English, probably to make sure

I understood his insult draped in foreign policy analysis: "What? Why you no friend of mine? Why you come here making war? Why no peace? You hate Senegalese people. Americans love war."

Something in me changes when I travel alone. I have an endless reserve of courage to speak my mind and to protect myself. At home, I smile at people who cut in front of me in line to avoid conflict, but as I get further from my comfort zone, I get more and more courageous. An insult to me will not go unchallenged.

I took off my sunglasses and looked Pop straight in the eyes for the first time. "I don't hate Senegalese people, I just hate you, Pop. You have been following me for ten minutes, even though I have asked you to leave me alone. You have been asking me personal questions and making me disgusting offers. You stole all the patience I had, and then insulted me when it was gone. I am here because I love Senegal and its people, but one day I will leave because I hate men like you."

I stunned him long enough to get a good five feet in front of him before he caught up with me again. "Mademoiselle, I am so sorry. I did not mean to make you hate me. I just wanted to be your friend. Please, come to my house for tea. You could share lunch with my family and meet my mother. You will see that I am not a bad person."

I tuned out his apologies and continued my shopping, ignoring him completely. I walked up to a stand that sold most of the things I needed and started reading my list off to the vendor. Pop was still hovering near, standing in a group of men a few feet from me. As I bargained for a decent price, he piped in a few times to tell the vendor to be nice to me, because I was his "friend."

The vendor and I finally agreed on a price, and I opened my purse cautiously to get my wallet. I could not find it.

Panic set in. I checked all the purse pockets. Empty.

I took everything out of my bag and shook it. I patted myself down. Nothing.

By now the vendor and the men standing nearby realized what had happened and offered their advice.

"Recheck your bag. Empty your pockets."

"Look around on the ground. Maybe it fell out as you were taking things out."

"Where have you been today? Where did you come from?"

"Was there anyone who followed you? Someone who would not leave you alone?"

I looked at Pop. Sure, he had bothered me to the point of losing my cool, but I could not remember his getting close enough to reach into my purse or pockets.

"Mademoiselle," the man repeated, "did anyone follow you today?"

Sheepishly, I hesitated. Stealing is so socially unacceptable in Senegal that thieves who are caught are usually severely beaten by the public, sometimes to death. But it was strange how Pop had followed me after I insulted him. Maybe the rejection had made him bitter enough to seek revenge and take what he still could from me. The one thing I hate more than blaming an innocent person is being taken advantage of.

"The only person who I have talked to today is ... him," I said, pointing to Pop. My eyes met his for the second time that day, and instantly I knew I was mistaken. He had taken nothing from me but time and patience.

97

My purse slipped off my shoulder, my confidence slumped. I glared down hard, burning an invisible hole in the concrete. Was I really going to have to apologize to this man? He may not have been the vengeful pickpocket I imagined, but he was still an obnoxious merchant with questionable sales techniques. Blaming him was a mistake, though. As I looked around the group of a dozen strange men, I realized he was the closest thing I had to a friend.

"Katie," someone cried from the other side of the street. "Katie! Hello! It has been a long time. Do you remember me?"

Before anyone could react to my accusation, we all turned to look and saw Amse coming across the street toward us.

"Katie. How have you been? What are you doing here?" He smiled brightly at me and I felt a flood of relief about seeing his familiar face. He gestured to Pop. "Have you met my brother, Pop?"

His brother! I sputtered for a moment in horrified embarrassment, then began talking quickly to fill the air, hoping the words of my explanation would push aside those of my accusation. I explained to Amse that I had lost my wallet. How everyone, including Pop, was helping me to find it . . . My words trailed off.

"Why don't you let Pop and me retrace your steps with you? Three sets of eyes will be better than one," Amse said cheerfully. He looked at Pop, who smiled at me, nodding.

We walked silently. Pop never gave any hints about the harsh words we had exchanged. Instead he kept his eyes on the street, scanning for my wallet. After an hour of walking, we arrived at the ATM, the starting point of my day. I leaned against the wall to rest, defeated.

"Hey, *toubab*," called out a man. "I've been waiting for you." He strolled over and handed me my wallet. I opened it up. It still had all of my credit cards and cash in it. "You dropped it as you rushed out of the ATM booth this morning, and by the time I picked it up, you had already walked out of sight."

Amse and Pop spent the rest of the afternoon with me, helping me find and bargain for all the things I needed and hailing a cab for me when I was ready to go. It felt good to be able to trust strangers again. As they helped me put my purchases into the cab, I thanked them profusely. Before I stepped in, I turned and faced Pop, searching for the right words. Pop waved his hands, silencing me. They were just sharing with me Senegal's *teranga,* he explained.

"*Teranga* is considered a long-term investment. If you welcome a person into your life, God will see to it that someone shows you the same welcome sometime in the future."

Amse elaborated: "It will be a reward for you or your family. Traditionally, a Senegalese mother welcomes guests into her house so that her children will be well received by others on their journeys."

I am on my way to my old house, keeping my promise to my host mother that I would visit as often as possible. As I settle back into the taxi, the driver turns to me and begins a familiar dialogue. "Where are you from?" he asks.

"The United States."

"Are you married?"

"No."

"Do you have a Senegalese boyfriend?"

Central American Dreams

Jennifer Bingham Hull

By the time I boarded the flight, I'd lost faith in everything except the power of dreams. I had a vision of living and reporting in Central America and was flying to Guatemala to attend language school. I'd traveled alone in the developing world before, yet suddenly the Spanish being spoken on the plane all around me sounded alien and intimidating. I felt conspicuous and unsure, the man in Manhattan with the marriage proposal and prospects still vivid. Surely it would have been easier to go his way, follow his dream.

It's one thing to have an epiphany, another to live it. When the sages say, "Jump and the bridge will appear," they don't mention the other bridges burned or that moment in midair. As we approached Guatemala City, I checked for my passport again, clutching my Spanish-English dictionary like a bible. In that space between the familiar and the foreign, you feel like your spirit could blow away with the first wind.

I was relieved when Guatemala City's lights broke the darkness, but struck by how dim they seemed.

From the airport I took a taxi to Antigua, the town in Guatemala's central mountains where the language school was located. Nestled amidst volcanoes and full of old, ornate buildings from its years as Spain's colonial seat, Antigua was beautiful. In the following days, I walked for hours, taking in the warm sun and bright colors. At night I felt it most—that strange sensation of entering a dream. One evening a Guatemalan girl greeted me. "I know you! You've been here before!"

"No, I haven't," I insisted, unable to convince her.

Drilling verbs all day was boring. I cut my classes down to mornings and spent the rest of my time exploring the city. Late each afternoon, I studied Spanish in the park. One day I noticed a tall Latino fellow there, arms crossed, gazing at the fountain.

A woman traveling alone learns to read men's faces like maps. A sharp edge at the mouth, an indirect gaze, a hard chin—all put me off like hazard signs. From previous journeys, I'd learned to seek out men with more open features, the way you learn, as a woman, to cross the dark street and walk under the lamppost. This man's expression was direct, his coffee-colored eyes clear. Eager to speak Spanish, I said, *"Hola."*

"Hola," he responded, eyes widening.

With the help of my dictionary, I discerned the outlines of David's story. After five years in Nicaragua's Sandinista army, he had deserted, fleeing his country in the last days of the American-sponsored Contra War. He had $20 and planned to enter the United States via an underground evangelical railroad. A relative was to wire him money to pay a contact. However, so far neither the cash nor the contact had arrived. If they didn't materialize, David planned to buy a knife and enter the United States illegally. *"Todo para todo,"* he explained. "You have to risk everything for everything."

I explained to David that I had a background in journalism and planned to report on Central America, selling stories to U.S. newspapers, once I got more Spanish under my belt. However, I spared him Joseph Campbell's line about "following your bliss."

Later, over dinner, all the dry verb tenses I'd studied sprang to life as David described his life. With thick black hair and a wide smile, the Nicaraguan was boyishly attractive and, at twenty-five, was six years younger than I. I didn't understand much of what he said. However, I connected better with him in broken Spanish than I had in perfect English with my man from New York. The lure of the foreign man is simple: He's so different. And for a *gringa* fleeing coldness, David provided an alluring warmth.

A few days after meeting David, an attractive American man invited me on a motorcycle ride in the mountains. The ride was thrilling, but I burned my leg on the motor. Within days the wound became infected. Relying on his first-aid training as a soldier, David cleaned the oozing pus from the burn and dressed it with one of my Kotex pads. The American waved as I limped around town. The Nicaraguan checked my injury daily for signs of infection. "He should have helped you with this," scowled David.

The former soldier was becoming hard to resist. When he wrapped his arms around me as we sat in the moonlight amidst Antigua's colonial ruins, I didn't try to. That night, David stayed in my room. A few days later, I quit language school and we moved into a $5-a-night pension room with rose-colored walls. David typed long, romantic poems into my laptop. "Look," he'd exclaim. "It just poured out of me!" Submerged in Spanish, I felt like a swimmer who had ventured from the pool's edge to its depths. Immersion is exhausting. Yet with each language, you do gain another soul. The soft, round syllables of Spanish opened my throat and something else that English, with its hard consonants, did not.

David spent his last few dollars not on a knife, but on roses for me. After that, I paid. This was okay. My Spanish lessons were now free and Guatemala was cheap, making the money I'd saved for the trip go far. But as compensation, David insisted on washing my socks. Soon he was cleaning our room and clipping newspapers for article ideas. We rented a motorcycle, and he drove me to interviews in Guatemala City. When the bike broke down, he took the vehicle apart, reassembled it, and drove us back to Antigua—all in the driving rain. Water pelting my face, I thought of the words of my mother, who'd just filed for divorce: "All a woman really needs is a handyman." And, I thought, in Central America, a gal could use a mechanic, too.

Weeks passed. I studied Spanish, visited Guatemala's tourist sites, and proposed a piece on the local political situation to U.S. newspapers. They weren't interested. In 1989, the big news in Central America was in Nicaragua and El Salvador, not Guatemala. To secure regular work, I'd need to move on. Meanwhile, neither the money nor the evangelist that David awaited arrived. "My dream is dead," my Nicaraguan lover noted gloomily one day.

My heart went out to David. However, I also sensed an opportunity. In Antigua, it had occurred to me that I might travel in the style of a man, rather than in that of a woman. Male correspondents never traveled alone. Bright secretaries filed their stories; wives cooked them hot meals. The bachelors had local girlfriends who translated, or bilingual sweethearts who flew in to take notes. "Men have a way of making themselves comfortable," a female correspondent once told me. Like other women reporting abroad, she traveled alone. My New York man's response to my Central American dreams still rang in my ear: "Sorry, honey, there's nothing for me to do there."

Yet if a man can get support while traveling, why shouldn't a woman? Clearly the buddy system has its benefits, especially in a place where nothing works and people are armed. Watching David repair the motorcycle had been a revelation. He could fix anything, had eyes in the back of his head, and maneuvered slowly around the potholes. Having experienced a few harrowing drives in developing countries, the last quality impressed me most. When I bought a jeep in Guatemala City, I asked David to be my driver.

"*Tus pasos son mis pasos,*" he wrote in my journal. "*Donde tu vayas, yo iré.*"

"Your steps are my steps. Where you go, I go."

My steps were less certain than David realized. Sitting on our pension roof, pondering my next move, I considered how far I'd traveled—and still had to go. I'd wanted to be a foreign correspondent ever since reporting in the Middle East in graduate school. The clip of foreign accents, the exotic scents, the exhilaration of traveling independently—the experience had captivated me. I'd vowed to do it again.

But since then I'd reported in the United States, most recently for *Time* magazine in New York. Working long hours on deadline in an office wearing nylons and pumps, I'd burned out so badly that I'd taken a medical leave. At the time, I hadn't completely understood why I'd gotten so ill and depressed. Now, like the shimmering volcanoes thrusting against Guatemala's sky, my upheaval stood in relief, making perfect sense. Wrong man, wrong job, wrong city—ignore your dreams, and life lines up falsely until an inner force finally rises in revolt. To resurrect my vision, I'd had to leave everything behind.

At last, my direction felt right. However, fear is insidious, making you balk at any situation even vaguely resembling a past threat. After New York, the thought of reentering journalism and writing on deadline terrified me. Like an actor who has developed stage fright, I dreaded performing—even though the scenery had completely changed.

To bolster myself, I pulled out index cards I'd inscribed with inspiring quotes. On the pension roof, watching the puffs of smoke rise from Antigua's Volcán de Fuego, I fingered each card like a talisman. "Whatever you can do, or dream you can, begin it! For boldness has genius, power, and magic in it," read one. I didn't feel bold. But another said, "Act as if." My Spanish had improved. I had wheels and a driver. The next step was to find reporting opportunities elsewhere in the region. With David accompanying me, I decided to investigate San Salvador.

El Salvador was then in the midst of a bloody civil war, and the atmosphere was understandably tense. I loved to walk at night in Central America, free from the sun's harsh glare—not an easy thing to do as a woman. Yet with David, I could walk for hours after dark through San Salvador—past the soldiers guarding barbed wire–laced military posts, past the bodyguards posted outside posh restaurants.

One night while we were walking, a man emerged from the shadows, and David quickly pulled me into a restaurant. "He was reaching for a gun," he said. After that, I examined men's hip pockets carefully.

El Salvador was fascinating but didn't suit me. And though David's street smarts proved valuable, on the road, the macho Latino and independent gringa clashed daily. "Nicaraguan women make better slaves," David huffed one day after I returned from an interview in San Salvador. "*Caramba,* you're both a man and a woman," he asserted another time. "Yes, sir," he answered when I asked him to change some money.

It was only after I gave him my wallet to pay a restaurant bill and he smiled that I understood. Though he wasn't really paying, it looked like he was, and to him appearances were critical. My handling the bill before had made David feel like a kept man.

A male traveler in the developing world can act as he pleases; men are expected to call the shots. A female visitor must negotiate the male ego. To remain allies, David and I needed to restructure our relationship. And so when we returned to Guatemala, I offered him a real job. Instead of footing the bill as we went along, I proposed paying David a salary to drive and assist me. He would move into his own room. We'd be partners, not lovers. He'd pay—with my money—at restaurants. David typed up a contract and we signed it, both relieved to be on firmer, if less rosy, footing.

It was the first job he'd ever had that didn't require carrying a gun.

Three weeks later, Violeta Barrios de Chamorro won Nicaragua's elections, ousting the Sandinistas and making it safe for David to return home. David was eager to see his family and show me Nicaragua. I wanted to get some leads on work from journalists there and investigate the country's political changes. After two long days on mountain roads, we arrived at his house in Managua.

My heart sank as we approached a dilapidated, gray, cinder-block structure. From the humble home, I could tell that the family was struggling to make ends meet. David's mother, Candida, greeted me warmly and led me to a room she'd prepared for my visit. A tattered cloth rose stood in a vase on the bureau. Candida usually slept in the room. To give me privacy, she'd moved into another shared by David's sister, brother-in-law, half brother, and three nieces. I'd planned on finding a pension but held my tongue and agreed to stay for fear of insulting her. I did refuse to eat the iguana, however, explaining that the Guatemalans' food had left my stomach sensitive, a lie that delighted the Nicaraguans.

David's house provided an education and an endurance test. My bed sagged, so I moved the mattress to the floor and got a little sleep, but not much. At 5 AM I awoke to babies screaming, diesel trucks roaring, and the Sandinista radio station blaring, *"Viva la revolución!"* At night, relatives explained how war had made their lives more difficult. Candida was struggling to live on $20 a month as a nurse. David's twenty-three-year-old sister, Elizabeth, who lived in the house with her husband and three girls, shuffled about in a nightgown stained with baby spit. Each night she injected herself with a vitamin concoction for her anemia. "A million times better to have your career, without children, than to have this," she said.

Traveling tests a woman's limits. When a mouse scampered across my face one night, I finally moved into a pension. With just a bed, a fan, and a single bulb suspended from the ceiling, it was modest. But it felt good to have a break from David and his family. My room opened directly onto the outdoors. The air coming through the door's wood slats was humid but soft. Stretching out in my underwear, I opened a book.

Then the door rattled, and I jumped up to see a man running away. How long had he been watching me through the door's narrow slats? Would he return? The room had no windows. Looking out through the slats, all I could see was darkness. It took me an hour to leave the room to talk to the pension owner, longer to fall asleep after he shrugged off my concern. No door has ever seemed so wobbly or thin. That night I vomited, prayed for deliverance, and slept with a can of Mace by my bed.

The next day, I met Carmen.

From Seville, Spain, Carmen spoke perfect English and rented rooms to journalists in an ample house in Managua. A spirited, voluptuous woman in her mid-thirties with long dark hair pulled high in a ponytail, eyes framed by black liner, and heavy, arching eyebrows, Carmen seemed connected to some powerful source of inspiration. Mornings she crooned to her green Chocoyero parrots. Afternoons she pumped iron. Evenings she charmed journalists with fiery displays of flamenco dancing, laughing in the darkness when the lights went out.

Carmen was so happy that I was shocked to hear her story. Just three years earlier, the journalist husband she'd accompanied to Nicaragua had abandoned her for another woman. Left with only a rusted-out car, Carmen had been devastated. "I was afraid that I wouldn't be able to survive," she explained. "But I stayed and confronted my fears, and now I'm a different person."

Carmen's confidence served us all. In the following weeks, David showed me around Nicaragua. I began doing interviews to sort out its explosive political situation, banking material for stories I hoped to sell. Then, in the spring, David and I accompanied Carmen and a German TV crew to northern Nicaragua. We were entering a Contra camp when a rebel soldier approached us, fingering his revolver. Angrily shouting war slogans, the man proclaimed himself the "advisor for democracy." The atmosphere was tense when Carmen, who was translating for the TV crew, walked up to the fellow and squeezed his arm.

"You exercise a lot, don't you?" she remarked.

"What?" he replied, blinking hard.

"How many hours a day?" she asked, squeezing his skinny arm again.

The question was absurd. Nervously, we awaited his response.

The rebel stood silent, then suddenly straightened up. "Three or four," he declared, releasing his revolver.

"And I bet you don't miss a day!" Carmen cried, defusing the situation with a brilliant bit of flattery.

We slept in the Contra camp that night, guests of the advisor for democracy.

Back in Managua a few days later, a departing correspondent gave me the contact information for *The Christian Science Monitor*'s editor and recommended to the paper that I replace him as their Nicaragua contributor. Another reporter who was leaving provided additional newspaper leads. Professional contacts finally secured, I now needed to commit to regularly covering one country and being a journalist whom editors could rely on for Nicaragua's news. I was in a good position to report from the troubled nation. After some initial struggle, I was finally making out the Nicaraguan accent. Managua lacked street signs. But being a native, David negotiated the city like the back of his hand. And the foreign journalists I'd met felt like old friends already.

Yet even amidst the magenta bougainvillea, I could not forget those cold Northern details: the stuffy air in that Manhattan office building, the antibiotics sitting by my keyboard, the ringing in my ear from phone interviews with distant people from different time zones whom I'd never meet. And while my view had changed, I could still see them: the men in the tower across the street, like bees in a hive in their dark suits and colored ties; the heavily harnessed carriage horses in Central Park blinkered to view only the narrow path ahead. You can travel very far and not lose a trace of the memories of fear and loathing.

I got press credentials. Carmen flicked her castanets and whispered, "Only you can give your power away." David hunted for gas one day, cornflakes another. Violeta Chamorro assumed office under a baking April sun. The rains came, carrying away the dust but none of the losers' bitterness. Then, on a hot July day, the Sandinistas called a strike.

A spark on a tinderbox, the protest quickly grew violent. Across Managua, leftist workers barricaded streets. Outside ministries, they pelted government supporters with rocks as the police fired back with tear gas. The Sandinistas shut down the ministries and the airport. Flexing further, they closed the borders, cut off international phone service, and turned off the lights.

People started shooting. I filed my first story for the *Monitor.* David negotiated barricades and burning tires to deliver a plate of rice, beans, and fried plantains. I did an interview with National Public Radio. Men fired machine guns outside my door all night. The cold Northern fear faded amidst the hot Latin tempers. The ground was shifting, but at least I could feel it under my feet. "You're crazy," David said, dropping me off at the right-wing radio station where fighting had broken out. "No, I'm not," I countered, feeling the confidence of a woman who is finally where she is supposed to be.

Amid the violence, I measured my steps carefully, retreating from the hail of stones, fleeing the barricade at the sound of gunfire. On the

111

street outside the radio station, though, I got too close to the action. Steps from me, men masked with bandannas crouched, taking aim at passing vehicles. The only other journalists there were war photographers; it was time to leave. Yet every exit was blocked. "Quick, go that way," said one of the photographers, spotting an opening.

Back in the jeep, I agreed with David. "The radio station is too dangerous. Let's get out of here."

Eager to get home to his family by dark, David dropped me at Carmen's. I filed my story, then went to visit my friend Mark, a *New York Times* reporter. Mark invited me to check out the radio station with him.

I knew how dangerous the area was. I'd already filed my story and didn't need to go back. But I didn't think about that. For once, I didn't think at all. Mark was far more experienced as a foreign correspondent than I. His driver, Guillermo, had covered the Contra War, as had Raul, the photographer who had come along. His office manager, Warner, was irritable, but I was delighted to accompany the men from the *Times*. And Mark was such a gentleman, giving me the front seat as he sat behind with Raul and Warner.

"I don't like this," Warner grumbled as we drove off. "They shot at a car there last night. I'm too young to die. I've never even seen my grandchildren."

"That reminds me of an old country song," laughed Mark. "I'm too old to die young . . ."

BOOM! The blast shook my skull as bullets smashed the front windshield and whizzed by my right side. *BOOM!* I dropped to the floor, trying desperately to move away from the stick shift so Guillermo could reverse the jeep.

"Move the car!" shouted Mark.

"I'm trying!" Guillermo shouted back, a sitting duck at the wheel.

"Oh my god," I muttered, crouching under the glove compartment, my shoulder suddenly burning.

Speeding into reverse, we encountered another barricade with more masked men. We were trapped.

"Get the car onto a lit street!" Mark shouted.

Lurching forward, then backward, Guillermo found an opening, and we sped around the barricade. Screeching down Managua's back streets, we finally emerged into the light.

"We're out of danger now," the driver sighed, pulling up to the Intercontinental Hotel.

Getting out, we surveyed the jeep. The windshield on the passenger side was smashed. Bullets had nicked my shoulder, grazed Mark's wrist, and whizzed through the back windshield. They'd apparently been fired from an AK-47 machine gun wielded by right-wing zealots who'd mistaken us for Sandinistas. Mark looked at me, amazed. Later, he said he'd imagined bringing my body back to the States.

The men gathered around the jeep. I stumbled toward a large hibiscus bush.

"Who was in the front passenger seat?" a journalist passing by asked.

"She was," said Warner, pointing to me.

"You're very lucky," said the fellow, shaking his head.

Nodding, I picked a pink hibiscus bloom and gave it to Raul. Being a photographer, I knew he'd appreciate its color too.

The *Monitor's* foreign editor wanted another story. I put him off, lay on my bed, and watched the light stream through the windows, amazed that I was alive and able to appreciate its luminous rays. David arrived and shook his head. "You could have been killed," he scolded.

Another editor called. I put him off too and took a shower, marveling at my previous concerns about deadlines and editors. Carmen was away, visiting Spain. In the garden, I whispered to her birds, hearing their bright song as if for the first time. The *Monitor* editor called again, desperate. Nicaragua was front-page news. "Well, okay," I said, examining the veins of green shooting through the palm leaves outside my window. *But don't expect me to care about it,* I thought, *as much as I care about smoothing lotion on my skin after a shower.*

It was easy after that: I no longer cared about pleasing editors. Proving myself and letting others determine my fate now seemed absurd. I continued to report on Nicaragua for two years. However, my stories served mainly as a vehicle for experience. Other matters struck me as more important than bylines—things like hearing roosters crow at dawn and smelling tortillas cooking on the corner.

Random acts of violence allow you to draw your own lessons. From the shooting, I determined that locals who've lost friends to war are better guides than those who report on casualties, that intuition suspended is power given away, and that the ground can shift under your feet but you can change too, leaving coldness for warmth and past fears for present appreciation. Digging bits of shrapnel from my right shoulder, I realized that writing is a gift, not a performance.

Thank god the masked man missed—and that he blew the timid woman with the First World fears away.

A year later, Mark left Nicaragua. I bought his horse. The boarding cost was so low that I couldn't refuse. As a girl, I'd taken riding lessons and dreamed of having a horse one day.

"What's the horse's name?" I asked the stable boy.

"*No Alineado,*" he replied. Nonaligned—not a name a Nicaraguan would give his steed.

"What's his original name?" I asked.

"*Candil,*" he said. "It means oil lamp."

"We'll call him Candil," I decided, thinking of how a small, flickering flame can illuminate a whole room.

Candil was a spirited stud and a quarter horse and—I quickly sensed—far too fast for me. Just trotting, I felt his untapped power. I'm a good rider, but no rodeo queen. I didn't dare admit it to the men around me, but I was afraid of my own steed.

Studs are not suited for "ladies," a male authority wrote.

"You're crazy," David remarked. "But don't worry. If Candil dies, we can eat him. Horse meat is good."

"What if you fall off and have to be hospitalized there?" cried my father over the phone.

What if, indeed.

Every few days I rode Candil, taking it slowly, unsure both of the horse and my surroundings. Farmers worked the fields near the stable, but there wasn't another foreigner in sight, much less a gringa in a white riding helmet. The men in the fields watched silently

115

as we rode by. Finally, after a few outings, I waved. Smiling, they waved back.

I rode near the stable for a while, then ventured farther into a village. One day, I discovered a valley and trotted Candil by its riverbeds. Back in the paddock, the stable boy scoffed, "This horse needs to be run."

"He will be," I said.

We cantered in the valley on the next outing, passing children on our return. "Gringo! Gringo!" they shouted.

Gringo? Did they think the horse was American? *"Este caballo no es de los Estados Unidos. Este caballo es Nicaragüense!"* I shouted back, making Candil's Nicaraguan origin clear.

Delighted, the children began chanting, *"Este caballo es Nicaragüense! Este caballo es Nicaragüense!"* Then the field workers joined in, and the refrain rang across the hills.

I felt at home in the neighborhood after that, though no less conspicuous.

The day arrived, warm but clear. Riding down to the valley, I hailed the field workers, then gripped the saddle as we approached the verdant, open expanse. "Okay, Candil. This is it. We can do it."

Candil trotted. I nudged him with my heel. He cantered. I clicked him on, and he broke into a gallop. Then, ever so slightly, I loosened the reins.

Flicking his head back, the stallion leapt forward. The wind whipped my face as we raced across the valley, leaving a trail of dust behind.

Half Dome in a Day

Amy C. Balfour

If you read enough chick lit, you start to think any crazy adventure is doable. As long as you have Mr. Darcy, the right purse, and a bit of goofy charm, you can scale any mountain, avoid obesity, and learn a self-affirming life lesson at the end of it all. Hurrah!

But where's Mr. Darcy now that I need him? He's not waiting beside the steel cables of Half Dome, that's for bloody sure. My purse is in the car, and I am all out of goofy charm. In front of me, two thick cables rip straight up the back of Half Dome, bordering the trail that'll lead me to the top of the most famous landmark in Yosemite. The cables hang a few feet above the rock, threading their way through parallel steel posts hammered into the granite. These posts tower above me, jutting from the Dome like human-size acupuncture needles. Thin wooden boards, three inches thick at the most, will be serving as rungs on this makeshift "ladder."

The final 650-foot climb to the top of Half Dome is the most notorious section of an already notorious trail. After hiking eight miles from Happy Isles in Yosemite Valley, this is all that's left. But I'm tired, I'm on the verge of chickening out, and if I were wearing red Jimmy Choos, I'd click my heels three times, hug the scarecrow, and think of the apple martini I could be sipping back in Los Angeles. But I'm in my boots, I'm sweaty, I've just climbed twenty-four switchbacks, and if I plan to scratch Half Dome from my Lifetime To-Do List, the time has come. Today.

The issue? I'm hiking alone. Solo. Table for one. "Alllll byyyy myyy-self," as the sad song goes. I'm between boyfriends, and my friends won't commit—one too many "Um ... er ... maybe later"s from people claiming to love the outdoors. A solo hike wasn't my first choice, but if I didn't start crossing items off the list, I'd be facing bungee jumping in Queenstown or rafting the Bio Bio at age eighty-five. It was time to pick some new role models. No Bridgets. No Bergdorf Blondes. Real women of the road and the sky and the trail. Did Amelia Earhart refuse to fly the Atlantic because she was solo? Did Karen Blixen leave her farm at the foot of the Ngong Hills? Did Christiane Amanpour turn around at the border of Afghanistan? Was I going to faint at the sight of two steel cables? Well, maybe. But not before getting a look-see. I'd scope it like one bad bitch of the trail.

So how does one bad bitch of the trail prepare? She reads every guidebook and website she can. She learns, for example, that the final slope up the dome is forty-five degrees. She can handle forty-five degrees. She'll start early, before 7 AM, to avoid afternoon storms. What else? Pack water. Check. Wear grippy shoes. Check. Notify friends of her adventure. Che—

"Dude, whatever!! I'm not gonna be responsible for telling someone to go pick up your carcass from the bottom of Half Dome!" my friend Amy IMed upon hearing my plan. "Whatever!!" I bet Christiane Amanpour doesn't have to put up with such disrespect. But I digress.

I approach the cables on this warm July Fourth weekend, scrutinizing my route to the top and wondering how the park literature could be so wrong. I tend to believe what I read, and on page sixty-six of the *Official Guide to Yosemite*, a well-organized chart includes the "trail" to the top of Half Dome. But isn't a trail something you walk "on"? Or backpack "over"? Not something requiring crampons, clips, and a living will. But who knows. Maybe "steel-pegged path of horror" wouldn't fit the space provided.

I look to my right. A large pile of climbing gloves rests beside the cables. Left by previous hikers, they are free for the borrowing and much recommended for getting a grip on the cables. I reach down, grab a pair of mittens. One red, the other yellow. Small rubber pads dot the palms and fingers, improving the grip. I slip them on, clench my fist. They're a little long. I am a bitch in big mittens. I turn, grab a steel cable in each hand.

The steel posts are hammered into the rock about six feet apart, too far apart to hold on to while stepping from rung to rung like I would on a normal ladder. I stare at the wall of granite in front of me. Just hold tight and pull yourself up. I throw my arms forward, gripping the cables tight. Like a puppy on a waxed linoleum floor, I scramble madly until my feet are directly in line under my shoulders. Whoa! John Muir's ass, this slope is forty-five degrees! Not only am I battling gravity and weak arms, but apparently I'm relying on inaccurate trail guides. Forty-five degrees?! Lynn Hill wouldn't climb this thing unassisted. This slope is at least eighty degrees if it's an inch. So now what? Do I hurl my hands forward and reach for the cables, hoping that in the split second my hands are free I don't slip? Or should I shuffle my feet ahead, then pull my body forward? I look up. The next set of posts is close. I inhale, hurl my right leg forward and catch it on the right post. The Fat Ankle has landed. I curl my leg around the post and heave my body into a standing position. If a crab and a tree sloth had a one-night stand, I could be their lovechild. The lovechild takes a breath. Looks down.

Okay, six feet. Not so far. But still.

The posts continue far up the dome, disappearing into the horizon like telephone poles on a vertical plain. I turn my gaze back to the rock in front of me. I throw my arms forward, pulling and scrambling. This is as bad as the flexed-arm-hang humiliation of seventh grade. But now I'm clinging to the side of an exposed rock. But now I'm wearing someone else's mittens. But now I'm in my thirties and wondering what I'm doing with my life and what would drive me to climb alone.

I hurl my leg up and around the next post, pull myself upright. I continue this routine until the hiker above me, in his shimmering sea-green basketball shorts, comes to a complete stop. I stop too, my feet balancing on a post as I take in the dizzying view of the valley far, far below. It appears I've driven all the way from Los Angeles just to get stuck in a traffic jam on the side of a 4,737-foot rock. Below me is a three-hundred-foot drop onto a granite ledge. If I fall, my plunge will be interrupted only by the screams of the hikers climbing below me as I knock them off the dome into thin air—a terrifying free fall of human dominos. If we bounce upon impact, we'll fall another three thousand feet before landing in a sweaty heap at the bottom of Yosemite Valley. And that's the good news. Once the jam clears, I'll still have 350 feet to ascend before reaching the top.

The *Official Guide to Yosemite* had also labeled the Half Dome hike "Extremely Strenuous." That's like calling the Donner expedition a family picnic. These last 650 feet are nothing less than "Potentially Fatal." It's hard to be a modern adventuress when you're relying on trail guides designed for Paul Bunyan. The hikers around me are dealing with the threat of death in a variety of ways. Most pause when reaching a pair of posts, taking a moment to catch their breath and assess the situation before setting off again. Others climb quickly, staying one step ahead of their fear. And then there are the few who freeze, causing backups like the one I'm in now. Maybe my friend Amy was right. To perish while crossing a hike off my Lifetime To-Do List would be ironic and just a bit sad. I look out over the rock and consider whether to continue, my only comfort coming from the knowledge that my mother has no idea where I am.

The sea-green basketball shorts start moving. The jam has cleared. Do I keep going or turn around? I'd flip a coin but I might kill somebody below. The danger of continuing is real, but I also feel the need to finish something, to accomplish a goal. My career back in L.A. is moving backward, sideways—any direction but forward—and climbing this damn rock is a challenge I might actually complete.

So I continue up, soon noticing a girl sitting on the slope, facing downward. Knees pulled to her chin, both hands clutching the cable above, she's immobile. Frozen with fear. I want to reassure her, but what if her fear is contagious? That would mean two wide-eyed catatonics blocking the trail. Or maybe I'd cause her to freak out and fall. I end up skulking by, pretending I don't see her. Passing her. Saying nothing. The devil wears hiking boots. Amy, the Coward of the County.

It's a strange little community we have here on the side of this big rock. The trail is so challenging that it's hard for anyone to focus on anything other than his or her own ability to hang on and climb. On the other hand, each of us realizes that we're dependent on those hiking around us. Someone else's decision to stop, turn around, or panic affects everyone else on the trail.

I guess I'll split the difference—I'll come back and check on her later, after making it to safety and getting my bearings. And yes, I'm rationalizing selfishness at five hundred feet, but I'm wearing mittens on a 650-foot steel ladder, for pete's sake. Give a girl a break.

A small ledge juts over the trail ahead. The only way to continue is to step up, out, and over this ledge. Half Dome wants its revenge for my selfishness. But I am tired. I am hot. And I have had about enough. I take a breath, a step, and give one final, gut-lurching lunge. I flop over the rock. Look around. Okay, I'm here. I stand, walk past a few posts before passing a big rock. I turn right. A barren landscape rolls gently in front of me. Hikers dot the five-acre surface, the scene resembling a backpackers' refugee camp with thirty or so "survivors" eating lunch, taking naps, and snapping pictures. I walk around a bit, then head to the edge. Look out over Yosemite. Verdant meadows. Gushing waterfalls. The wonders of God's bounty.

Hmm. Now what? I'm psyched to have made it to the top, but with no one to talk to, visions of steel cables intrude on my thoughts like incessant drumbeats of doom. Will I freeze on the way down? Can I be rescued from the side of the rock? Will buzzards pick my bones clean? Note to self: *Consider bringing travel companion on next trip to share nagging neuroses.* I take another look around.

Yep, time to go.

I return to the cables. Most hikers leaving the top of Half Dome walk facing forward, down the slope. Some grab one cable with both hands and shuffle-jog along the outside of the trail, while others sit on the rock and scooch forward, sliding their posteriors over the rock while gripping the cable above with their hands. I look down, but experience such paralyzing vertigo that I realize there's no facing forward for me. I've got to face the rock, letting my feet go first as I grip the cables. This works well, and my primary obstacle is the horde of hikers climbing up. Since there's only one set of cables, those of us climbing down have to share the limited space with those climbing up—which makes for a tangled, stress-filled mess. As I descend, I notice that the girl I'd seen "frozen" on the rock has disappeared. I haven't seen any rescue choppers, so I'm optimistic she made it down in one piece.

Dropping onto the ledge, I rip off my mittens. I am Amelia Earhart landing in Ireland. I am Karen Blixen farming coffee in Nairobi. I have hiked the Dome. I am alive. I am invincible. I am . . . whistling Dixie at the dashing outdoorsman in front of me. Mr. Darcy of the Cables is waiting to start his climb. Where were you fifty minutes ago? We smile, exchange pleasantries. And what a smile it is. I grab my pack, departing with a spring in my step and a rock in my shoe.

And my self-affirming life lesson? You can't always believe what you read, be it a trail guide or chick lit. But I can tell you this: Whether you're a Bridget or a Blixen, a Bergdorf or a bitch, when it comes to Half Dome, be sure to pack enough water, get an early start, make sure your arms are in shape, and let your friends, but not your mother, know where you're going. And most important? Wear your grippiest hiking boots, and don't let the steel cables overwhelm your resolve. Whether Manhattan, Nairobi, or the backwoods of Yosemite, it is all in the shoes and the attitude. Hurrah!

Three Minutes
of Freedom

Lara Triback

I arrived in Buenos Aires on the first of January 2005 on a pilgrimage I did not fully understand. I wanted to learn tango, and the lessons I'd been taking over the previous year had taken me as far as they could. Although I had developed a basic aptitude on the dance floors of Boston, I was still left on the sidelines by the best dance partners, whose musically sophisticated leads I coveted. I was filled with a hungry urgency, dancing nearly every day with a desperation that refused all pleas for moderation. There was a feeling and an experience while dancing that I could get near, but couldn't quite reach. The smell and imagined taste of it drove me madder and madder, leaving me snuffling obsessively in every corner to hunt it down like a hungry dog.

In the end, I decided to offer an unequivocal surrender: I gave my notice at my dead-end office job and bought a ticket for Buenos Aires. I crammed my belongings into three small bags and boarded the plane.

It was ninety-three degrees when I arrived at Monica's. In the dark, high-ceilinged apartment were four tiny bedrooms, each the size of a large closet. Monica provided affordable rooms for students of the nearby language school, where I would be taking Spanish classes. My effusive, affectionate host mother maintained a large presence in the household and nearly smothered me when I presented her with the expensive perfume she had requested days before I left the United States. I slept in a twin-size bed that had been hers, and I couldn't imagine how she had ever fit her large frame into it.

The perpetual thick fog of cigarettes and sweet perfume, the twenty-four-hour blare of Argentinian television, the accompaniment of a shrill, yipping dog, and the remarkable lack of privacy would test me mightily. (In my first few days of residence, Monica burst into the bathroom to wrestle with the bucking washing machine, completely unfazed that all the while I was sitting on the toilet.) But in exchange for cheap room and board, I was willing to put up with a lot.

On day three, I planned my first tango outing. I consulted my Tango Dance Map, listing in a blurry, microscopic font, at least twenty-five places to tango at any hour of the day, every day of the week. Tuesday night: El Beso.

Next, transportation. Buenos Aires has an impressive and extensive network of local buses, called *collectivos*, that avoid the main streets and follow arbitrary zigzag routes in order to hit every side street in the city. I studied my supersize *guia*, filled with colorful grid maps on one side and corresponding bus routes on the other. Matching up the bus route numbers near Monica's apartment with the numbers listed on the grid near El Beso, I found the bus that, for thirty cents, would deliver me to within three blocks of my first *milonga*, or tango dance club. I left myself ample time to get lost, and Monica, able to name any of the hundreds of bus routes without blinking, provided specific directions for me to dutifully follow. Armed with my thick bus-route and tango maps, I donned my prettiest pink summer dress and headed out for my first night of tango.

Boarding the bus, I told the driver exactly where I wanted to get off, studied the route, compulsively checked it against my tango map, and forty-five minutes later arrived exactly where I had intended to go. With an air of victory, I strutted the three blocks to the address, and voilà! Within moments, my triumphant pride evaporated into panic as I discovered that I had misread the tango map and traveled to a *milonga* that took place on an altogether different evening, on the other side of town. And now it was an hour later, dark, and I didn't have a clue how to get where I needed to be.

A woman I accosted in panicked and stuttering Spanish suggested I take Bus #86 to Avenida Rivadavia 0 and walk from there. I waited for ten minutes until I spotted Bus #86 approaching. Relieved, I stepped to the curb with my arm raised, smiling, to flag it down, but it raced past me. Five minutes later, another Bus #86, another failed attempt to wave it down, and another, and another. I began to walk in the direction my buses had disappeared in, feeling increasingly despondent and desperate. Finally I enlisted the help of a fellow bus traveler, who, sensing my desperation, successfully flagged the bus down for me simply by standing in front of it, forcing it to screech to a halt.

I paid my fare and asked the driver to let me off where the woman had suggested. He shrugged his shoulders, signaling he'd never heard of such a street, and stared straight ahead. I approached a policeman sitting up front and asked, *"¿Rivadavia Cero?"* He responded curtly, "I don't know. Ask the bus driver." I pulled out my map and waved it in his face. He still refused to help. Now panicking, I tried to read the map and confer with the driver in my broken Spanish, as the bus raced down the street to an unknown destination. Finally I recognized a street name and demanded to be let off, and the driver eagerly complied. I began to walk, trying not to be overly conspicuous with my oversize foldout map and rapidly wrinkling party dress.

What I hadn't realized was that this was one of the major avenues that runs the length of the city. Two hours later, makeup smudged, eyes wild, and hair tousled, I arrived at El Beso.

A waiter greeted me. "Reservation?" I didn't have one, but possibly out of sympathy, as I looked both slightly insane and on the verge of tears, he directed me to a small table near the dance floor. I observed that the most popular dance partners were tall and blond, with impossibly enormous breasts poking out of the sides of their skintight dresses. Two hours passed, and I danced with three people. I felt self-conscious and awkward on the dance floor. I walked home and was in bed by 3 AM, exhausted and unwilling to admit to myself that I was glad the night was over.

Previous visitors to Buenos Aires had warned me not to accept a first dance until I was assured that the man asking was a skilled dancer. A new dancer's reputation is immediately established, and potentially destroyed, if she is observed dancing with an incompetent partner. At my next *milonga*, I turned down dances and sat for two hours. At 4 AM, one of the young locals finally asked me to dance. I tripped over his lead, and it didn't feel good. I hit my pillow at 4:30 AM, feeling defeated and exhausted once more, not wanting to dance again, and scheduled to attend four hours of Spanish class the following morning. If all else failed, at least tango would teach me the virtue of patience.

The following Wednesday, I attended an informal *milonga* at La Viruta and finally experienced my first tango fix. I accepted a head-nod invitation from a young Argentine. The moment he embraced me and inhaled slowly, with my body pressed against his, it felt as though I were sinking into sweet, warm butter. He exhaled and we landed gently, softly, and began to move. Although his technique was subtle, he succeeded in making my body comply with every movement, every syncopation, every weight shift. My legs felt completely relaxed, flying in all directions under his artful navigation. I lost track of time. My feet were killing me. It was 3 AM and I was ecstatic. This was why I had come.

On my way home I dodged drifting garbage and dog shit. The smell of rotting vegetables, cigarette smoke, and diesel filled the air. I was morphing into a creature of the night. My average bedtime now fell between 3 and 4 AM. With ever-darkening circles under my eyes and untameable, tricolored hair, I had begun to resemble a woman I did not know, but had always envied and maybe feared.

A few weeks later, I made my pilgrimage to the local tango shoe mecca, "Comme Il Faut." A pair or two (or three, or ten) of this particular brand is the must-have of every *tanguera*. These limited-edition shoes were snatched up from the shop as quickly as the women stumbling toward them in four-inch heels could grab them. I've never had a shoe fetish, but upon fondling this new foot candy, I realized that I was nearly drooling. Once my shoe size was determined, I hungrily awaited the delicate surprise lying inside each plain white box brought before me. First came the violet with a twist of lime, then the tangerine-orange with frills, followed by bright gold snakeskin with black velvet, then a pair with a psychedelic print, topped off by furry fuchsia leopard spots. I finally settled for a pair of high-heeled copper-and-blue leopard-spotted delights.

I swapped suggestions with a chatty Swiss woman (Green or red? Four-inch heels or three and a half?). After she made her purchase, the subject of accommodations came up, and she charmed me with tales of her friendly host family, significantly lower rent, and promises of increased sanity. The rooms were clean, the faucets did not leak, and there was no laundry hanging over anyone else's patio and no stupid biting dog. At my disposal would be a fully equipped kitchen, free Internet, and, twice a week, tango lessons in the living room.

I purchased some purple flowers in a futile attempt to mitigate Monica's disappointment over her lost source of revenue. As soon as I broke the news of my moving, she stopped calling me her *"hija"* and *"chica"* in her affectionate, singsong way. Instead, she shrugged her shoulders in irritation and said coldly, "The language school will send someone else to take the room." The next morning, while schlepping my bags across the floor and out the door, she offered the following blessing: "You are moving to a bad neighborhood. You'll probably get robbed." *Hasta luego.*

I moved to a bright, sunny apartment filled with smiling faces. Within minutes of my arrival, my housemate, a young Colombian tango dancer, grabbed me for a waltz in the kitchen. His teacher soon appeared for their daily private lesson. The living room furniture was pushed aside, and the two men danced together for several hours. As I observed the two sweaty, hot-blooded Latino men in close embrace, nose to nose, arms and legs wrapped around one another, I looked on with giddy bemusement, wondering what strange and lovely pansexual Oz I'd been deposited in.

Out dancing, my ego continued to be crushed on a nightly basis. I began to feel as though I were on a tango cruise ship. Even when I traveled out of town to dance, the same faces followed me everywhere. There were nights when I would sit for hours without an invitation to dance, and then I would have a beautiful dance that eradicated any feelings of self-doubt. But afterward that partner would ignore me and never ask me to dance again. How wonderful it would be if, before adding my name to the dancer blacklist, my partner would say

something like: "I would love to dance with you again when _____
[fill in the blank]." For example: " . . . when you don't feel like one hundred pounds of rotting albatross in my arms," or " . . . when your feet
no longer flap like canoe paddles on the dance floor." I craved this
feedback desperately. It would give me something to work toward. I
asked my dancer housemate for his professional opinion about what
I needed to work on. He turned his vapid, doelike eyes toward me,
clasped his hands behind his back, smiled, nodded, and said: "Your
steps, your embrace, and your posture. But you dance very well." *Gra-
cias por nada.*

Nearly every day I wanted to quit, and then I experienced something
that taught me again that this was the dance of the gods, lovers, whores,
the old, the forgotten, the brash, and the desperate—a dance of trans-
formation and painful, ecstatic magic.

There was a man named Oskar whom I saw every week, perched by
the bar at Salon Canning with a drink in his hand and a cigarette dangling
from his toothless mouth. The brown, leathery skin on his face was covered in black patches and hanging in folds, and his black-and-gray hair
was unkempt and bristly. He reminded me of a man I saw in a documentary on tango who polished gravestones of the rich for pennies in order
to attend dances in the evenings.

One night Oskar invited me to dance. Although his features were
repulsive, his eyes were kind, and after weathering so many personal
rejections from the young and the beautiful, I eagerly accepted. I closed
my eyes and embraced him. He pressed my chest close to his and placed
my right hand over his heart. When the music started to play, Oskar

began to sing. As our feet moved in time to the music, his raspy voice belted out words of love and pain and loss and longing from deep within his gut, and I understood them all. After each song ended, he would whisper in my ear, *"¿Bien?"* and I would reply, *"Sí, Oskar, muy bien."* When the set of three songs ended, he gently kissed my moist cheek and escorted me back to my seat.

I returned to El Beso one Sunday afternoon to attend a women's technique seminar taught by a popular Argentine teacher. In exchange for eighty pesos and three hours of our time, we would learn all the secrets to dancing tango well. Every participant in the class was a foreigner, as the high cost of the seminar outpriced the budget of native dancers.

Our teacher divulged to eager ears that a woman must imagine a tube of water starting at her vagina and flowing through her fingertips, spouting out her head and over the head of her partner. "Water plus the lioness within equals tango," she said. This teacher, a diminutive, chubby older woman, would be passed on the street without notice. But as soon as the "water plus lioness" entered her body, she appeared so regal and elegant that no one could shift their gaze from her. Her demonstration of foot embellishments while grasping a rusty chair held the entire class of women in awe of her grace.

I had begun studying with Guillermo, an exceptionally musical and dynamic mover on the slick dance floors of Buenos Aires. He was nearly a head shorter than I, but he transitioned from lightning to lugubrious in nanoseconds and interpreted the nuances of the music with his feet like

133

a ten-toed orchestra. I worked with this teacher three times a week, and after each lesson my dance technique improved significantly. I could now sustain a weightless connection, maintain my axis, and glide around the dance floor at breakneck speed.

Still, I struggled to attain the effortless grace of the most accomplished dancers. The focus of the dance is the feet, and my flat, nonarched paddles struggled consistently to recreate graceful, swift-moving, toe-tapping adornments. I've always suffered from holding excessive tension in my hips, which made learning to flip my legs in a swift boleo a nearly impossible task. I had been attempting to break a bounce in my stride, resulting from an inability to shift weight in my hips at the appropriate time, and Guillermo asked me to perform a simple exercise, involving stepping backward while pulling up the hip on the standing leg and then using that leg to propel the movement backward. Easy for some, but to me it felt like hacking at an iceberg with a salad fork.

I suddenly felt self-conscious. My hips felt as though they were filled with a paralyzing ball of energy and refused to budge. Having years ago learned anatomy, I could picture my skeletal structure and the muscles connecting to the bone and urged them, fruitlessly, to move. I felt like I couldn't even walk right. My eyes filled with tears and I sank to the floor. Guillermo asked if I wanted to take a break, but I shook my head. I got up and continued to attempt the simple elevation of the hip and extension of the legs. At his gentle urging, my hips suddenly began to move with ease, while tears silently streamed down my face.

Guillermo wiped my tears, declared me "crazy like his mother," and we danced. For the first time in my life, my hips had the sensation of weightlessness, and I felt free.

Many Argentine men dance only with their partners or their cluster of friends. Another crop of Argentines dances almost exclusively with foreign women. A man of this caliber is often on the prowl for a potential student to charge an exorbitant rate for a private lesson, or for a tasty dessert to devour after the *milonga*. Once he has eaten his fill (usually the span of one evening), his craving has been sated, and he will no longer invite her to dance. If the woman refuses the man's invitation for a "coffee after the *milonga*," he will become insulted and will never ask her to dance again. It's a tricky game.

During a crowded *milonga*, I boldly took a seat at a table occupied by three Argentines. I had sat at that particular table when I first arrived, but it was usurped at some point during the evening. My feet were tired and I wanted to rest, so I pulled up a chair and plunked myself down. A tall, slim man with a spiky crew cut and a profile that reminded me of a turkey turned to me and said hello. He wore a black T-shirt and suspenders, and his right hand intermittently adjusted himself between his legs.

"How are you?"

"Fine."

"Where are you from?"

"The States. I'm here to learn tango."

"I thought you were from here."

"No. Do you dance?"

"Oh no," he said. "I just enjoy the music."

I spied the new issue of the local tango magazine, listing all events for the coming month, being circulated at the far end of the room, and I jumped up to grab one. My conversation companion begged me to bring him one, and I did, under the condition that he save my seat. When I returned, he thanked me profusely, pushed the man away who had taken my chair, and flipped the magazine to one of the last pages. He gestured toward a full-color photo that occupied a third of the page, featuring his mug with a raised eyebrow. The ad read: BACK FROM BARCELONA: THE LION ATTACKS! PRIVATE LESSONS ONLY.

He leaned toward me and said, "I invite you, for *free,* to take a class with me. *At night.* You give me your information and I tell you where to meet."

I laughed and said, "But we're here. At a *milonga.* We can dance right here."

"No, no, no. I'm on vacation. I dance twelve hours a day. I offer you a free class at night. Give me your information."

I slapped him affectionately in the arm and replied, "Nothing is free." Then I burst out laughing. I couldn't stop.

He looked me in the eye and asked, *"¿Estas contenta?"* (Are you happy?) *"¿Que quieres?"* (What do you want?)

What did I want? Didn't I want first and foremost to improve my dance? To be invited to dance by the natives? Didn't I want to improve my Spanish, to have an opportunity to dance with professionals, regardless of whether it was under unprofessional circumstances? Didn't I want

136

desperately to find, to have, *the* dance? The transformative dance I could look on forever after as the three minutes that changed my life? Didn't I want to be whole, to find love, to discover some connection between parts of myself that remained estranged, something in my heart that was disconnected, like my hips from the rest of my body? Or was the drug of the tango enough?

What *did* I want? Why was I here?

I leaned forward, met his gaze, and said, "I want nothing. I have everything I need." And with those words, I collected my shoes and my water bottle and moved to stand at the far side of the room.

The Dis-Orient Express

Eileen Favorite

While I paced the platform at Chalons-sur-Marne, my backpack was hurling through the French countryside on the Orient Express. It was 1 AM on a cold December night in 1984. Coatless and shivering, I stared down the empty tracks at the wires and dim lights that stretched for miles, thinking of my gargantuan backpack wedged comfortably on a coach seat beside the kind Frenchman who had promised to watch it for me three hours before.

I was twenty. I was Junior Year Abroad Girl. This was not a moment of international intrigue. This was another episode in my version of "Lucille Ball Does Europe." As I paced the platform, a prickly vanity kicked in and I worked to affect a cool nonchalance by rolling my eyes and looking at my wrist, which held no watch.

A series of false moves and impulsive gestures had resulted in my standing at the train tracks alone in the dead of night. I had arrived at Gare de l'Est in Paris that evening just before nine. I was going to Munich to visit my boyfriend for Christmas. That afternoon, I'd wandered the Parisian streets lost, mainly because I'd mistranslated the expression *tout droit*, which means "straight," as "totally right." Every time someone told me to go straight, I went totally right and wound up going in circles. I discovered that Sunday in Paris meant that all the stores and museums were closed. I visited Notre Dame, dismayed by the pacing tourists who pointed at the ceiling in the middle of Mass. I decided to kill time in a café, but when my coffee arrived in a tiny espresso mug, I downed it in three minutes. A Midwestern girl, I lacked the cosmopolitan entitlement to occupy a seat without ordering something else. Down to my last few francs, I shouldered the backpack and killed time by skipping the *métro* and hoofing it to the train station.

My visit to Paris had been both a revelation and a disappointment. My high school film-strip expectations were met: the usual landmarks wowed me, as well as the Jeu de Paume and the Louvre. I had the sparkling moment of wonder that I, a suburban girl with eight siblings, was actually face-to-face with the *Mona Lisa,* and other low moments of feeling overwhelmed by everything I didn't know. The friends I visited at Versailles, competitive architecture students from Illinois, were too busy with final projects to give me much time. And none of them spoke French. I often found myself alone in Versailles townie bars, speaking my half-assed French with older men who tried to coax me back to their apartments. I wanted an entrée into Paris, but not through the bedroom. However human the scale of Paris, the cobbled streets led to shining apartments with golden lights that struck me as fortresses meant to keep me out. By Sunday evening, I was ready to move on.

When I arrived at Gare de l'Est, the Orient Express awaited with open doors. Let's clarify one thing. The train was nothing fancy—no *wagon-lits* or elegant dining cars. The Cold War Orient Express of the 1980s was a regular old train with filthy windows and stained chairs, which merely followed the romantic Paris–Budapest route with a stop in Munich. I trudged down the aisle with the massive backpack strapped to my waist. I hadn't mastered the art of traveling light.

Contained in that backpack were the *accoutrements* of my artsy makeover. I'd only recently discovered the wonders of thrift shops. Having worn school uniforms for twelve years—plaid skirts and vests, white blouses with yellowed armpits, v-neck sweaters, knee socks, and saddle shoes—in college I found picking an outfit every day a challenge. Unable to compete with the Kappa Alpha Thetas with their wardrobe expense accounts, I sometimes longed for my Catholic-girl ready-made. When I'd discovered the Unique Thrift Shop in Markham, Illinois, located in a sprawling, abandoned A&P, the long racks of clothes organized by color made me feel like a millionaire. I could afford anything in the joint! I spent hours that summer assembling my Eurotrash look. The collective value of my backpack may have been $40, but it harbored not just clothing, but my fledgling identity.

I carried a box of adapters to accommodate my travel hair dryer, iron, and Bausch & Lomb contact cooker, as well as a four-pack of hot rollers I used to pouf up my short-on-the-sides, long-on-top Flock of Seagulls do. The Oxfam Shop in Dundee, Scotland, where I attended university, had become my new couturier. The backpack held a hand-knit black pullover, a pink-plaid tunic, a purple wool cardigan, a paisley scarf, chartreuse Capris, a pink linen dress, a black cowl-neck velvet dress, and satin old-man PJs, as well as twenty pairs of socks, ten pairs of underwear, four Shakespeare paperbacks, tights, strappy gray boots, a handful of bras, and a preppy scarf and John Lennon biography for my boyfriend. Complicated straps of varying lengths dangled from the backpack, which I didn't know how to adjust for greater support and comfort. I looked like a D-day parachutist, and it would be years before I understood why Parisians laughed and asked, *"Tu cherches le debarquement?"* ("Looking for the landing?")

Sweating, I plopped the backpack into a seat next to a thin, middle-aged Frenchman who looked like he was fighting the flu. His lids hovered over his dark brown eyes and he smelled like cigarettes. He kindly agreed to watch my backpack and hot-pink double-breasted cashmere coat (a $5 find), while I ran outside to find a phone booth. Since the train didn't depart for another twenty minutes, I had time to call my boyfriend and tell him my exact arrival time. Our initial plan, detailed in a letter I had written two weeks earlier, was that he would meet every train from Paris on Monday morning. Now that I had boarded, I could confirm my arrival time. I took with me the satchel made from rubber tires I'd bought at Les Halles the day before. It held my money, passport, travel clock, Interail pass, Walkman, ten homemade tapes, my journal, and my beloved Thomas Cook train schedule. In other words, it too weighed enough to herniate a disc.

The station air cooled my sweat and made the lambswool sweater scratchy against my skin. At the end of each track was a pay phone, and I hurried from one to the other, lifting the receivers to discover that not a single one worked. As I turned back to return to the train, I counted the number of tracks, unsure which was mine. A train began to pull out of the station, so I ran after it. I had been gone for only five minutes, but the Orient Express was leaving early! The satchel thumping against my thigh, I ran faster, yelling, *"À Munich? À Munich?"* A train employee pressed the door open with her elbow and yelled, *"Oui!"* I jumped, grabbed the handle of the door, swung onto the first step, and jumped into the train.

When I finally regained my breath, I snapped open the sliding doors and headed for my seat. I walked through the first car, but nothing looked familiar. Where was the flu-stricken Frenchman? I passed through one car, then another, until I reached the dining car, where a bored girl in a polyester uniform smoked a filterless cigarette. I bolted down two more cars, doubled back, confused. Had I been facing in the direction of travel or backward? I moved faster, steadying myself on the seats as the train rocked. Back through the dining car again and into the next coach. The people looked familiar, but simply because I'd seen them a minute before. I had boarded the wrong train.

I ran to find the attendant, my sophomore-level French flying out the window as I blurted in English, "I'm lost!" When I explained the situation, the attendant shook her head. "We cannot stop the train for you."

I didn't expect her to stop the train. She presumed I was a presumptuous American who, in the words of one of my English classmates, "expected to be catered to." I had noticed that something about me often garnered annoyed looks in Europe. Whether it was my bright pink coat or the mattress-size backpack, I didn't know. I'd wisely tucked my black beret in my bag, having observed that only old men wore berets in Paris. It was not a great time to be American in Europe. Our nuclear missiles were stockpiled all over Western Europe, ready to be launched at the U.S.S.R. should Gorbachev make any funny moves. Reagan's landslide reelection didn't help, and the dollar was ridiculously strong (as low as $1.10 to the English pound). So even I could be mistaken for that dreaded class of human: The Rich American.

"Wait!" the attendant said. "This train follows the same path as the other! It will arrive in Chalons-sur-Marne at 1:00. The Orient Express will get there at 1:15."

"I can switch trains there?"

"*Mais oui.*"

I took a seat and studied the gospel of Thomas Cook. It was true. The train I'd boarded like a comic action figure followed the exact same path until Munich. If, and it was a big if, nobody had stolen my backpack by now, a middle-of-the-night reunion was possible! I simply had to remain calm and kill the next three hours. I saturated my brain with *Purple Rain* and R.E.M.'s *Reckoning*, read and reread the timetables, and squinted at the dark countryside that looked like Wisconsin with an occasional illuminated château in the hills.

When the train was three stops from Chalons-sur-Marne, I went to stand by the door. Enduring the jostling stops and blasts of winter air offset my anxiety in a fine masochistic fashion. If only my shoulders were weighed down by my backpack! When the train pulled into the station, I hopped off and moved toward the stationhouse with two other passengers. The sight of a couple hugging stopped me. I was too nervous to seek shelter in the warm stationhouse. As the train pulled away, I looked up into the cloudy, dark sky. A minute later another train roared into the station. It was 1:09. I willed myself still. The Orient Express wasn't due until 1:15. I was learning. Trains never left early. They may leave late, but they never leave early.

The platform clock had long lacy arms that *tick, tick, tick*ed. The couple had boarded the new train, and I was alone on the platform. I started to cut my losses. I still had my passport and Interail pass. I could replace the clothes, sort of. I felt a pang for the velvet dress, which I'd planned to wear to the Munich Symphony. But the loss of the clothes wasn't what troubled me. It was the sheer embarrassment of having made such a clumsy mistake. I was an amateur traveler. Alone on some French train platform, in the middle of nowhere, it struck me that no one in the entire world—neither my parents nor my friends—knew where I was. It felt as if I could step into some void and disappear. What if I fell on the tracks and were crushed by the train? Who would return my body to my people? My backpack would continue its solo trip, perhaps be detonated on the Hungarian border. What if I were abducted, taken into the black night? The edge of the platform felt like the edge of the world. I may have been connected through rail to hundreds of other destinations, a few minutes from a phone, but it still felt as if I were on the brink of an oblivion that comes with genuine solitude. If a girl stands on a platform but nobody knows she's there, does she really exist?

The rumble of the approaching train snapped me out of my existential pondering. It was 1:15, and right on schedule the Orient Express shuddered to a stop. I climbed on board. As I moved down the aisles, I was stunned to find them crowded with people. The air smelled of sweat and piss, and the windows dripped condensation. People slept on the floor because every seat was taken. I moved through one car, then another. Finally I saw it. While French teenagers curled in the aisles, my backpack sat like a fat, entitled Yank in the chair. I lifted up the backpack and slid into the seat beneath it. I hugged it; I planted a kiss on the zipper. I had fumbled, but I hadn't dropped the ball.

The sickly Frenchman awoke and squinted at me. I smiled back, wondering where he thought I'd been for three hours. I wished that he had looked out the window to see me standing out there on the platform. He might have thought I was a mysterious time traveler who could snap her fingers and vanish, and then, like magic, reappear beside him.

In the Land of Athena

Gail Hudson

My daughter, Gabrielle, sticks close by my side, eyeing the armed guards and sniffing dogs as I stop to check and recheck our passports. My mind clicks through the details of our itinerary. I have a hotel lined up for our stay in Athens and have even arranged for a cab driver to meet us at the airport—safety nets that I never considered throughout my years of bohemian travel. Footloose trips before I had children. Before I became the safety net.

As soon as we pass through customs, we spot a young Greek man holding up a sign with my name on it. He introduces himself as Tomas, then grabs all four of our bags and stacks them under his arm as if they are loaves of bread. His thick black hair tumbles down the back of his suede fringe jacket, and two large silver hoop earrings dangle from his ears.

"Where in America you from?" He is winded from the exertion, but smiling.

"Seattle. It's on the West Coast...."

But before I can explain further, Tomas stops in his tracks and drops all our bags on the sidewalk. He makes a *namaste* gesture with his hands and bows to me. "Home of the King—Jimi Hendrix," he says.

"Yes, the King," I say, holding my hands prayerfully and bowing in agreement.

"And home to Nirvana," he adds, hoisting the bags into his arms again and continuing toward the cab.

"Hendrix is the King and Cobain is the Prince."

I am dazzled by the sudden wash of Aegean sunlight, by this Seattle-savvy Greek rocker and my ability to keep pace with his banter. Gabrielle walks silently beside us.

When we're settled in the cab, Tomas looks at me through his rearview mirror. "You been to Greece before?"

"Two times," I offer, noticing his thick eyelashes and earth-brown eyes.

"You come before and you didn't call me?" Tomas makes a sad face in the mirror and winks. My god, he is actually flirting. "When was your first time?"

147

"I was still a teenager." The window is open and my long hair is swishing about my face. I lean my head back and breathe in the warm, sensual air.

"What year?" He smiles. Nice teeth, very white and straight.

"Let's see," I begin reluctantly. "I think it was Christmas 1973."

"Ahh, 1973," Tomas says, breaking eye contact. "The year I was born." He adjusts the rearview mirror and shifts his gaze to my daughter. "What about you? You go to many nightclubs?"

Gabrielle giggles. "Not really."

My drifting daydream skids to a halt. I roll up the window and sit up straight. "She's thirteen years old. And she doesn't *do* nightclubs."

"Ohhhh, you two are mother-daughter," he says, slowly catching on. "Alone?" he adds, turning around to address me. I shift slightly on the vinyl seat, which is sticky and cracked.

"Yes. My husband and son are back in Seattle."

We are silent for a long stretch of minutes as the sterile strip-mall scenery gives way to small residential neighborhoods on the outskirts of Athens.

"It's nice, a mother and daughter coming to Greece together," Tomas says finally. "Tell you what, I take you to see where I grow up."

He pulls off the highway and into a maze of narrow streets. "My neighborhood," he says, gesturing toward a cluster of small apartment buildings with white sheets flapping on clotheslines. He breathes in deeply. "Can you smell the tangerines growing on the trees? It reminds me of my mother." Pointing to an empty lot of busted-up cement, he says, "That's where I played soccer as a boy. Every day my mother would call for me." He makes his voice high-pitched and singsong: "Tomas. Tomas. Time to eat."

We study the remains of his childhood playground with tufts of weeds pushing through the cracks. Our first Greek ruins.

December 1973, a few months before my seventeenth birthday. I have arrived in Athens with my mother and brother. It is the first Christmas after my parents' breakup. My mother, who has never traveled outside the country without my father, has impulsively decided to take us to Greece for the holidays. Why Greece? It is warm in the winter (at least on Rhodes, the southernmost island we plan to visit), and the airlines are running cheap holiday airfare.

And why not Greece? Isn't a life of spontaneous travel and adventure something that's available to a woman of the 1970s? My mother, who did not want the divorce, is wearing her hair longer, sporting high-heel boots and stylish suits. She's even started driving a red Fiat convertible.

We arrive at the Athens airport after midnight. It is officially Christmas Eve. "We don't even have a hotel," my mother confesses to the cab driver as we climb in the backseat.

"No problem," he says. The driver takes us to a hotel beside the Plaka—the old city at the base of the Acropolis. The floors are marble and a crystal chandelier hangs in the lobby. It smells of coal heat. At first the owner seems resentful that he's been roused out of bed to check in guests. But when he sees the situation—a striking American woman traveling alone with her children—he becomes overly solicitous, fussing over my mother's luggage and insisting that she get some sleep and not hassle with her credit card or passport until later.

On Christmas morning we awaken before dawn and hike up the hill to the Acropolis. When I step through the royal entryway and see the ancient city spread out before us, I begin to cry. I have never seen anything so beautiful and lasting.

In 1973 visitors are allowed to walk and climb over all the ruins, touching everything. I keep returning to the magnificent Parthenon. My mother joins me and looks skyward to where the ceiling once was. My brother, Jim, a Yale college student with a thick hippie beard, wanders over. He is holding the Blue Guide to Greece—an intellectual guidebook that he has been studying ever since we made our plane reservations.

Jim informs us that this was a temple to the goddess Athena. "She was born right out of her father, Zeus's, head," he says.

I tell him this makes Athena sort of like Jesus, born from an immaculate conception.

But my brother says Athena was actually more like Mother Mary, since Athena was also a glorified virgin. In fact, the guidebook calls her Athena Parthenos—Athena the Virgin. But she wasn't a good-girl kind of virgin, he tells us. She was a rebel—not willing to conform to the rules of womanhood. She refused to marry, refused to have children, even refused to have a lover.

"Sort of like an early women's libber," my mother says, lighting up a Virginia Slim.

My brother shows us a picture of Athena in his Blue Guide. I ask why she's wearing a helmet and carrying a spear. "Because she was a very important warrior," Jim says. "You really should start reading Homer."

He goes on to tell us that Athena was a defender of justice and fought only when the battle seemed worthy. She was considered wise, which is why there's an owl perched on her shoulder—her special symbol.

And that is how we spend our Christmas sunrise, sitting amongst the pillars of the Parthenon, watching the sky turn from pink to pale blue as Athena's city awakens.

I have returned to Greece because my daughter has turned thirteen. More specifically, I thought it would be a good idea to offer a marker for this particular stage of life. If we were Jewish, she'd have a bat mitzvah. If we were Catholic, she'd be confirmed. But we don't belong to any organized religion, except for having a loose affiliation with the local Quakers. Nonetheless, I want Gabrielle to have some recognition of her passage from child to young woman. About a month after she had her first period, I went into her room and asked what she'd like to do to celebrate this time of life.

My daughter lifted her gaze from *The Mists of Avalon* and looked me in the eye. "I am not having one of those crone and maiden menstruation parties."

"No blood parties," I promised.

"If I could do anything?" She looked at me sheepishly. "I'd go to Greece."

Gabrielle sat up tall beneath the white canopy of her bed. She told me how she would give anything to see the Acropolis and the Parthenon. Let's make it a special mother-daughter trip, she said, our own private pilgrimage to Athena.

Why was I surprised? Ever since she was a little girl, she'd been captivated by the Greek myths, especially the goddesses, and especially Athena. I had been thinking of throwing her a dinner party, and now I was desperate to swing a trip to Greece. I had just received a modest inheritance from my grandmother. Why not invest it in the feminine lineage?

So here we are in Athens, a week before Easter in the year 2000. After Tomas drops us off at our hotel, we immediately head out to the Plaka for some food. It's a warm Sunday afternoon and there are only a few tourists on the streets. As soon as we enter the labyrinth of the ancient Plaka, Gabrielle's face opens in awe. She takes in the faded stucco buildings with brightly painted wooden shutters, potted flowering plants, and carefully washed marble entryways. Tendrils of wisteria flow everywhere. The air smells of garlic cooked in olive oil, mixed with oregano and rosemary. And the light, earthy scent of Acropolis dust whirls and settles everywhere.

"I had no idea it would be this beautiful," she says.

As we stroll past the tourist shops, the accordion players, flower sellers, and kiosks, the men begin staring at us, eyeing us up and down in a blatantly appraising way. A few make clucking noises—some follow us for a few paces, calling out, "Hello, I love you!" Before long, the whistles and kissing sounds become relentless.

"Ohh-kay," Gabrielle whispers. "This is getting weird."

When we sit down in an outdoor café in the main, tree-shaded square, a group of men walks by, smiling and staring at us in unison. "American beauty!" They throw us kisses, and Gabrielle buries her face in her hands.

"I'm too young for this," Gabrielle says, shaking her head.

"And I'm too old," I say.

As she eats her first Greek salad, swirling peppered cucumbers and feta cheese through pools of golden olive oil, I tell her the men don't see her age. They just see her loveliness.

"Well, it feels like they're harassing us," she says.

I have to agree that it seems more like harassment—something we've had many conversations about as she's navigated the awkward lewdness of middle-school boys. As the bouzouki music drifts through the café, I try to put it into a cultural context. I talk about the influence of American movies and MTV. Maybe the Greek men think it is okay to treat American women as sex objects, since so many of our movies and music videos do.

"But even so, this seems really disrespectful," Gabrielle says. "It doesn't make sense. I thought they worshipped women here."

I don't know what to say. Here is the place where goddesses once reigned supreme. The place where the original mother goddess, Gaia, gave birth to the world. To this day, Greece is still filled with images of feminine deities. How can the divine be feminine, but women so disrespected? I tell my daughter that it's confusing to me also.

What I don't tell her is what happened to me when I was sixteen.

My mother, brother, and I stay in Athens for three days before heading to the island of Rhodes. Once the shops reopen after Christmas, I venture into the Plaka alone. Browsing the souvenir stores, I spot a white cape hanging on the wall. The shop owner tells me it is made from lamb's wool. He drapes it around me and says "Liv Ullman" as I look in the mirror. I burst into a huge grin and count out $20 worth of drachma. With the cape still wrapped around my shoulders, I step into the cool, evening air. Walking the streets of the Plaka in my new cape, I notice men looking appreciatively at me. I pretend I am the regal goddess Athena, attracting the adoration of her mortal fans.

On the night before we leave Athens we have dinner in a traditional *taverna*—a casual, café-like restaurant. The family rules are different here in Greece. I am allowed to smoke cigarettes with my mother and drink wine in restaurants. The waiters discreetly wink at me as they light my cigarettes and fill my wineglass. Ordinarily I am invisible to grown-up men, but here they pay so much attention to me. Instead of feeling my usual awkward, pudgy-cheeked self, I start to see myself as beautiful and sophisticated, in that Greek-goddess/Swedish-movie-star kind of way.

A young Greek man walks over to our table and introduces himself as Mikhael, a friend of the owner. He tells us he speaks English well and likes practicing with tourists. His thick, wavy brown hair is styled in layers, and he wears tight, European-cut flared pants and a form-fitting shirt that is unbuttoned to reveal much of his slender chest. Before long he is sitting at our table, ordering us carafes of house wine and amusing us with disappearing-coin tricks.

My mother's laughter seems willing and relaxed tonight. It's been a long time since she's looked this happy, and I am grateful to Mikhael for making us feel so special and welcome. When the folk dancing starts, he puts his arms around the other Greek men's shoulders and begins to spin and stomp, clapping his hands and snapping his fingers. After a while Mikhael pulls my mother onto the dance floor, and I watch in awe as she stomps and twirls amongst all the Greek men. Before long my brother and I are dancing, too.

Meanwhile, Mikhael continues to fill our glasses with wine. By closing time we have drunk enough to make us stumble out the door.

"I will walk you back to your hotel," Mikhael offers, throwing an arm around my brother, Jim, and another arm around my mother. "Come! You too, Gail," he says, tucking me into his body with an affectionate squeeze. When we reach the hotel, my mother and brother groggily make their way to the front door. One moment we are all together, and the next I am alone with Mikhael on a darkened street at two o'clock in the morning.

He quickly presses his face into my neck and reaches a hand up my shirt. I pull away.

"But we are going to make love," he says, as if this is already fated.

"No." I step backward. "I can't."

"Yes, you can," he steps toward me and wraps his arms around me. "We are alone now."

"No, it's not that." I try to wriggle away again, only now he has me in an iron-tight grip. "I'm a virgin," I blurt out, surprising myself with the absurdity of this defense.

"A virgin," he says in amazement. This time he pulls away so he can search my face. "No! Really? An *American virgin,*" he adds, as if this were an oxymoron.

I nod vigorously, still uncertain whether this will help or hinder the outcome here.

"Wait," he says, turning away from me and stepping into a nearby alley. Through the dim street lighting, I see him unzip his pants and turn away. I try to sort out what's happening. Does he have to pee? It takes me a long moment to realize what he's doing. Still drunk from the wine, still a good-girl virgin, I obediently stand there, not even thinking to make a breakaway run. When he is finished, he walks back to me.

"Okay. Now you go to sleep." Mikhael sighs, puts his arm around my caped shoulders, and walks me up the steps of our hotel. He kisses my hand, tells me he loves me, and then walks off into the city night.

When I enter our darkened hotel room, my brother and mother are in a dead sleep. I am careful not to wake them. Lying between the starchy sheets, it occurs to me that I could have been raped or kidnapped, even murdered. But it doesn't occur to me to be angry at my mother and brother. Instead I feel ashamed. I did something wrong, something stupid. I got too worldly, too happy, too big on myself. I decide not to tell my mother and brother what happened. Besides, tomorrow we leave for Rhodes—Athens will be behind us.

On the island of Rhodes, we stay in a seaside village called Lindos. Everything is painted white and there is not a cloud to be seen. Right away I go to the small public beach, slather myself with Bain de Soleil gel, and cultivate my first December suntan. When I step into the Aegean, the water is so clear I can see my toes, even when I am standing up to my neck.

I notice that grown-up men don't look at me in the same way here.

156

In fact, they don't look at me at all. Only the women and children seem to acknowledge me. As the days pass, I begin to feel safe enough to walk the backstreets of Lindos by myself. By the end of the week, I have ventured onto the hilly trails that led out of town, walking until I find the sunniest and most hidden place to sunbathe. Alone on the Aegean cliffs, I read from my brother's copy of *The Iliad*.

On New Year's Eve, we go to a *taverna* and the owner's children serve us lamb stew and glasses filled with retsina, which we agree tastes like Pine-Sol cleaner. After dinner the three of us decide to race back to our little villa. The rules are these: We each go home a separate way. Whoever wins gets to stand on the rooftop of our villa and howl at the moon. My brother pretends to fire a shot into the air and we take off. My sandaled feet slap on the deserted cobbled streets. Almost every window has a single candle burning on the sill in honor of New Year's. I feel hysterically joyful, running hard, not missing a step on the dark bumpy streets. Inside my knapsack is a bag of tangerine-flavored hard candies. I suddenly decide to toss pieces of the cellophane-wrapped candy through the streets so the village children will find them in the morning.

I am the first to reach the villa. I lift my sun-freckled face to the moonlight and howl with delight.

Years from now I will wish the trip could have ended here. But instead we returned to Athens for our connecting flight to the States. On our last evening in Greece, my mother sends me to the Plaka for a bottle of red wine to bring back home and some yogurt for the next morning's breakfast.

At first I feel excited to be Athena again, proud to enter the evening with my cape and island suntan. But then the men start looking at me in a creepy kind of way and I remember about Mikhael. I am relieved to enter the brightly lit market and buy a plastic tub of goat's milk yogurt and a bottle of red wine. On my way home, it starts to rain, and in the dark labyrinth I become confused about how to find my way back to our hotel. The streets are becoming narrower and emptier. A car pulls up alongside me with two men inside—men who look to be my father's age.

"English? English?" the passenger calls to me from his open window. I look straight ahead. *Don't look. Ignore them.* My feet move faster on the cobbled street. "Help!" one of them yells. I look over and the men laugh together. The passenger licks his lips and waggles his tongue. I walk faster. The car scoots forward, then stops just ahead of me, and a door swings opens. The man in the passenger seat steps out, rubs his groin, and urgently gestures for me to get in the car. "Quick. Quick," he says. There is no one else on the street but the men and me.

I start to run. But almost instantly my sandaled feet lose their grip on the wet cobblestones. I fall down hard on my tailbone, my white cape slamming into the wet soot of the street. The red wine and yogurt crash onto the cobblestones—a pool of creamy white mixing with a river of dark red. Again, the men are laughing—this is all too funny.

I scramble to my feet. "No!" My voice sounds like a three-year-old's. I run again—it takes me almost an hour to find my way back to my mother, my sandals slopping in puddles of water the whole way. Bursting into the hotel room, I cry hot tears as I tell my mother about the men.

Hunched over the bathroom sink, we try to hand-wash the black smudge from my new cape, but it won't come out. "I hate to say this," my mother says while she scrubs, "but this is exactly why women should never travel alone."

Gabrielle wants her pilgrimage to include the island of Crete because of the artistic Minoans who dwelled here almost four thousand years ago. They were one of the earliest civilizations known to revere a feminine deity.

After we land at the ferry dock I find a rental car lot that offers us a red Fiat convertible, uncannily like the sports car my mother drove. When I sit behind the wheel, I can't help but compare myself to her. Even though I've vowed to be a more vigilant parent than she was on our Greek journey, a part of me envies the freer, more reckless attitude that she somehow possessed.

Driving out onto the twisting road, I want to shed my maternal worries and simply relax into the sensuous glee of traveling in a windy convertible with no destination and no road map. But what I feel is the burden of being a mother nomad with a teenage daughter. I know all too well what can go wrong. In fact, I feel more alone and vulnerable than I ever have traveling solo.

Just the night before, when we were still in Athens, Gabrielle and I walked to a restaurant called Socrates Dungeon. It was twilight and there were only a few cars on the street. Suddenly we heard a guttural moaning sound coming from a stairwell. We looked over to see a hefty older man with his pale pink penis exposed as he masturbated furiously. I grabbed Gabrielle's wrist and we didn't stop running until we reached the restaurant.

Ever since then, Gabrielle's been asking me, "Is this happening because I'm wearing tight jeans?" Or a sundress? Or a fitted shirt? And finally, "Is it because my breasts are too big?"

"No, no," I tell her, "You can't take this on. It's about them, not about you." But still I see the doubt on her face. And it frustrates me. This is not the coming-of-age message I want her to experience.

I am not, by nature, a warrior mother. I am a soft-spoken woman, having been born from the head of an impeccably mannered Southern gentleman and the womb of a mother who avoids conflict at any cost. More than once I have pondered what it would be like to politely ask these men, "How would you feel having your daughter treated this way?" But even if I had the language, I doubt if I would have the nerve.

After a number of wrong turns and several squabbles, Gabrielle and I navigate our way to the southern end of Crete. The following morning we are the first to enter the ruins of Phaistos, the ancient Minoan palace that sits amidst the lushness of olive groves and flaxen grasses. As my daughter explores the four-thousand-year-old ruins, I see her straddle the cusp between child and woman.

One moment she is a young girl with dirty knees and a faded Mariners T-shirt, lying unself-consciously in the soil so she can see through a small crack into the children's sleeping area. Turn around, and she's a woman walking grandly down the promenade with her head high and arms extended.

"I'm a high priestess holding my charmed snakes in each of my hands," Gabrielle announces, smiling wide, her braces flashing in the morning light. Still so young and yet, biologically speaking, old enough to be a mother.

Eventually we come to a grassy altar where the goddess Rhea was worshipped. I open the guidebook and read Gabrielle the story of Rhea: She had it good as a daughter—born to Uranus (supreme god of the sky) and Gaia (the big-time goddess who created the earth). But she had it bad as a woman. For years her cruel brother, Cronos, repeatedly raped her and then ate their children as soon as they were born, having foreseen that one of his offspring would overthrow him.

Finally, the grief-stricken Rhea goes to her mother, Gaia, and crawls back into her womb, asking for advice. Gaia doesn't know how to protect Rhea from her brother's brutal assaults, but she does have an idea for protecting Rhea's children. She suggests that Rhea hide her next-born child in a cave and give Cronos a stone wrapped in the baby's swaddling clothes to eat.

So when her son Zeus is born, Rhea follows her mother's advice, and the trick works. Cronos swallows the stone. Little Zeus is raised by two sister nymphs, who feed him goat's milk in a cave on Crete.

Meanwhile, Rhea is fed up with her bully brother Cronos. Again she returns to her mother's womb, asking for help. The two of them hatch a lovely little plan. When Zeus is old enough, Rhea will give him a sword to castrate his father and then slice open his stomach to free all the children he swallowed. Zeus grows up, does the dirty deed, and out pop some of the most powerful figures in Greek mythology: Demeter, Poseidon, Hera, Hades, and Hestia.

I close the book. Bullying men wreaking havoc with their penises. And always the mother protecting the child. No matter where we go, the themes chase after us.

161

When the sun gets high and hot, we settle into a shady spot and Gabrielle begins painting the palace with her new watercolor set. She informs me she was an artist here in a previous lifetime. Pointing to a cluster of red poppies sprouting through the stone cracks, she says, "I would have used those petals to make my dyes." The two of us are quietly content for hours—she moving her paintbrush across the paper and me scribbling my pen across the page. She interrupts our silence to tell me, "This is the moment I came here for."

Late in the afternoon, we head to a nearby beach for a swim. What the trailhead didn't tell us is that this beach is actually an oasis for nude sunbathers. For a moment Gabrielle is mortified, but I convince her to join me in some topless swimming. As we wade into the clear blue water, she marvels at how blissful it feels, stretching her naked torso in the salty womb of the sea.

The next day, when we are touring the Minoan palace at Knossos, we study the painted friezes of black-haired, bare-breasted Minoan women.

"What if all the women in the world decided that they wanted to walk around like that?" Gabrielle says. "Maybe our bodies would stop being some kind of sexual thing and we wouldn't get harassed so much."

All I can think is, *I wish it were that easy.*

On the ferryboat back to Athens, I feel relaxed, having let my guard down after a week of carefree swimming, sunning, and palace touring where the men barely bothered us. But now my daughter comes to the bench where I am reading in the afternoon sunlight.

"There's a man who's scaring me." She thinks he's a ferry worker, and he's been staring at her and following her around the boat. Just now he was standing outside the bathroom door, waiting for her to come out.

I tell her to sit with me for a while. "If he follows you up here, I want you to point him out." Sure enough, seconds later he approaches us and leans against the boat railing, blatantly—no, forcefully—fixing his gaze on Gabrielle as if he had every right to intimidate a thirteen-year-old girl this way.

What's my daughter going to take home from this trip? A stained white cape or a sun-freckled face lifted to the sky?

"Stay here," I say to her. I get up from the bench and walk toward the ferryboat worker. He is smoking a cigarette and takes on a mantle of nonchalance as I approach. My heart is hot in my chest. I step in front of his face and position my body closer to his than I am really comfortable with.

"She is my daughter," I say, pointing to Gabrielle. I make my voice loud, though I can hear its quivering undertones. He draws a long inhale from his cigarette, and smirks. And that smirk calls up a rage in me. I point my finger inches from his moist, suntanned face. "You stop following her." I jab my finger toward his nose. "You stop bothering her. You stay the hell away from her."

The other passengers put down their books or stop their conversations to see why this woman is shouting. Onstage now, he shrugs and shakes his head, as if to say, *I don't understand what you are talking about.* But I stand my ground, staring into his eyes. He is the first to break eye contact. He drops his cigarette onto the deck, crushes it thoroughly, and saunters out of sight.

On our last day in Athens, we wake up early so we can be at the Acropolis when the grounds first open. Before we left for Greece, Gabrielle agreed to have some kind of low-key coming-of-age ceremony on the Acropolis, but she didn't want to plan it. "Surprise me," she said.

So now I lead her to the temple of Athena Parthenos and ask her to dig a shallow hole in the ground. I reach into my purse and pull out a small velvet pouch that I filled with three objects before we left for Greece.

"This is to symbolize your babyhood." I make my voice ceremonious as I place her first baby tooth into the ground.

"This is to symbolize your childhood love of horses." I place a silver horse charm in the hole.

"And this is to symbolize the womanly wisdom of Athena." I place a big, fluffy bard owl feather into the hole. Just then a gust of wind lifts the feather high into the air and swirls it amongst the pillars of the Parthenon before sending it into the crotch of a bewildered German tourist.

"Perfect," Gabrielle says. "Hey, I have something to add." She opens her watercolor case and pulls out a red poppy—colored disk from the row of colors. She crumbles the red paint into the dusty soil and mixes it with her finger. "To symbolize the artist in me."

"And the blood that now spills from your body." I make my voice as cronelike as possible. Gabrielle rolls her eyes.

We cover her shrine with the fine, dusty soil. I want to say something profound, but all I can do is silently pray. *Guide her. Protect her. Help her find her way.*

For our taxi ride to the airport, we are delighted to see that the

164

agency has sent Tomas. After we tell him the highlights of our trip, I go out on a limb. "The hardest part was the men following us, trying to pick us up, harassing us."

Once again I watch his dark eyes through the rearview mirror. For a moment he looks confused, uncertain how to respond. "I am sorry the men bother you here," he begins sincerely. "You know, we Greek men, we love women. Me, I love women even more than I love my guitar, even more than I love my mother."

I resist the urge to tell him this last statement makes no sense. Instead I look out the window at the sprawl of high-rise hotels on the outskirts of the airport. We pass a billboard with a blond, blue-eyed woman in a strapless gown selling Metaxa liqueur.

Tomas breaks the silence between us. "I think maybe the problem is we men don't know how to love you women so good."

Before I have a chance to respond, Gabrielle jumps in. "Maybe the problem is you men don't know how to respect us women so good."

We both turn toward her commanding voice. She calmly holds Tomas's vulnerable gaze in the mirror. Her posture is erect, almost regal, as if Athena herself is sitting beside me.

I relax back onto the cracked vinyl seat and roll down the window. The warm air whooshes into the car, sending everyone's long hair flapping in the wind. Together the three of us inhale the fading scent of sea water, Acropolis dust, and tangerines.

Iceberg

Alison Culliford

In terms of the remote places of the world, Labrador is up there with Timbuktu. Few people could actually place it on the map ("Scotland? Somewhere near the Falkland Islands?"), and my compulsion to go there would have struck my friends as inexplicable even under normal circumstances; going there on my own, six weeks before my wedding day, they saw as pure madness.

Some journeys, however, feel like fate. I had spent three years planning this one, since being tipped off by an enigmatic borehole engineer in Dar es Salaam about the icebreaker traveling up the Canadian coast to villages cut off for nine months of the year by snow and ice. Since my career as a travel writer had taken off after a fruitful trip to Georgia with my fiancé, Mark, one exciting trip had led to another. An inflight magazine gave me carte blanche to find quirky and original stories, with little regard for how near they were to the airline's flight destinations. After years of slaving in offices as a sub-editor, the world, as an oyster, had just landed on my plate. Having never really done the backpacking thing, suddenly I was traveling club class to fulfill my wildest dreams. This trip had everything that a great travel piece needed—a cargo ship, icebergs, whales, and a meeting with people whose lives were radically different from my own—and I definitely needed a break from wedding planning. Besides, boats had always held a certain magic for me. I loved the way the vessel becomes your temporary home, floating in a no-man's-land detached from mundane realities and forging ever onward to a world of possibilities, accompanied by the camaraderie of one's fellow travelers. I had to go now, at the beginning of July, to catch the first ferry of the year and meet the hardy inhabitants emerging from their winter isolation.

Mark was happy to see me finally doing something I loved. His own lifestyle was not dissimilar. He had just spent two months filming in Liverpool and Iceland, seemingly oblivious to the wedding-planning hell I had been going through. In Iceland he'd walked on a glacier in bare feet. In a moment of shared wonder, we both squinted at transparencies held up to the pale London light. "You see, the ice isn't white, but blue," he said.

In the few days we actually got to spend together during those months, there didn't seem time to express my feelings of drowning. Maybe this was just how it was; after all, it was I who had wanted to get married. Since his suggestion for the venue had been vetoed by my mother, he had left it to me to sort out, and the wedding had become almost a taboo subject. I was battling alone, trying to please everyone, not offend anyone, and pull off an organizational coup that would win back his affection and create an illusion that it had all been done effortlessly.

As I waded through white silk, white tulle, white envelopes, a white-painted former theater where we were to hold the reception, the search for a lime-green Citroen DS, and the scary reality that planning a London wedding solo on a budget of £2000 was a very tall order, Labrador became my promised land. I fantasized about disappearing into the snow and ice, and about no longer having to deal with tablecloths and entertainment licenses, guest lists, and the well-meaning but unrelenting telephoning of our two mothers. Tundra was all I longed for.

Getting to Labrador took three days and three planes, each one smaller than the last, till I boarded the twenty-seater that flew from St. John's to St. Anthony, at the tip of Newfoundland, over patches of water looking like spilt gold. I had been booked into a kind of rustic honeymoon suite at the bed-and-breakfast there, and when Mark called to wish me a good trip I felt pangs of loneliness and regret. Why had I come all this way with a stinking cold when I could have been curled up in front of a DVD with him? What exactly was I searching for? On previous trips I had been annoyed that he would call me to report domestic trivia; this time I craved the reassurance of his voice, which I would not hear again for another two weeks. I had to cut the call short, however, as Bonnie and Ed, a Canadian couple who were also going to be traveling on the *Northern Ranger*, had invited me to eat with them. "So how are your cod cheeks?" asked Ed about the local delicacy I had ordered.

"Like the leftovers from a British chip shop, scooped up and refried after lying in grease for a week," I replied.

"Get used to it," they both laughed.

The trip up the coast involved stopping off at some twenty points to deliver goods. Two local guides were assigned to the cruising guests to tell them more about the lifestyle and nature they would encounter, but aside from that, the schedule simply followed the drop-off points, which could occur day or night. In between there would be hours to spend swapping life experiences with the other people on board. Being seaborne is known to break down social barriers—the reason why nineteenth-century heiresses were so carefully chaperoned on their Atlantic crossings. The *Northern Ranger* was no *Titanic,* but the handful of cruising guests (paying around $2,000 each), the locals traveling from village to village in economy class, and the crew all chipped along just fine. "Bet ye caan't unnerstan wh' wr saayin'," joked the sailors. "Bet oi caan," I replied. "Ye taak jus loike wr oim fram." They sounded like the neighbors I grew up with in the southwest of England—despite the fact that their ancestors had arrived here at least two centuries ago.

As we pulled out of St. Anthony's little harbor, the first person to strike up conversation was Carl Wheaton, bristly, red faced, with bright-blue, watery eyes. A lobster fisherman on his "holidays," he was traveling up the coast to see a friend in Makkovik, bedding down nightly in the lounge with his bottle of rum and Coke. Carl pointed out the massive containers that would be unloaded at each port on this, the first voyage of the year after the ice melted.

"What's in them?" I asked.

"Pop, mainly," he replied, and he wasn't joking. Most of the ferry's hold was packed with cans of Coke, along with freezers (who in God's name would need them here?) and snowmobiles. "And see those? Lobster pots," he explained, going on to give me a full briefing on the cod moratorium of 1992 and the government's outrageous policy of sending people from Quebec to build a road and uranium mine. The subject of the uranium and the road brought dark looks from all I met along the coast.

I stayed on the deck for quite a while, filled with a sense of excitement and liberation, and my fellow travelers turned out to be a fascinating bunch. There was Bruce, who stood at the bow in rain, shine, or blizzards, clutching his GPS. He was taking his wife (he flew, she drove) on a long-promised visit to the territories he had worked in as a radio operator in the 1950s. "There were dogs running loose everywhere in those days. The Reverend Peacock was trying to reteach the Eskimos to make snow houses. Never found out if he succeeded. The Hudson's Bay Company wanted them to buy timber, so they persuaded them it was better to build log houses. But snow houses have an advantage, you see: The toilet is inside, a hole in the ground. They only last three weeks or so, just fill it all in. Very practical. I slept in one quite a few times."

Mariah, a sixtysomething divorcée from Cleveland, Ohio, was on a three-month solo journey with her camera. She was keeping a diary of her trip on her laptop, whose screensaver bore a message from her son: "There are no rules in life, Mossy, just do what feels right."

Then there were Alice and Marion, from St. John's itself; Boyd, traveling up the coast to look for communities to develop for tourism while doing some whale watching with his ten-year-old daughter; a lovely Catholic priest; our local Labrador guides, Kirk and Lisa; Otto and Billy, the chefs; Ernest and Lewis, seaman and mate; and the ship's entertainer, who led a Newfie sing-along in the lounge every night.

On these four hundred miles of inhospitable coastline, the coldness of the climate is matched by the immediate warmth of its inhabitants. Our first port of call was Red Bay, where a sixteenth-century Basque whaling ship had been discovered a few years previously, and a museum built around it. Chris Bridle, a young former fisherman, proudly showed us around and described the incredible feeling of discovering that the area he believed had been colonized for the first time by his grandparents had actually been the site of a massive whaling station four hundred years before. At 10 PM, we'd got him out of bed with a cold to greet us. "Anytime you call, we're open," he said cheerily. Meanwhile, with shouted directions and much feverish activity down in the hold, the pallets of beer, diapers, buckets, and crab pots were being unloaded onto the shore, and we had time to exchange just a few words with the excited locals, who included a mother and daughter who had traveled fifty miles to greet the ship.

At the daytime ports, we arrived to a hero's welcome. Children ran over the roofs of warehouses and dived into the oily water, while, disburdening themselves of their cabin fever, their parents rushed up to us to chat with the familiarity of old friends. Never has so much been said in so little time. At Port Hope Simpson, an old guy of ninety reeled through his life story in three minutes flat, expressed his loyalty to the British royal family, then proposed marriage. With few opportunities for work now that fishing was in crisis, the inhabitants made the most of the small opportunities for trade that the *Northern Ranger's* visits offered. Here in Port Hope Simpson, hand-knitted socks, dream catchers, and pottery were laid out on trestle tables in the street, and Kitty, the vendor, openly explained that some of the makers had Down syndrome, the result of inbreeding.

The *Ranger's* visit was a chance not only to meet outsiders, but for everyone in the area to get together and swap news after the winter. Despite the isolation and lack of work, few people showed much enthusiasm for the road-building program. They were proud of their independence and history of hardy survival, close-knit communities that saw no reason for things to change and wanted respect, rather than handouts, from the government. And yet unlike many isolated communities, these folks were incredibly candid and friendly, as curious about us as we were about them. Perhaps the fact of our being part of the functional cargo ship gave us a more natural entrée into their lives.

Most of the villages—Mary's Harbour, Port Hope Simpson, William's Harbour, Pinsent's Arm—were little more than a single street extending along from the wharf, with populations from three hundred down to seventy, all of whom, it seemed, were there waiting for the boat. The buildings were temporary-looking structures of corrugated iron and wood, nailed together and painted in blue and green, the handiwork of people with lots of time and few materials. Farther up the coast, where the indigenous population was stronger, creativity was expressed in the driftwood sculptures and painted sealskin displayed in their little gardens. Still, you couldn't help wondering how on earth they filled the dark winter days.

More memorable than the look of the places were the people and their stories. Kirk's accounts of growing up in little Port Hope Simpson, skating on a frozen lake, and summers fishing in William's Harbour were evocative. We stared into his family's deserted summer house, unused since 1984, and saw peeling wallpaper, a baby's high chair, and a bike. Farther up the coast, at Postville, we met his granddad and were proudly told the story of how this amazing old survivor chopped four fingers and his thumb off with a saw, wrapped them in a handkerchief, and flew to Goose Bay, then St Anthony's, to have them sewn back on. His neighbor, Douglas Jacques, showed us his huskies, like chained wolves with their pale blue eyes, and told us about his exploits in the cross-Labrador dog-driving race. "I'll probably be the last champion 'round here," he said. "Youngsters would rather drive a Ski-Doo."

I watched with Carl, who showed an avid interest in the cargo, the coming and going of the goods. Pinsent's Arm got the first delivery of pop. The insulation found a home at Charlottetown, a village swarming with black flies, where former trapper and local author Bob Powell runs the general store. His story was extraordinary—World War II virtually passed him by as he fought his lone battle against nature, including getting his leg stuck in a trap and almost starving to death.

As we plied up the coast the local passengers changed from mainly Scots and Irish ancestry to Inuit and Innu (Native Americans). I met a young Inuit family traveling up the coast to show their baby to the wife's parents for the first time, a perfect little family group, the mother's smiling face reflected in that of her gurgling daughter. Childhood friends, he was from Hopetown and she from Rigolet. *Will it ever be like that for Mark and me?* I wondered. Could life be that simple once the stress of the wedding buildup was over? At the same time, I feared the boredom of daily routine. I wanted Mark to soar with me, to experience through words and images all the things I had experienced, to push the boundaries of existence. Maybe I was asking for too much.

We were nearing London's latitude, and outside, snow was blowing in flurries around the ship. The captain took us up to the bridge, from where we could see Bruce with his GPS, undaunted, charting every inch forward to the frozen North. Later that night we were all in the lounge for the sing-along, when suddenly, the cry went up: "Iceberg!" I rushed outside, and as we moved through the fog like an elfin pinnace, a magical, magnificent berg passed by, blue in the dusk, the tip of a mountain of mystery and purity.

All the next day we traveled among these majestic bergs, which seemed just beyond arm's reach. Staring into them was mesmerizing. One after another, they progressed on their preordained journey that had started one thousand years earlier when they broke off the ice cap. I photographed them through the long lens Mark had bought me for this trip, and thought of him, walking on glaciers in his bare feet. I wanted him there, but I wanted him to be different, more engaged, more in tune with

174

my inner being. Each photograph, like each detail of the wedding planning, was a gift of love to him, yet I felt I could never get close enough to really see inside. Perhaps if I penetrated the heart of the iceberg, I would achieve the sense of oneness that I craved. Yet the more I stared into the deep blue crevices, the more I reveled in my solitude. At last, far removed from the pressures of others' expectations, the constant deadlines and demands, I centered on myself: who I was, where I was going. And where I wanted to be going now was north, north, ever onward, until we reached the inconceivably massive frozen block from which these great ice gods were messengers.

After the icebergs, something changed in my mentality. I stopped worrying about getting back to London, the politics of the wedding, and the mountain I had to climb just to get back to a position of normality and accepted the fact that I could not communicate from the boat. I just went with the rhythm of the voyage, immersing myself totally in the sights, the sounds, and the stories of people I met. Naturally, as experiences were swapped over cod cheeks in the canteen, people got to know that I was planning to get married. They asked about my fiancé and how we'd met, and expressed joy at the forthcoming happy event. They talked about their relationships, their marriages and divorces, children, travels. "Mark's one very lucky man," they said. And the more I talked about it to these complete strangers, the more I felt distanced from the event, as if it were someone else, not me, that they were referring to.

"There are no rules in life, Mossy, just do what feels right." The phrase chanted itself like a mantra as I lay in my windowless cabin with my dream catchers hanging redundant from the bunks, listening to the throb of the engine and the occasional crash of a block of ice. Increasingly desperate thoughts oppressed me. Could I have the courage to do what Mossy had done, to jump ship so late in the day?

As we neared the last two villages on the run, the atmosphere on board took a darker turn. I'd been warned about this by the sailors: "We got stoned at Davis Inlet," they'd told me at the beginning of the trip, and at the time I thought they were talking about smoking marijuana. But no. They had literally had stones hurled at them by angry villagers who blamed the boat for bringing alcohol into their community. After Rigolet the kitchen staff battened down the hatches—no alcohol was to be sold from now on. And yet this didn't stop bootleggers from flogging gasoline to the Innu, the tragic victims of a desecrated culture. In 1992, six children had burned to death here in a house fire. More recently, two teenagers had doused themselves with petrol and set fire to themselves. We watched in silence from the ship as the goods were set down here as quickly as possible, the seamen who were forced to disembark visibly scared. As we motored off, we saw a child of seven or eight sniffing gasoline on the shore, possibly the saddest image I have ever seen.

Nain was a little more optimistic. Suicide and substance abuse were still a big problem here, but we learned of moves to rebuild pride in the community, such as the Aboriginal Peoples Television Network to be stationed here. At the Moravian Mission, an Inuit man who rejoiced in the name Johannes Markhews Lampe showed us the 1900 chapel and its bizarre collection of brass musical instruments with their own hand-knitted jumpers. Though missionaries were responsible for many of the problems of these communities, the Moravians, uniquely, respected something of the indigenous culture and preached in Inuktikut, resulting in this strange, hybrid central European and Inuit culture. Johannes told us people had been forced to uproot and move to Nain in the 1950s in order to get healthcare. "They turned to alcohol to forget the beautiful land they had turned away from." Every summer he takes his mother back to the cabin thirty kilometers inland where she used to live, to replenish her spirit.

Nain was meant to be the end of my journey, before I flew back to Goose Bay and eventually to London, but fog intervened. The small plane might be grounded for up to two weeks, I was told. If I got back on the boat, I would have four more days at sea before Goose Bay, where I could try to get a standby flight back home. There were ten minutes left before the *Northern Ranger* was due to depart. Should I take a chance and get off in Nain? Seemed like an interesting place, and I was curious to see what the locals would make of the missionary from Bible Belt Ohio, who was the only other person due to leave the boat here. At least I should let Mark know I would be back late. I rushed to the post office and dialed on a clunky 1970s phone. Voicemail. "Stuck in Nain because of fog. Will be late back, not sure when," I said. And dashed to get back on the boat.

A weird sense of anticlimax engulfed me. The previous night, the other passengers had had a send-off party where Ed had written a song about my getting married. It had brought me to tears. They welcomed me back on the boat—"We're so happy, we didn't want to lose you"—but I was all at sea. I spent the next four days in limbo. The voyage had ended for me, yet I feared the future. *Stop! I want to get off!* my inner voice cried. But all around was fog. Solemnly, I wrote an SOS, put it in a bottle, and threw it over the side. When I eventually arrived home, things had disintegrated. Unable to understand my message, Mark had thought I was in Maine, which at the time seemed to me a limp excuse for not even getting up off the sofa to welcome me. He felt betrayed by my nonappearance. I felt injured by his coldness. But more than this, the moment with the iceberg had made me militant. I wanted my life back, and even though the wedding plans were almost tied up, I felt resentful about the months during which I'd battled alone. I ended it in the worst and most cowardly way possible: by sleeping with someone else. Three days later we canceled our wedding.

I lost my dream catchers but still have a few shards of labradorite, a glistening mineral that I keep as a talisman, and a pair of children's moccasins whose future owner is as yet undecided. The following winter, just before setting off to start a new life in Paris, I looked down on Labrador from the air en route to New York, and in the paths of the frozen tundra, where sea and earth become one, I saw my own destiny in retrospect. It had become abundantly clear over these last few months that I had made the right decision: marriage was not right for me.

Although I often wonder what it would have been like had we taken the journey together—would marriage ultimately have cemented, rather than divided, our relationship?—this solo voyage had unleashed a need to be free that was like a force of nature, destructive and unstoppable. Despite the fallout, I will never regret it.

The Trek to Thirty

Aarti Sawhney

I secure myself into the diminutive plane's seat and press my face against the window. Surrendering to the narrative that is about to unfold, I temporarily forget all the anxiety that has preceded this moment. We take off suddenly, and the slowly steadying plane bounces me about to its erratic beat. Sprawling, suffocating Delhi seems to dissolve before my eyes. Compressed neighborhoods give way to the crisp, geometric forms of Punjab's cultivated acres. My eyes strain to locate Chandigarh, the city where my grandparents died. On our biennial trips to India during my childhood, we would travel there from Delhi in a caravan of relatives.

Fields of wheat, rice, and mustard collide against sudden foothills, forcing my reminiscences to retreat for the time being. The sharp demarcation between the plains and the mountains is so distinct I can trace it with my finger.

Our path contours the weary and older, but greener, Himalayas. Eventually, we make our first stop. Nearly scraping a few treetops, we pounce on a narrow landing strip. A couple of passengers get off and a new one boards; the casual swap makes me smile—it feels like we are on a bus.

Beyond Shimla, the trees are lost among young, robust peaks. As a child, I often stayed up late watching mythological Hindi films set in the Himalayas. Peering down, I imagine Bollywood's charming gods maintaining world order and settling scores in those tranquil, awe-inspiring ranges. Soon I too will wander along that rugged terrain in an attempt to do something significant—I'm just not sure what, exactly.

On the ground several hours later, I arrive at my final destination for the day: Solang Nallah, a tiny, picturesque tourist stop, located in the hills halfway between Manali and the source of the Beas River. My rickshaw pulls up in front of a compact, yellowing concrete inn with a red corrugated roof. Hotel Iceland is a smaller and sleepier place than I had imagined. I had also expected to be expected—but other than the ubiquitous lazy mutt, no one approaches or wags a tail.

Across the way there seems to be a more functional guesthouse. I walk over, peek in, and offer a tentative greeting to a young, mustachioed man who is finishing his lunch. He is neither surprised nor disturbed by my presence.

"Do you know Khem?" I ask.

"Yes, of course, from Hotel Iceland," he replies.

"Any idea where I might find him?" I ask, somewhat encouraged.

"Khem?" he repeats.

"Yes."

He shakes his head emphatically, and my heart sinks.

"Where is he?" I inquire, fighting off panic.

"He's gone off with some Japanese people. He is showing them the mountains. They want to make a ski resort in this area."

I'm shocked by this news. My cousin had arranged for me to stay with his friend Khem, and he is nowhere to be found. Things seldom go according to plan in India, but hospitality is a cardinal cultural rule. How could a cousin's friend abandon his promise to look after me?

Lacking any other alternative, I return to Hotel Iceland and meet Raju, a twelve-year-old boy. His vague notion of who I am gives me some comfort. He confirms that Khem is away but assures me that Gokul, Khem's cousin, will come by in the evening to look in on me.

I have no choice but to wait and trust.

Raju takes my bags and leads me to a small, tidy concrete room with an attached bathroom that is as simple as it is clean, much to my obsessive-compulsive relief. A thick, dusty screen on the room's only window obscures a dazzling view.

"Are there other guests here?" I ask somewhat perfunctorily.

"Nope, nowadays there isn't anybody," Raju answers, confirming what I already know. As he explains that Hotel Iceland is essentially closed for renovation, I realize that the absence of other tourists will at least benefit my Hindi.

Raju sets off to prepare the lunch he has just asked me about, and I remain on the balcony. A perfectly placed chair allows me to contemplate the view, as well as my situation. In my head, two versions of my reality battle it out like little over-the-shoulder cartoon angels and devils.

Version Number One: *Isn't this great? I am surrounded by forests, snowcapped peaks, and glaciers. It will be so nice to have some peace and quiet after noisy, crowded, in-your-face Delhi.*

Version Number Two: *This sucks! I'm the only guest here. How will the time pass? Is this even safe? I'm sure these people think I'm crazy. What on earth am I doing here?*

Feeling scared and lonely, I revisit the events that brought me to this moment.

A frequent hiker and occasional backpacker, I had always assumed I would find myself on a Himalayan trek during one of my almost-annual trips to India in my twenties. Yet for a variety of reasons, it never happened. Some years I visited during the wrong season. Some years I lacked company. And every year it was just hard to get away from my very large and very hospitable family.

As my thirtieth birthday approached, I began to take stock of my life in the unfortunate way of neurotic TV-show characters. I found that my life at "almost thirty" was very different from what a younger me had imagined. I started to catalog all of the things that were missing: A partner, a job I liked, and a place of my own topped the list. And then there were smaller, though equally vital, deficiencies. Each year I had fewer adventures that pushed my limits, and fewer friends who were available for the commitment and spontaneity those adventures required. I wasn't fluent in Hindi. I hadn't written anything. And I had never done that Himalayan trek.

Feeling empty and dissatisfied, I decided to make some changes. Eventually, I would discover that those changes needed to take place inside; but at that time, it seemed easiest to just discard everything on the outside. So I left the two best roommates I'd ever known, quit my job, and went to India, arriving in Delhi a couple of weeks before my thirtieth birthday.

Within a few days I started to ask around about the possibilities of arranging a trek—now my symbol of hope for a better, more satisfying life. I called some travel agencies, thinking that perhaps I could join an already-scheduled group.

"Sorry, ma'am, it's not possible. If people are traveling with their friends, why would they want a stranger to join them?" Or, "Sorry, ma'am, this year we have no bookings. Because of U.S. warnings, people are not coming this season." These were the typical responses to my inquiries.

I tried the Internet and found that most companies charged a minimum price for four trekkers. At my aunt's suggestion I contacted a government tourist agency. They offered a glimmer of hope, but upon learning that I was a woman traveling alone, they changed their tune.

With the season drawing to a close, my relatives tried to convince me to delay the trek. "Plan it for next summer. We can all go together." They had no idea what this trip meant to me, and I wasn't about to tell them. I feared that sharing concerns about my life with my family would invite unwanted "helpful" advice or action. The last thing I needed was a series of lectures, or awkward introductions to "eligible boys." I nodded politely as they tried to dissuade me, but continued my investigation with the same poor results.

After two weeks, I was ready to give up. I started to consider other ways to spend my time in India. I got the schedule for a yoga class. I researched different travel options. Then I met Tumpy, a second cousin previously unknown to me. Tumpy had apparently spent much time trekking, traveling, and writing in Himachal Pradesh's Spiti Valley. I explained my dilemma to him, and before I knew it he was on the phone with a friend.

"Khem? Hi, how are you? Yes, it's been a long time. Listen, I have a cousin who wants to go on a trek. Can you arrange something for her?"

They talked for a few minutes more before Tumpy hung up. Grinning at his own helpfulness, he informed me, "It's all set. Just let me know when you make your booking for Manali and I'll give him a call."

As simple as that, my problem was solved. When you know the right person, India is a place where anything is possible.

Remembering my intent and the initial difficulty involved in arranging this trip, I resolve to stay positive for the moment and cling, however tenuously, to Version Number One. Over lunch I start to feel better. The dining room is clearly the center of life and activity at Hotel Iceland. A few young men help serve my meal and then eat their lunches, absorbed in the cricket match on TV. I am not much of a cricket fan, but today I welcome the life it breathes into this quiet place and the attention it draws away from me.

I explore the village a bit and feel even more at ease when I befriend a Nepali brother and sister who own a little shop with a phone booth up the road. She is surprised to find a woman traveling alone, and more surprised to learn that I have come all this way to pay money to walk in the mountains. He understands it a bit more, having worked as an assistant guide once. A devoted younger brother, he tries to explain my purpose to his sister.

"You see, where she lives they don't get to see mountains like this. They travel everywhere in cars. For them it's nice to walk up something new."

She nods, but seems unconvinced. As I listen to her brother's description and consider their perspective, the absurdity of my venture is embarrassingly obvious.

In the evening Gokul comes, as promised. After the requisite small talk, I ask him about my trek.

"We can walk to the source of the Beas River," he suggests. "If we start early, we can come back the same day. Otherwise, we might have to spend the night."

I nod and almost agree to his suggestion, but then I muster up the courage to speak out.

"Actually, I want to spend the night."

"Okay, no problem."

"Actually, I want to spend a few nights . . . I want to go on a bigger trek."

Gokul does not seem pleased with my plans—and I fear that he was dumped with the responsibility of taking care of me against his will. However, after we talk for a while and agree on a price, he becomes more enthused.

The following morning we meet in Manali and buy more food than I can imagine consuming in a few days. We arrange for the horses and meet Hiralal, our guide, to whom I am instantly drawn. He is skinny, quiet, and incredibly handsome. His infinite eyes, set deep within the sharply molded landscape of his face, look away each time I stare.

Our trek begins two days later, with a steep ascent from Prini village, near Manali, just above six thousand feet. The path is challenging, if not particularly scenic. Passing through several settlements, we remain connected to civilization throughout the day. As we climb I keep my gaze glued to the trail in an effort to avoid all the fresh cow dung. Occasionally we pass locals, who stare at me before exchanging a few words with Gokul in Kulvi, the local language. I wonder if they are mocking me for paying so much to walk the path they are obliged to walk daily.

After two hours of hiking in silence, we stop for what I think will be a break. We sit on an enclosed grassy area outside a cozy, one-room structure, where tea is served to us within a few minutes of our arrival. I am happy to be resting, until I learn that we are done for the day.

Apparently, Hiralal has to return to Manali because some foreigner is missing his sleeping pad. I'm not exactly sure how he is involved in this, but it's clear that he is going to go back whether I object or not. Knowing that I have to spend five days alone with these two men, I decide not to piss them off the first day, though I do feel cheated that my trek is being delayed, and that we will spend our first night out near people and cows.

I am also annoyed, because the American in me wants to push my body to its physical limits. But I say nothing. I sulk for a while, considering the long afternoon and evening ahead, deciding that this would be a good time to have a companion with whom to chat or play cards.

Several hours later, fully settled in our tea-stall home, my disappointment at arriving so early has faded. The afternoon passes with ease, and I become grateful for the opportunity to absorb the rhythm of life in the tea hut. I take several walks, lie in the sun, and chat more comfortably with Gokul. There is a constant stream of activity—shepherds, cows, and horses flow as freely as the tea.

The evening air brings a chill, which prompts Gokul to start cooking dinner. Crouched close to the stove, he tells me amazing things. I hear about the first time he traveled by plane, saw the ocean, and went, petrified, to the big city.

"Do you know that in Bombay, the sun sets behind the ocean?" he asks.

"No, I've only been to Bombay once, a long time ago," I reply.

"My whole life I had only seen the sun set behind the mountains. It was amazing to see it set behind the water," he continues.

We talk about travel, and I am surprised to hear him speak so positively of tourism's impact on his homeland.

"People's thinking has become broader—they are more aware of the importance of education. Most of the village children go to school, especially the girls," he boasts. "The youngest girl to climb Everest is from my village."

As Gokul is completing his description of village life during the different seasons, Hiralal returns from his second climb of the day. I think about how hard his work is, and I am no longer upset by our delay. He is a soft-spoken, delicate man. I imagine that the high-maintenance foreigner gave him a hard time, and I feel apologetic for the degree of maintenance I require.

He joins us for a candlelit dinner in the tent, now converted into a kitchen. We chat over a complete Desi meal. Our intimacy forces me to recognize the limits of my Hindi. While I understand most of what Gokul says, I cannot respond with any depth or sophistication. I agree or ask another question each time he finishes. It is good to listen for a change, especially to someone who has many insights and experiences to share.

After dinner I understand, from their short exchange in Kulvi, that the two men are getting ready for some post-work drinking. Though we have grown more comfortable with one another, I don't want to push appropriate limits. I decide to retire to my tent.

As the candle's flame reflects in their glowing, tanned faces and in our steel dishes, it occurs to me that even though the hike was disappointing, I did experience great beauty today. I know I can neither photograph this moment nor reminisce about it later with a companion, so I sit a few more minutes and just absorb it. For the second time today, the absence of a travel partner forces me to be more present in the moment.

On day two, we encounter a young woman who has come to retrieve her herd of cattle. They refuse to follow her commands, so Gokul and Hiralal dutifully stop to help while I, now accustomed to delays, watch in amusement. One rogue calf gives them a run for their money and they wind up chasing him around in circles. A great deal of laughter heralds a wonderful day ahead and reminds me of how lucky I am to be in such good company.

This young woman is at ease with our group, and she roams freely and without fear in these hills, which, I am beginning to realize, are a special and uniquely safe place for women. I wish I could call my mother at this moment and tell her not to be worried, as I'm sure she is.

The rest of the day is green, and perfect. Our hike is long and exhausting. We skirt meadows, cross rivers, and lose ourselves in a forest, only to emerge out onto an inviting grassy area that we choose as our resting place. Taking advantage of my solitude as the men set up camp, I sketch the view ahead. Rocky, treeless, and dramatic, it promises exciting things to come.

Our dinner is similar to that of the previous night: Gokul talks, Hiralal and I listen. Tonight he is more political than personal. He denounces corruption, extols communism, and even endorses temporary dictatorship for India. He expresses some frustration over what he labels the "foolishness" of some of his family members.

"They spend lots of money when the magician comes to town. They are so impressed by his cheap tricks, but they never wonder about the real magic. What makes an airplane fly or the telephone work?"

The next day is *the* day. We are to cross the Hamta Pass. Just above fourteen thousand feet, it will be the highest place I've ever been. For breakfast, I force myself to down butter-soaked toast. With heavy stomachs, we climb for four straight hours. The views are stunning, but as the grade becomes more severe, I can only concentrate on each step.

Gokul and Hiralal stop for a bite, but I can't even think of eating the hard-boiled eggs offered for lunch.

"How much longer until we get to the pass?" I ask, trying to sound casual.

"Not too much—maybe forty-five minutes, an hour?" Gokul responds.

I am momentarily comforted that we've completed 80 percent of the climb. But then I start to worry. *What if he forgot to account for my slow pace? What if it's more like two hours? I'll die. . . .*

Our path is now covered in snow. My tired feet provide tenuous grounding, and I start to doubt my ability to last another hour. After about fifteen minutes, the trail curves to the left and winds between two narrow peaks—the Hamta Pass is within view!

Gokul encourages me to hurry, now that we've reached our destination well before he said we would. He couldn't have orchestrated a more euphoric arrival.

The pass's elevation is marked with a small sign. Other trekkers have left their marks too. I study the etched initials on the jagged wall flanking the trail and take pictures with my rented camera. Posing with uniform smiles, each of us seems equally pleased. Though Hiralal and Gokul have been here before, and will come here again, I fantasize that in some way this trip is unique for them as well.

We trade a glacial landscape for desertlike terrain as we descend the other side of the pass. Our day has been long, but we keep a fast pace. The weather looks like it might turn, so Gokul decides to continue past our original destination in the hope of finding a warmer spot. Happy that this challenging day is becoming even more intense, I follow along on jellied legs.

We find an adequate spot just before dusk. A small hailstorm batters our hastily constructed camp shortly after our arrival. Gokul responds by making french fries and soup. We thaw out temporarily, but a cold night is followed by an even colder morning.

The previous mornings were frosty too, but we always woke up to a bit of sunlight within view. Initially just a narrow strip of light on one of the hills, it would gradually expand as the line that separated warmth from shade descended the mountain. Once the sunlit patch got within our reach, I would walk to it and plop down, pointing my face toward the sun to warm up.

This morning, however, our valley is tucked away beyond the sun's reach. The cold does not help my aching muscles and stiff bones, which will remember yesterday's descent for some time. They resist movement until I fuel them with extra cups of tea.

After a slow start, we eventually complete our descent. Entering the Spiti Valley, we are reunited with the sun in a place that looks like the moon. We cross the gushing Chander River on an improvised bridge (really just a pole wedged between rocks). I have no fear as I leap toward Gokul, giving him full responsibility for my safety and, if I want to be dramatic, my life.

Beyond the river it is a short walk to Chattru, a random point on the road that services Spiti during the summer months. Chattru consists only of several contiguous *dhabas* (food stalls), but still, like so many empty areas we trekked through, it has a name.

We celebrate the end of our trek with hefty fried *paranthas*. Gokul and Hiralal nap while I sit and write to the sounds of a transistor radio, wondering about the lives of those who make their home here, up high and far away, cut off from the rest of the world for several months of the year.

I order countless cups of sugary tea and begin to get antsy. We are waiting for the bus that will take us to Manali, but, of course, there is no fixed schedule.

After sitting for three hours, I finally see it in the distance. We rush to ready our things and say a sad goodbye to Hiralal, who will spend the night at Chattru before beginning his solo trek back with the horses.

Gokul and I stand at the side of the road and wave at the bus, which passes us without slowing down. My eyes expand and my hands beat the air. Gokul is unfazed.

"It must be full. I guess we'll have to spend the night here," he declares.

"What? How can that be? Won't they send another?" I demand.

"No, not until tomorrow."

"But what if that one's full too?"

Gokul shrugs. "Maybe we can pay someone else to take us."

I sit by the road, my gaze fixed on the horizon, and pray for a ride. It's a while before anyone stops. Two truck drivers refuse to take us (contrary to Gokul's prediction). Now that staying seems inevitable, I rethink my reluctance. I get ready to settle into comfortable clothes for the night, just as an overstuffed Mahindra jeep pulls up for a snack. Already carrying five passengers and heaps of luggage, it seems like an impossible option for us, but Gokul approaches the driver, a corpulent Sardar from Punjab, anyway.

Just as I've learned to accept that things seldom go according to plan, I am also learning that often, right when you're about to give up hope, something surprising happens. The jeep's passengers rearrange their luggage to make room for us and our gear as I look on, incredulous. The men pile into the rear cabin and I am offered the front passenger seat. Rather than feeling guilty about this privilege, I consider it an early birthday present. Lowering the window, I prepare to spend the last few hours as a twenty-nine-year-old watching the vistas reveal themselves to the sound of joyful Punjabi rhythms.

Lightened

Barbara Sjoholm

Copenhagen's Central Station very early on a dank December morning: cold enough to keep your coat on, not cold enough to ignore the stench of stale beer and vomit. Later this Saturday the cavernous main hall would surge with travelers. Now drunks were sleeping it off on any bench where you might want to sit, and disheveled clusters of men or men and younger girls lurched around where they'd spent the night, still having acrimonious conversations fueled by drink. The few people in the café seemed melancholy and burdened, as if traveling to funerals.

I nibbled a croissant and sipped strong coffee with cream, cursing myself for getting here almost an hour before my train. All because I'd been determined to save money and take the city bus, rather than call a taxi and arrive just before the train departed for Hamburg. All because of my obsession with not missing a departure. I was always early—the curse of the firstborn child, so they said. Yet this morning my unease seemed disproportionate; I wasn't otherwise unhappy. In fact, I'd had a wonderful, though often solitary, time the last three weeks in Denmark, researching a subject I was passionate about, the life and times of Emilie Demant Hatt, the painter and ethnologist. Today I was homeward bound. I was taking the train to Amsterdam, where I'd spend two nights before leaving on Monday for Seattle.

I'd always liked Amsterdam, but now it seemed a foolish decision to have added a stay in that city to the end of the trip, when really all I wanted was to be magically transported home to my familiar warm bed, with the down comforter up over my head. I pushed my croissant away, unable to finish it for sudden nausea. Instead of recalling the many absorbing things I'd learned about Emilie Demant Hatt, I remembered another Dane, one who wrote books titled *Fear and Trembling* and *The Sickness Unto Death*. Kierkegaard was always having existential moments like this. The oily look of cream floating on black coffee could do that: make you queasy enough to doubt the existence of a positive creative force in the universe.

I got up from the café table, unable to finish my breakfast, and began slowly rolling my suitcase around the hall. I tried to put a spring in my step and a cool expression on my face—the woman traveler's persona that says, *Don't even think about messing with me*. But I hadn't slept well and my movements seemed glacially slow. My suitcase weighed a ton, packed as it was with books, notebooks, a fat Danish dictionary, and winter clothes and boots. My leaden old laptop was strapped to the top of the rolling suitcase, and in my small daypack I had the really important notes and writing. I even had a purse with me this trip, hidden down at the bottom of the daypack. I'd spent a good deal of this trip in libraries, where a purse was the only thing you could take into the reading rooms. I hadn't wished to wear a fanny pack and advertise that I was American when I took out my ID.

When did I become the kind of woman who traveled with a purse, even a hidden one? With so much luggage? I remembered many trips in the past when I'd zipped around Europe with only a small red backpack, red so I could keep an eye on it. Even more recently, traveling around the North Atlantic several years earlier and writing about women and the sea, I'd managed to keep my wardrobe small, my burdens light, by discarding clothes and shipping books home as I bought them. But this trip I hadn't been a traveler so much as a researcher based in Copenhagen. I hadn't bothered to ship books or papers home, and now I felt the weight of everything I had with me. I was a walking—make that staggering—mini-office suite. It wore me out to think I'd be dragging all this stuff around for the next three days, along cobbled canal streets and up and down those vertiginous Dutch staircases.

It was early to get down to the platform for the Hamburg train, but I decided I might as well. The atmosphere along the tracks was, if anything, even more dispiriting than the central hall upstairs: dark, sooty, stinky, freezing. The strange sick feeling in my gut deepened, vibrated through my body. *Who am I? Why am I here? Where am I going? Why do I have to go?* I often experienced panic around getting to airports and bus and train stations on time; it was the stuff of nightmares, these departures, and though in real life I never missed a flight or train, that wasn't true of my dreams.

In my anxiety-laden travel nightmares, I never managed to get to the station or airport on time. My suitcase was always too small, and I kept wasting valuable time trying to pack far too much in. I didn't speak the language to ask directions and often wandered dark and unfamiliar streets. The taxi driver didn't know the way or brought me to the wrong station. And often in these dreams, a big round clock hung on the wall, moving painfully slowly, but always moving forward to the hour of departure: *tick, tock, tick, tock.*

It didn't help to know, intellectually, that my nightmares were most likely about death, or that generally once I actually got on the plane or train, I was fine or more than fine: cheerful, relaxed, forward-looking. Yes, I'll take a newspaper, and a Diet Sprite, thanks.

A young German couple with backpacks came along the platform and stood smoking right nearby. I moved away, bumped into a man all in black, with a hat pulled down comically over his forehead. His skin was unnaturally pale, his eyes ice blue, and those eyes shifted away when they caught mine. My hand tightened automatically on my suitcase, with the heavy old laptop sitting on it. Every night for three weeks I'd written up my notes on women artists of the late nineteenth and early twentieth century. Now I mustered a little of the woman traveler's tough persona. No one was going to take this laptop from me.

197

The laptop had sustained me the entire visit, been a daily companion. I'd felt my solitude at times—yes, sometimes it had been lonely to come out of the Royal Archives when the reading room closed and walk through a city growing festive with Christmas decorations. But it had been a pleasing sort of loneliness. I often walked all the way home to the tiny studio apartment I was renting from a piano teacher, Magrit, and shopped a little in the small Turkish market near the house in the district called "Potato Rows," for the English-style streets of terraced brick houses. As my soup or pasta cooked on the hot plate, I turned on the computer and the lamp and was happy. Now I took the laptop off the suitcase where it had been strapped, and put it between the heavy black boots I was wearing.

More and more people had arrived on the platform; still, I felt uneasy. Above us the clock ticked inexorably but with stunning slowness. I wanted the train to come, because I wanted to be on it and finished with my fears that something really dreadful was happening or about to happen; and I wanted the train to be postponed, so that I could have a reason to just walk away, back upstairs, and completely change my plans. Two minutes, one minute, and now we heard the engine's heavy, hot, metallic rush toward us and saw the coach windows flashing by, the conductors jumping off, the doors opening. Usually, from anxiety, I was one of the first passengers to find my correct coach and my seat. But now I stood, almost paralyzed, while everyone else flowed around me. I couldn't remember where my seat was, or even the right coach number. I paused to take out my reservation slip from my purse, the purse I'd securely hidden at the bottom of my small daypack. Still I stood there. *Don't get on that train.* Was I having some kind of premonition? Was the train going to crash? Should I warn everyone?

I jammed the purse back into the daypack, grasped my laptop in one hand and the suitcase in the other, pushed forward, and hoisted myself onto the train. Everything seemed too bright, the colors of the vinyl seats too loud. The aisle was narrow and everyone was struggling to find seats, dragging luggage back and forth. My reserved seat was in the middle of the compartment, on the aisle. I tried to breathe calmly, but I was almost hyperventilating in panic. Finally I found my seat and set down the laptop carefully and my suitcase, shrugged off my daypack, momentarily surprised to find it zipped open.

The surprise turned into shock. My purse was gone. Had it fallen out? I retraced my steps, then rushed back to my seat, looking on the floor, saying wildly, "My purse, my purse." Everything was in that purse—credit cards, passport, tickets for the train and international flight. The train whistle sounded. I grabbed my suitcase, laptop and was out the door again. A minute later the train was gone and I stood on the now-empty platform, holding my laptop to my chest.

Why was it that I felt so incredibly relieved?

Every day about thirty thefts take place in Copenhagen's Central Station, from pickpocketing to brazen mugging. Most of the thefts are highly organized, carried out by gangs, often from Poland, I was told. During the hour I spent in the police station, two other women came in. My case was more complicated than theirs—they were Danish—because of my missing passport and plane ticket, but also because one of my two Visa companies routed me to someone in Panama with a thick accent and we spent fifteen minutes trying to understand each other. Someone had already tried to use my credit cards. I woke my girlfriend, Betsy, from a sound sleep and told her the bad news. At that point I still imagined I'd be able to get a new passport at the U.S. embassy and take a later train to Amsterdam. I didn't mention to Betsy, not in front of the patient desk officer who was letting me use the phone, how I felt as if I'd been pardoned from a death sentence.

Of the many places in the world to be robbed, Denmark must count among the best. A girl at the minimart had first led me to the police station; afterward she took me to a place to leave my luggage for free. Although I didn't have a single krone, I still had a punch strip for the bus and metro in my coat pocket. How light I felt stepping onto the subway car, with no purse or daypack, no identity or money to worry about any longer. How unburdened I felt stepping out of the metro and strolling down Dag Hammarskjölds Allé in the early morning light. The American embassy wasn't far from where I'd been staying in the Potato Rows; it was almost across the street from a library where I'd often checked email, and I'd seen the Stars and Stripes flying and felt my usual ambivalence. We were again at war and disliked for it, and there was nothing I could ever say to anyone here to apologize enough.

The day had brightened, though it was still cold. Just as it had been almost impossible to breathe deeply and be mindful in the train station, so was it easy now. I looked in wonder at the helmetless Danes on their sturdy black bicycles in the bike lanes, pulling their tiny children behind them in trailers. I admired the nineteenth-century architecture of the apartment buildings. The air tasted cold and crisp in my lungs. It felt so good to stride along the street. I swung my arms, delighting in the sense of not carrying anything. I hadn't lost my notes or my laptop. Passport, tickets, money—they were just bits of plastic or paper that could be replaced.

The marine out front of the embassy told me it was closed for the weekend and that I'd have to come back Monday morning. "But I have a flight from Amsterdam Monday morning!"

"Sorry, ma'am."

I walked away in a daze, penniless, without an identity, my mind scrabbling to figure out the next step. I walked over to Magrit's house on the street in the Potato Rows. Although her apartment was booked that night, she gave me coffee, sympathy, and a $100 cash loan. And that was the beginning of a strange and wonderful two days. I suddenly had time to eat in the vegetarian restaurant I'd always wanted to try, to visit the small sculpture museum I'd missed, to walk the streets taking photographs like the tourist I'd previously been pretending not to be. The Mermaid Hotel, where I'd stayed a couple of times before, welcomed me back without a credit card. My story of being robbed was sad and interesting to all, and except for telling Betsy my strange experience on the platform, I didn't share my relief, or my enormous happiness, at having two more days in Copenhagen. Yes, it cost me lots more money. I had phone calls to make, a wire to pick up at Western Union, a new passport to apply for. None of this bothered me; I was unusually serene. And when I left on Tuesday, flying direct from Copenhagen to Seattle, I only felt the usual amount of flurry getting to the airport and on the plane.

I have often wondered since about that train to Hamburg. I never heard it crashed, but that doesn't mean it might not have if I'd been on it. I've wondered if I averted a tragedy somehow—and if I saved the lives of hundreds of people, including my own. Or perhaps my fate would have been less spectacular. I might have eaten tainted food in Amsterdam, brushed a sick stranger's hand, or been run over by a tram. From time to time, even though I swear I'm not really superstitious, my Irish blood stirs and I seem to know something I should or shouldn't do. When I think that way, it's easy to believe that the nausea and horror I felt were strong enough to override reason. That I subconsciously engineered a way to not travel by train that day, even to the point of displaying my purse and setting it carelessly in my daypack.

At other times I think that's self-deluding nonsense. That's when I recall taking my purse out in the café to buy the croissant and coffee and then burying it, in view of everyone around me, in the daypack. I was probably followed down to the platform by someone who saw me, distracted and sleepy, as an easy mark. I remember the man with pale skin and ice-blue eyes, who had the look of the grim reaper in his black clothes and pulled-down hat. After thirty-five years of travel, there's one thing I do know: Other people are watching you, even if you're not watching them. And I *had* noticed him. I had just been too preoccupied thinking about Kierkegaard to really register him as a threat.

The mind is always inventive; we shape and turn and twist memory to serve our egos. It's more subtle and flattering, perhaps, to think of myself as psychic rather than stupid. Yet the memory of nausea, of *fear and trembling*, stays with me and I know I haven't made up the sense of panicked horror I felt to see the clock ticking above me and hear the train rushing into the station, though surely, in retrospect, the clock was digital and had no hands. The hands came from my dreams.

If there's a deeper reason I was relieved to see the train steam off without me, perhaps it had to do with an email I had received, at the library across the street from the American embassy, a few days earlier. A colleague who was becoming a friend had written to tell me she had cancer. In fact, she'd had recurrences for fourteen years; it was now spreading. I'd cried at the library computer when I'd read her letter, with its lack of self-pity, its bravery, its determination to live and to thrive. Jan's death was a year in the future, time enough to get to know her much better and to believe that somehow she might survive; yet perhaps a shadow of her coming absence passed over me that morning at Copenhagen Central.

Departures in search of new or unknown places, for all their connotations of pleasure and exploration, have inevitably had something of my night terrors attached to them. Travel, along with bringing the possibility of unexpected joy, can also seem a harrowing of the soul, a tempting of fortune. I set off on my journeys wondering if I really will be able to return home. When I do come back, with tales of humorous misadventures and delightful chance occurrences, I feel emboldened to dream of traveling again, to take part in a play, partly of my own devising, that dramatizes fate and offers the possibility of escape. Departures are leave-takings, but generally they end in arrivals. In between there's the chance to let go of all that baggage, all those fears and worries, to travel light.

I still wonder if I escaped death that day, or only imagined that I could. But just as often I think of walking, carefree and unburdened, down the streets of Copenhagen, breathing in the cold morning air, nothing in my hands or on my back to weigh me down, nothing to carry any longer.

Shokran

Alice Carey

When I was a young girl I loved a popular song called "You Belong to Me," and at an early age I vowed I'd see all the exotic places mentioned in that song.

By the time I was fifty I had "flown the ocean in a silver plane" and "watched the sunrise on a tropic isle." I had even "seen the marketplace in old Algiers," but I had yet to see the place I wanted to see most. I had yet to "see the pyramids along the Nile."

Then, in 2002, I got my chance. My husband, Geoffrey, was going to be in Cairo for a United Nations meeting, and I decided to tag along. The only hitch being I'd have to be on my own during the day for an entire week, as UN conferences go from sunup to sundown. The week we were slated to go was also the week that coincided with the first anniversary of 9/11.

When Geoffrey told his colleagues his wife was planning to wander around Cairo on her own for a week, he was met with strong admonitions from the primarily female staff. They intoned that it was dangerous for a Western woman to travel alone in Egypt, especially (though no one put it in so many words) if that woman spoke with an Irish brogue and sported a head of brightly hennaed red hair. She would need a driver, a guide, someone who knew the city, to be with her all the time and—if the need arose—protect her.

But I was having none of it. The prospect of wandering along the Nile in Cleopatra's footsteps was so intoxicating, I was bursting with excitement—an excitement I could experience only as a woman alone.

Since Islamic dress code requires women to cover all their hair and wear long, loose-fitting clothing, I knew it would be best if I conformed. But I wanted to do it my way and in my own style. Coming to this realization so easily is one of the perks of middle age. When I was a young woman, I would have rebelled. I'd have railed to the God of Islamic Fashion: "Listen up there! This is the 1960s and I'm a modern gal. I wear what I want when I want to and that's all there is to it. Like it or lump it, I'm wearing what suits me in this torrid Egyptian weather." But that was then. And this is now. And I am now wise enough to know which wars are worth waging and which aren't. So I accept the Islamic status quo completely. I cut off all my hair until it is marine-boot-camp short and I pack a flat-brimmed straw boater to hide what's left of it. I buy a series of long-sleeve Brooks Brothers men's cotton shirts and several pairs of long white linen pants. And voilà! I am completely covered—my way.

When the plane touches down in Cairo in the middle of the night, everyone is up and around. On the drive in from the airport, I see women and children reclining under palm trees, eating roasted corn, a popular snack, and large cones of Day-Glo—colored cotton candy. Do Egyptians sleep? Well, they do, but not like Westerners.

Next morning, first thing, I head for the hotel's roof garden, hoping to see the pyramids. And I do, but barely. The pyramids are not anywhere near the city. They are way, way up the Nile. And I can barely make them out—three little triangles baking in the dusty morning sun. It will be a while before I can really see them.

Yet there's the Nile. The Nile! Not as pretty as I hoped. But there it is: a Stephen Dedalus "snot green" Nile, all dolled up with sea grass and white-and-purple water hyacinth, leisurely making its way through the city upriver from Luxor, Aswan, and its source, Burundi.

To my surprise, there is no one around on the street and it dawns on me that my New York habit of a cup of coffee, a newspaper, and a croissant eaten in a café may not exist in Egypt. What's more, morning as I know it does not seem to exist either, in that most people are still sleeping after having been up all night.

At the time I was making notes for a new memoir. And because I did not bring my laptop with me (I was writing by hand in copybooks), I needed a place to go to write, preferably outside. Perhaps on the Nile esplanade on the other side of a very large thoroughfare across from my hotel, where there were a few scattered park benches.

But first a word about Cairo traffic: Traffic runs continuously on a six-lane highway in the middle of the city, designed to keep commerce flowing and pedestrians terrified. There are no traffic lights at all (even in the middle of town—say, around the Egyptian Museum).

Picture me then, please, in the disguise of a latter-day Rosalind— unadorned and with hidden hair—in her Egyptian Elyria, standing by the side of an autobahn (with three lanes whizzing north to Alexandria, and three south to the pyramids), hoping to get to the Nile and realizing there is no easy way to cross this road.

I get scant comfort from the few pedestrians scattered about waiting for a break in the traffic. Traffic that consists of trucks and hundreds of teeny-tiny black cars with lots and lots of baggage and boxes tied on top, and an occasional open door with people hanging on for dear life— albeit happily—laughing and chatting.

After a few minutes of observing pedestrian mores, I see that people just jump in and cross the highway when there is a lull in the traffic, which isn't often. It's then I realize that the safest way to cross the highway is to follow a woman dressed in the *hijab*, to whom some deference is given. Or to follow a person on crutches—of which there are many. (I cannot help but wonder if legs are broken as a result of crossing this very highway.)

My baptism by fire commences when I elect to follow a man with a clubfoot and crutches. I leap into the traffic and soon I am where I want to be—on the Nile, where under every palm tree old men sit on benches, smoking and listening to cigarette pack–sized transistor radios.

On close inspection I see that palm trees are not as shady as I thought them to be, so I have to find a really shady bench, which I do. A bench commandeered by an old man, who I'm sure thought of it as *his* bench.

The old man looks like a deeply wrinkled Ben Kingsley. He is very chic and immaculately dressed in beige, from his shirt and slacks to his radio and cigarette. I approach, smile, slightly bow, and sit down to write, which I fake. What I really want to do is stare at everyone.

A faint breeze blows off the Nile. The palm trees shiver and Egyptian morning radio natters on. Soon the old man is joined in a serious bout of cigarette smoking by a few smiling cronies who are (I think) amused at his female benchmate. (After a few days in Cairo, I realize that females don't sit alone with men on benches in public places. Yet it is a pleasant place to write, and my ritual continues every morning.)

In the evenings, when Geoffrey and I take late-night walks after late-night dinners, we would occasionally meet one of the old men taking a walk as well. He would smile and slightly bow to me, pound his fist on his heart, and say, "*Shokran,*" which means thank you.

Around eleven o'clock my tourist day begins. And for the first couple of days, as I wander around the city, I confess to looking over my shoulder. Sad but true: When people say bad things can happen to you, you tend to believe them. Yet I feel protected as I wander through Cairo, glad to be covered up from the blistering September heat.

In the massive Khan el-Khalili *souk*, I avoid small bands of English tourists who are not covered up, for fear I'll be marked as one of them. How foolish they look in their I'm-going-to-the-mall-leisure-wear outfits. Moms looking like Goldie Hawn. Daughters like Britney Spears.

Their look is notable not only because of the way they stand out, but because of the way they are treated by shopkeepers, who think them cash cows. Whereas I . . . well, I just slip through the cracks, much like the women in *hijab*. No one thinks I have any money to spend.

I make my way to the spice market, with its heaping pyramidal piles of herbs and spices that would rival Lady Macbeth's desire for "all the perfumes of Arabia."

It's in a shady section, sheltered by a series of ancient walls and brightly colored cloth canopies. Piles of orange saffron, golden curry, ochre cumin, and orange chilies are everywhere; also, stacks of oregano, thyme, and rosemary still on branches. Bay leaf branches as well. Large jars of preserved lemons sprinkled with black mustard seeds, and soaps, and aromatic oils—oils to do what, I don't know, as everything is written in Arabic.

Amid this lovely exoticism where the magic of scent prevails, my nose leads the way to my little secret. My surrender to vanity—the henna stall, where a gaggle of old women in *hijab*, some with veiled faces, are hanging out, chatting and eating pistachio nuts from paper cones.

As the men on the Nile have their place, this is the women's, and the man in charge seems slightly bored. Yet at the sight of this person in front of him with no visible hair, he brightens and says, "American?"

"Irish American," I say, and he smiles more broadly.

I point to a pile of henna and say, "Henna?" To which he smiles and sweeps his hand over five or six other piles, naming in Arabic what I think must be specific henna colors.

The women's interest picks up. The man speaks to them. They stare at me and smile slightly. I'm sure they are thinking, *What hair?*

To buy the right henna color, I realize I will have to show them my hair. So I walk over to the women, smile, and remove my hat to reveal my short haircut.

"Henna," I say, tapping my head with an index finger. "*Rouge* henna, *rouge*." Why I resort to French, I don't know. But at the time it seems more postcolonially appropriate than English.

"Ahhhhh," sighs a woman as she leaves her bench, grabs me by the wrist, and brings me directly up to the proprietor, to whom she speaks in Arabic.

"Five kilo . . . ten kilo?" he jokes. I say three, whereupon he scoops out a huge mound of mustard-colored henna and weighs it on an ancient brass scale. Then he takes a packet of what look like cinders, puts it into another paper bag, and gestures "for you" while the old woman indicates I must rub some onto my hair before, or after (I don't know which), I henna it.

Permeating the calmness of *my* Cairo, the specter of the first anniversary of 9/11 screams from headlines in Arabic newspapers that divert my eye as I wander through the *souks*. And when the days get too hot and I have wandered too far afield to return to my hotel on foot, the taxi driver who brings me back thanks me for being in Cairo and having faith in "his" country. He asks what I think of "his" city. I always say I love it. Then he says "shokran" and thumps his chest in a trusting gesture, as do I.

Complimentary high tea—a proper British high tea—is served every afternoon on the "executive" top floor of my hotel, from which there are wildly contrasting views of Cairo. Out front the Nile is snaking its way upriver from the pyramids baking in the evening sun. This is Egypt. On the other side are the Cairo slums. This is Egypt as well.

I sit outside on the terrace in the heat, preferring not to be inside in the freezing air-conditioning with men smoking cigars. You see, I've surrendered willingly to the Egyptian heat, pollution, and decay. I haven't seen a blue sky since I arrived. The ochre, dusty light reminds me I am in Egypt—Egypt, where I want to be.

The young Egyptian waiter (who speaks good English and wants to go to Paris) thinks me funny, sitting outside. And he too thanks me for being in Egypt.

"But why is your country so mad at us? We are good people."

I have no answers.

He tells me he lives "down there," gesturing to the slums. And I feel bad. I've walked around the slums and seen for myself the contrast between the nearby Hiltons-of-the-Nile and this jumbled, intense neighborhood where some houses do not even have roofs.

Yet here I am, this white Western woman, romancing the pyramids. And here is this young man, happily serving me in a class-structured elegance (Would I like a fresh pot of tea? The strawberry tarts are ready.) that does not come easily to Americans, who all like to believe ourselves to be equal to each other.

Every day I take the city by foot, sometimes not returning for six hours. I look for what's left of the famous Shepheard's Hotel. Nothing. I ride the Cairo Metro (financed by the French) and sit with veiled Cairene women and children in the women-only car. I walk around the perimeter of a leafy isle in the middle of the Nile—Gezira Island—and admire the old French colonial mansions, now mainly ambassador residences.

And I sit by the Nile in the morning, marveling at its lovely slowness and greenness that does not beckon me in to swim, but to boat. Perhaps in a lovely linen- and hide-covered felucca, like Cleopatra.

I am not a souvenir hunter, but I would like to buy myself something special to remind me of my week in Cairo when I was alone and dependent on the kindness of strangers.

As the Cairo kids admire my style with an occasional shy smile and the bolder "look at that one" gesture, I admire theirs. Young boys wear long cotton garments with v-necks and short sleeves that look like nightshirts. These shirts are so graceful, so cool, so pretty in sky blue or yellow stripes, or fawn or white with navy piping, that I want one for myself.

This is what I will bring home to New York. Yet I have no idea where to buy one, or what they are called. I didn't see any for sale in the *souks*. However, in my wandering around the Gezira, I spy them in a ladies' haberdashery window. There they are—lots of them—hanging outside the store, side by side with what I like to call "naughty-lady nighties."

Cairo abounds with nighties. Throughout the *souks* and in store windows all over the city, baby-doll frillies in delicious Crayola colors flutter in the breeze. Girlie, naughty in a 1950s-cheesecake way—"Oooooh, Mr. Billings, I didn't think you could see into my window"—all have built-in, pointy padded bras and are sold by men to women covered in *hijab*.

My week is nearly up and it's blisteringly hot. I buy an orange juice from a nearby vendor and contemplate how I am going to navigate a store. Stores aren't *souks*. There will probably be a formality I want to neither rupture nor insult. Also, from my peek in the door, I note the electricity isn't on and it is female run—another challenge, as the little shops in the *souks* are run by men.

Also, I need to be back in my hotel at two in the afternoon to join New York through television, for the 9/11 first anniversary ceremonies at Ground Zero. So screwing my courage to the sticking point, I enter a dark store that reminds me of European stores in 1940s-era black-and-white films.

There are several woman in *hijab* resting, napping—none of whom seem interested in dealing with this creature, for indeed, under the circumstances, that is what I look like standing there. But soon a young woman comes out from the back and sort of smiles, and I think this is a start.

I say, "Hello . . . *bonjour,*" hoping my French will be understood, as English generally is not. The girl smiles and brings over one of the older women, who, on her way, switches on a single lightbulb dangling on a cord from the ceiling. And I am indeed back in the 1940s.

In Ireland we would call this a drapery shop, for not only are there *hijab* of every color, description, and size hanging from the walls, but there are wonderfully gaudy colored bedspreads and silky pillow shams more prewar oriental (lots of pagodas and the phoenix rising from flames) than Egyptian.

There are also sheets and dishcloths and blankets, men's underwear, baby clothes, an occasional pair of jeans, socks, or sneakers, and veiling of every color. But more than anything else, naughty nighties abound, adding a touch of Technicolor to the chiaroscuro that is this store.

But I don't see what I want. I will have to bring one of the ladies outside to the street where I can point, which I do. But even with my hand pointing to what I want specifically, I am misunderstood.

The lady says, "Ahhhhh," and we go back inside, where she presents me with a tangerine-and-chartreuse naughty nightie. This interests the women, who gather around and say, "Ahhhhh" as well. Clearly, this is the ritual I do not want to upset.

"*Non, non,*" I reply. And the Rolodex of what-can-I-say-now starts whirling madly in my head. Then it comes to me. I will invent a lie that will be clear, unassailable, and get me what I want without having to break gender barriers.

"*Très jolie,*" I say, fingering the nightie. "*Mais je désire une chemise pour mon petit garçon.*"

And again I bring the woman outside and point to what I want.

"Ahhhhh," she responds again, going back inside, where she goes to a shelf and points to what seem like hundreds of young boys' nightgowns.

"Ahhhhh," I say, pointing to a yellow one, which she pulls out, shakes, and holds up in the air. But it's way too small for me.

I smile and indicate by gesture that my *petit garçon* is bigger. Then she pulls out a blue one that would be perfect for a boy-giant.

215

By now I realize, much as I did in the spice market, I will have to reveal myself and in some way tell these women I want to buy an item of clothing for myself that is designed for a young boy.

"Madame," I say pointing to the blue garment. "*Je désire cette chemise pour moi.*"

Silence descends. The women look at each other and start talking in Arabic. I could have walked out the door then and there, embarrassed for making an ass of myself. But I really do want this garment and I am going to stay the course, no matter how foolish or sexually deviant I may appear.

Another woman approaches, offering me a raspberry-and-violet nightie, to which I smile and say, "*Merci, non.*" And I point again to the boy's dress, whereupon the young girl enters the conversation. I don't know what she says, but whatever it is, very soon a pile of these garments is in front of me and the women are holding them up to my body to gauge the proper height.

I buy three of them.

It's nearly two in the afternoon Cairo time (nine in the morning in New York) when I get back to my hotel and switch on CNN. I sit on the floor looking at a scene I know all too well, for I was there a year before. I saw it all from my block in Greenwich Village.

Children sing. People pray. Bagpipes wheeze. Names are read. And the sky is blue. Just like it was last year. It's all too much, and I shut the television off.

I must get out of this freezing room. I must go to the Nile, where no harm will come to me. It's the hottest day so far, and I'm knackered from both the heat and the hard-line memory of 2001 that I did not really need to experience again.

I must go to the Nile.

I stand on the highway, waiting for the right minute to jump into the traffic—now far more congested, it being midday.

I stand by the side of the road stymied, tired, slightly swaying from the heat. I've lost my ability to jump into the traffic because I keep seeing images of people faced with that unimaginable decision to jump into the void a year ago.

I stand and I sway. There is no one around. No woman in *hijab* or man on crutches to lead me into the fray. And truly, I am scared, for I know that to be where I want to be, on the Nile, I'll have to risk my life.

Suddenly a man—a very handsome man with a mustache, dressed all in white—comes out of nowhere, grabs me firmly on the wrist, and drags me across the highway. Leading the way, he does not loosen his grip, weaving in and out of oncoming trucks and minivans, until we get to the other side.

Only then does he release my wrist. He faces me, says *"Shokran,"* and thumps his heart—as do I. And he's gone.

Shokran. How simple, how elegant, how equal: Two people, a man and a woman, a Muslim and a Christian, alone on the Nile, facing each other and saluting each other by thumping their hearts.

And yes, I did really get to "see the pyramids along the Nile." They are breathtaking.

Shokran.

Avoiding the Road to Wellness

Kate Chynoweth

Last fall, in what I thought was a great stroke of luck, I landed a job to travel to Arizona and write about a couple of famous wellness resorts in the desert. The job had a couple of minor drawbacks, of course: I had to pony up for the flight and rental car after my editors refused to bother, and on top of that, the pay was low. Fortunately, reimbursement in the form of hot-stone massages and holistic pedicures sounded worth it. If I was lucky, maybe I'd even find the "soaring spirit" and "authentic me" that the brochures promised. Certainly, I wasn't looking forward to the noxious dose of Southwestern mysticism. But nobody could *force* me to wrassle with my demons during chakra work or skip wine with dinner. Finally, it seemed, I'd scored a work trip where I could also relax. And that was something I desperately needed.

Just so everyone else was clear on my goals, I called the PR people helping to arrange my itineraries. Politely, I made it clear that I wanted more pampering than no-pain-no-gain self-improvement. This outreach, I thought, had succeeded. When I looked over my final schedules, the treatments had promising titles such as "Thai Massage," "Energy Glo," and "Deluxe Pedicure."

One unfortunate side effect of paying my own way was that I'd been unable to afford a direct flight to Tucson, my ultimate destination. But the drive south from Phoenix turned out to be beautiful. The weather was clear and dry, with temperatures in the eighties. Back in Pittsburgh, it had been a cold and dank early November, the drifts of leaves moldering on our unkempt lawn like scarlet letters that marked our house as one under new and overwhelmed ownership. The late autumn sky had settled low over the city like a shroud of old coal dust. Here, the air was so clear, the landscape sprang forth in 3-D. The curved arm of a towering cactus by the highway pointed my way, like a friend urging me along on the journey.

Nearly ten hours after I'd left my own kitchen, I finally stepped into the air-conditioned comfort of the first resort's brightly tiled Southwestern-style entryway. I felt grateful for the smiles of the attractive staff as they pinballed me efficiently through the check-in. Within minutes of my somewhat tardy arrival, they'd put me on the path to the Wellness Dome, where I'd receive my much-anticipated Thai massage. The huge campus, like the staff, was immaculately groomed. Posted signs led me along freshly raked sand trails that meandered past tall succulents with prickly leaves that looked remarkably Seusslike.

When I reached the front desk, a trim blond attendant handed me a pile of fabric and a locker key. "During your treatment, you'll be wearing this," she said.

I stared at the fabric, which looked like the equivalent of three sets of king-size sheets. "All of it?"

She nodded.

"It must be quite different from regular massage if you wear all these clothes," I said, feeling regretful that I hadn't lucked out with a hot-stone—a favorite of mine—as my first treatment.

"Right," she said. "It's more like intense stretching."

Feeling as kinked up as I was from my early flight and the long drive, this sounded a bit ominous.

"Don't worry," she said, reading the concern that crossed my face. "It's incredibly energizing."

My masseur, Denny, was a towering man with a mane of dark hair pulled back in a low ponytail. He looked like a 1960s folk guitarist crossed with Paul Bunyan. Even though his fabric outfit was draped more gracefully than mine, I couldn't help but feel like we were at a toga party for two.

He smiled and handed me a cup of cucumber water as I sat on the massage table.

"Have you ever done yoga?"

I nodded.

"Great," he said. "The Thai massage modality is similar in some ways to yoga. But the stretches are much deeper because I'll be gently kneading and pushing your muscles to help you move into the postures."

Deeper stretches than yoga? I wondered if now was the time to mention that I hadn't done a downward dog recently—in, say, the last year—but decided against it. I'm one of those unfortunate people who hates to disappoint anyone, particularly doctors who ask how much I drink and smoke. Apparently, massage therapists fall into that same category.

"It sounds energizing." I repeated the desk attendant's words firmly, hoping they might be true rather than believing them.

"Wonderful." Denny paused, as if needing to let the wonderfulness of it all sink in. Then he got started.

First he tugged my legs, raised my arms overhead, and pulled at my wrists and ankles in a series of basic but slightly uncomfortable stretches. For the first twenty minutes, the experience wasn't entirely painful. But even though he moved with rhythm and purpose, it wasn't nearly as relaxing as being gently massaged with warm oil or hot stones. I felt a sense of relief when these stretches stopped.

Denny said, "Are you ready to move into the hips?"

I felt a sense of doom as I realized that he was just getting started.

"Sure," I said.

"Just try to breathe deeply," he said. "The hips are the body's emotional center. Releasing tension there can also yield some pretty powerful feelings."

I nodded.

Alas, what happened next was not like any stretch I'd ever experienced—it felt like a Mac truck slammed into my pelvis. And that's the last thing I remember before passing out.

When I came back to the light, Denny was standing over me, his thick black eyebrows knitted together in concern. He handed me another cup of cucumber water.

"I'm so sorry," I said. I felt guilty, as if I'd insulted him.

"Don't be," he said. "Try to breathe."

"I'm a writer and I'm covering this for a magazine," I blurted out. "Maybe I can't relax because I'm working."

"No, I think it's because your hips are incredibly tight," he said. "I was barely putting pressure on the joint."

From the last bit I could remember, I begged to differ, but I didn't say so out loud. I was still trying to catch my breath. The air I drew in seemed to catch at my throat, rather than flow into my lungs.

"Please don't answer this question if it feels presumptuous," he said, his brown eyes soft and crinkling around the corners with the hint of a pretty believable *"trust me"* smile. "But are you going through an emotionally difficult time right now? I rarely see people hyperventilate and black out during massage."

"I thought I just fainted."

"I think you hyperventilated first and *then* you fainted. Hyperventilation isn't always the gasping sort of experience that people imagine. It can be a quiet thing. I noticed your hands curling up, which is a common reflex to lack of oxygen. You may have had an anxiety attack."

"Travel writing is more stressful than people think," I said, a bit defensively. "The last time I traveled for a spa magazine, my editor hadn't really cleared the comp, and the place wouldn't give me my car keys until I agreed to pay a bullshit charge of more than a thousand bucks. Maybe I haven't purged that demon."

I tried a lighthearted laugh, but it sounded forced even to me.

Denny sat down on a teak bench opposite the table. "Can I massage your feet? I won't if you think it will make you anxious."

"Better not," I said, worried that a foot massage might open up some other Pandora's box. "Maybe I'll just try to recover."

"Fine," he said soothingly. "Is there anything else you feel like sharing?"

I calculated that if this massage turned into talk therapy, it would be the most expensive session in the history of the world—$250 for an hour. So why not really unload on the guy? But the truth was that I just wasn't sure where to start. In the last four months, I'd gotten married, given up my job and apartment in Seattle, moved with my husband from Seattle to Pittsburgh of all places, wondered if my new marriage was failing while he devoted himself to his medical residency, bought a fixer-upper house (our first), undergone painful surgery to repair a bizarre hole that gaped open in my abdominal wall, and learned that my beloved father had cancer.

"Nothing that I can think of," I said.

I could tell by the way Denny looked at me patiently that he was not buying it. *You're a train wreck*, his eyes seemed to say.

"Is this your first time to the Southwest?"

I nodded.

"I hope you don't mind me saying this," he said. "But I think this work assignment wasn't random for you. I think you were given this trip as an opportunity. We're close to a powerful energy vortex in Tucson. People come here from all over the world to find wellness."

"So I've heard," I said.

"They say this is the age of anxiety," he said. "I think that's why more and more people are drawn here."

"Well, it's also very beautiful," I said. "And it has great weather for hiking."

He nodded, but I could tell he was disappointed in me. Ten minutes later, the session ended and I backed out of the room, trying not to look like I was thrilled.

That night at dinner, I felt lonely. After asking in succession for a wine list (there wasn't one, because the resort was dry); salt (it was never put out on the tables, I was haughtily informed); and bread (sliced gluten-free whole grain was the only option), I tried joking with the waitress.

"You guys take denial seriously," I said.

But she just smiled politely and backed away.

I sipped my unsweetened iced tea and wished I had my husband's knack for enjoying solitude. When I'd met him, he'd just come back from six months traveling alone in the mountains of Peru and Bolivia. "It's like my brain is sharper when I'm on my own," I remembered him saying. "The memories I have from my trips are so clear."

I stared at my minuscule piece of grilled salmon and steamed julienne vegetables, gracefully arranged into low-cholesterol food art on my plate. For me, traveling alone—especially on this trip—felt like the opposite of a great education. I felt tired, irritated, and oddly upset. It didn't occur to me until much later that this solo dinner was the first time in a long time that I hadn't had someone there to distract me from how I felt, or someone to cover it up for.

Forty-eight hours later, departing on the second leg of my journey, I felt limp and exhausted. Few of the treatments had turned out as I'd hoped. The Energy Glo treatment was with a woman who played loud birdsong music while she moved her hands over my "energy centers" like a maestro conducting an orchestra. Tragically, she never even touched my stiff lower back. In another session, I'd been asked to select tiles in different colors and shapes by a psychologist who told me that I was creative but emotionally blocked. The cranial-sacral massage had yielded a splitting headache. In fact, the only decent pampering I'd experienced during my whirlwind stay had been the pedicure. And even that had been slightly marred when the woman doing my toes informed me that the dark spot under my right big toenail wasn't a bruise, but growing mold spores.

By the time I checked out, I felt like an escaping prisoner. Optimism seized me as I gunned my old rental beast down the narrow, winding roads away from the handsome campus. Finally, after dietary deprivation and New Age torture, I was about to go to a *real* resort. I'd read the glossy brochures for my next destination the night before, and it offered a wine list and dessert—with sugar! I couldn't wait to indulge.

Alas, the dinner I dreamed of was not to be. By the time I turned off the freshly paved road that had carried me away from town, past the suburbs' outer edge of pale wooden house skeletons and empty future mall lots, I was lost. It turns out that you can't rely on a world-class resort to provide signage; by the time I arrived, the dining room was closed. Fortunately, in my room, I found a split of white wine and a splendid fruit basket, complete with a giant chocolate chip cookie to welcome me. Biting into the sweet, crumbly cookie and sipping the chilled sauvignon blanc felt more rejuvenating than anything I'd done so far.

Before bed, I drank a glass of water—I'd been told during my Energy Glo session that I didn't hydrate enough—and checked the next day's frantic itinerary. At the sight of my first appointment, I tossed the paperwork aside and poured the dregs of the wine into my glass. It was one of those horse-whisperer excursions that I'd been seeing flyers for since I'd landed in Phoenix. This was the latest big thing at these Southwestern spas, the idea that an hour with a horse and a spiritually centered trainer could change your life. Oprah had done it and testified, and, of course, the world had followed suit.

Needless to say, as a person who is skittish around squirrels and even pigeons, I'd felt apprehensive when my editors had strongly suggested that I try this equine experience. My fears were exacerbated by the fact that I hadn't ridden a horse for nearly two decades, after an ill-fated trail ride in North Carolina at the age of eight with my mother, during which my mount had thrown me. But there was nothing for it: This was work. So the next morning, I dressed in the best equestrian outfit I could find and headed out, wearing wrinkled cargo pants and a green T-shirt with a spray of balsamic vinaigrette stains across the chest.

As I approached the group's morning meeting place in the entry hall—a stone slab table that reminded me of where the talking lion gets slaughtered in *The Chronicles of Narnia*—I immediately had second thoughts about my outfit. A leggy blond sporting a pink cowboy hat and a tight white T-shirt stretched across a Pamela Anderson–style chest shot me a pitying look. *Whatever,* I insulted her silently. *You're about to get covered in horsehair.* I joined the woman and her much-older husband in orbiting the handsome young cowboy who I guessed was our guide.

"Here's the straggler," he said, flashing me a whitened smile from under the brim of his Stetson. "Everyone else is in the van, so let's get going."

As I squeezed into the last space on the back bench seat, I was already sweating, as much with fear and anticipation as from the stuffy air inside. But once I had the chance to take in my companions, a sense of relief washed over me. Half of them were wearing glitzy Western-wannabe outfits, and I couldn't believe the resort was about to unleash dangerous equines on this plastic-surgery set. Whatever the cowboys were about to dish up, I told myself, would likely be pretty easy to handle.

We were greeted as we stepped out into the dust by a tall cowboy in his sixties with deep crow's-feet around his eyes, dirty jeans, and dirtier boots. With an authentic horseman's gait, he led the way to the corral. The horses had looked tall when I stepped out of the van; now they loomed much larger as we approached, their nostrils flaring wide at the sight of company.

The old cowboy gave a few short instructions on how to lift a horse's foreleg, clean its hooves with a curved pick, and finish by brushing its flanks.

"Horses understand true intention," he said, demonstrating on a tall, sleek black horse. "Don't act nervous, and always approach with authority. They'll lift that foreleg for you if they know you mean business."

I felt my hands sweating at the thought of getting that close to a horse's leg. But then, I told myself, the cowboy had made it look easy enough; the horse had lifted its leg up on its own, making its hoof available before the man even leaned in with his pick.

The old cowboy assigned two people to each horse. I didn't know what was worse—that my partner was a Rush Limbaugh lookalike who introduced himself as "Tex," or that our huge, snorting bay was the horse I'd targeted on first sight for avoidance.

"You go ahead first," said my companion, attempting gallantry.

"Thanks," I said, wincing.

I took a deep breath to calm myself down, walked over, and leaned in toward the horse's leg as the cowboy had done. The horse ignored me. Not even a ripple in its flank reflected my presence. I flushed with embarrassment and wished that Tex wasn't behind me, impatiently waiting to take his turn.

I stood, retreated, straightened my shoulders, and approached the horse again. Again, nothing. I looked across the corral and saw a slim older woman with silver hair successfully cleaning a hoof. But I tried several more times and couldn't make it happen. The fifth time that I failed, I stayed crouched down on the ground and started tugging on the horse's leg. I was so frustrated now that I wasn't even scared of getting kicked.

"You think you're stronger than a horse?" The old cowboy's deep voice had a derisive undertone.

I stood up, red faced. "I guess not," I said. "It's just that the horse isn't paying any attention."

"You have to change your approach," said the old cowboy. "A horse only responds when you're honest. Are you honest?"

He walked up to the horse and, as the previous creature had done, the bay lifted its leg, offering up its hoof before the cowboy even touched him.

He turned to me with a stern look. "Intention," he said. "Keep trying."

He took Tex's elbow and guided him across the corral to a horse that had already been successfully handled by two people. I stood there feeling like a failure, got up my nerve, tried again, and failed.

I retreated to a safe distance from the horse's hind legs, and then the sound of sobbing drew my attention across the dusty corral. The blond in the pink cowboy hat was bawling. Not whimpering or shedding a few tears, but all-out, ugly crying. Even from a distance, I could see the mascara running down her cheeks.

I heard the old cowboy say, "What are you, a little girl? A crybaby? Deal with it." Then he stalked away to another victim.

Her sobs got louder, and I felt close to following her lead. But I steeled myself to try again—and failed for about the tenth time.

229

The old cowboy approached. "Well, how do you feel?"

"Embarrassed," I said.

"Why? Do you think the horse cares?"

"Everyone else can do it," I said.

"Embarrassment is worthless and gets you nowhere," he said. "Forget it. What else are you feeling?"

I stared at him and tried to conceal my anger.

"I get the feeling you're not good at showing people your emotions," he said.

I flung a silent *fuck you* in his direction, proving his point.

"You're not embarrassed, you're mad. So why don't you show it? You should use your anger to show that horse who's boss. You're acting like a little girl who's too scared to show her feelings."

I stared at him defiantly. "Is that shitty line about being a little girl the only one you have?" I looked over toward the blond, who was leaning into the chest of her male companion. She was still sobbing. "It works well."

The old cowboy didn't quite laugh, but he looked just on the brink of it.

"Oh, stop talking and just do it," he said.

Without a word, I turned around and marched over to the horse with a new sense of rage. I'd barely reached its side when, just like that, it lifted its leg and offered up its hoof. It felt like a chunk of heavy, fine-grained wood in the palm of my hand. I used the metal pick to carve out a few chunks of embedded dirt and stood up to see the old cowboy grinning broadly.

"You're just out of practice, see. The next time you feel angry, try showing it. It might just change everything."

230

"I feel so empowered," I said sarcastically. "I'm sure that getting mad will cure my dad's lymphoma."

His amused expression didn't change.

"You're an asshole," I said.

His smile broadened like it might crack his face open.

"See?" he said. "Now that's more like it."

He walked away.

When I got back to my room a couple of hours later—after more interminable corral exercises—I collapsed on the bed and cried. I choked and snuffled and sobbed until the six-hundred-thread-count pillowcases were soaked and stained. I hadn't shed any real tears in months, but now grief spilled out of me. It was my father, yes, but it was also everything else. But just because the old cowboy had helped me get to catharsis didn't mean I wanted to thank him. The exercise had made me feel worse, not better. And unlike most of the pathetic seekers who came here, I wasn't ready to mistake provocation and a subsequent emotional outburst for healing. Not that I had time to reflect much, because just then, I caught sight of the time and groaned. It was time to go. I had a treatment. It was called Spirit Dancer.

Soon enough, I was back in the familiar position on a massage table, lying flat on my back, this time breathing through my mouth because my nose was stuffed up from all the crying. The practitioner, a weathered woman in her fifties with a dirty-blond ponytail, looked down at me with deep-set light-blue eyes and introduced herself as Dakota. Of course that was her name.

"Is there anything you'd like to share before we get started?"

I sat up, pulling the sheet with me.

"I don't know what this treatment's all about," I said. "But I can tell you that so far this week, I've hyperventilated and blacked out during a massage and cursed out the local horse whisperer. So I don't really know what might happen."

She smiled and looked like she might laugh. "At least you're honest," she said.

I liked her, I decided—even if her name was Dakota.

"I don't want to catch you by surprise, so let me explain how this will work," she said.

"First, we'll do a purifying smudge with sage and sweetgrass. Then I'll lay hot stones on your chakra points, and you'll open your own energy pathways during a meditation." She held her downturned palms above my chest and motioned slowly, as if patting the head of an invisible toddler. "Your energy is extremely high over your heart chakra, which represents emotion."

"You guys should have a meeting," I said. "In Thai massage, they tell you the emotional center is your hips."

She laughed. "I guess everyone has their take."

She held up a large brown-and-white feather. "After you meditate for a half hour on your own, I'll remove the stones and use this feather as part of a purifying sage smudge."

My inner cynic wanted to take the bait—I mean, come on, *a feather?*—but I was so surprised to hear that she wasn't going to give me a massage that for once I didn't bother.

"It's an energy massage," she said, as if hearing my unspoken question. "Not a physical one. While you meditate, try to circulate your energy and bring your heart chakra into alignment with the rest."

She pulled large, smooth black stones from a plastic bin of steaming water and placed the first two beneath my upturned palms. I inhaled the rich scent of sage and the honeylike smell of sweetgrass while she balanced the stones elsewhere, too—on the tops of my arms and legs, behind my knees, around my feet. Their penetrating heat felt almost dangerous, but it pacified me, too, like a very hot bath. I heard her leave the room and relaxed further, slipping into a peaceful, near-waking dreamstate. My consciousness drifted. I wish I could say that I had some fantastic, empowering vision of myself as a she-wolf, or experienced total emotional self-mastery. But it wasn't anything like that. All I know is that I lost track of time. And when Dakota returned and I opened my eyes, I felt lighter. It was like waking up from a nap and noticing the dull headache you've had for hours is finally gone, without a trace.

She removed the cooling stones, dropping each one back into the plastic tub with a satisfying *thunk,* and relit the sage bundle. Using the big feather, she brushed the fragrant smoke over me in a kind of ceremonial, rhythmic way. I closed my eyes because I knew it was supposed to be solemn.

When she finished, she squeezed both my feet and said, "Take your time getting up."

"Thanks," I said.

"Your energy feels very balanced," she said.

I felt vaguely embarrassed. At the same time, I did feel calmer, somehow smoother around the edges. As I pulled on my clothes, I had to wonder why. Maybe I'd been in the Southwest long enough that I wanted to believe. Maybe the old cowboy had done me more of a favor than I knew. Or maybe I'd just finally found a brand of Southwestern spiritualism that worked for me—one where I was alone, without a huge man in Thai swaddling clothes trying to reshape my hip joints or a horse wrangler giving me guff. Sure, in addition to solitude, I also apparently needed smoking sage and a large feather to brush away the bad juju. But I didn't have to tell anybody about that part.

Aphrodisias

Carol Perehudoff

The man had bristly silver hair and a faded black suit. He picked up an albino rabbit from the table and held it in front of a tray with slots. In each of the slots was a folded piece of paper. The rabbit darted forward, picking a slip of paper from a slot with its mouth. The man handed me the paper. It was fortune number nine.

A very new topic will give you an opportunity to get a big amount of money. You will forget the worrisome days as if you never had. It is necessary to go on a short trip for your health. You will meet one of your old friends.

I nodded and handed the man a fistful of Turkish lira. I'd been waiting for this fortune for a long time. I'd tried to buy it off a guinea pig in Sofia, but the other journalists I was traveling with wouldn't wait. So when I saw this rabbit in Istanbul, I knew I'd been given a second chance.

I was sure the fortune would be apt—rabbits don't lie. And I *was* planning a short trip—a trip within a trip, really, as I was already in Istanbul. I just didn't know where to go from here. When your boyfriend suddenly leaves you and the trip you'd planned together is off, you're a bit lost for direction. Before Gabriel had disappeared from my life, we'd arranged that I'd stay two weeks after my press junket, meeting him in Budapest, where he'd just moved. That was before he'd cut off contact with me. Not even a goodbye. Just because he'd cancelled our trip—and, presumably, our relationship—it didn't mean I had to change my travel plans, I reasoned. What was I going to do back in Canada except mope? No—I'd listen to the rabbit and continue on solo.

I reread the fortune as I walked down Babihumayun Caddesi. *A very new topic will give you an opportunity to get a big amount of money.* That was no mystery. I had just completed a weeklong rail trip through the Balkans with five other travel writers and planned to sell the story to a newspaper. The idea that I would get a *big* amount of money for it was laughable, but it would be more in Turkish lira.

As for the second part, *you will forget the worrisome days as if you never had. . . .* Maybe that meant the problem with Gabriel would be resolved, though I doubted it. It had been a month now, without a word. No reply to my emails. And, since he'd been in the process of moving from Germany to Budapest, I didn't even have a phone number for him. Maybe it meant I'd simply forget about him, maybe after I went on my "short trip for health."

I stopped to run my fingers over some rich red carpets hanging off a stone gate near Topkapi Palace. Dust, mingled with the faint scent of cinnamon, hung in the air. It wasn't as if I were totally heartbroken. Long-distance relationships are hard to maintain, and he'd been living in Germany while I was in Canada. Even at the best of times Gabriel was a difficult, moody man. We had almost nothing in common, other than a love for walks in the woods and boat rides, and slightly reclusive tenden-cies. Yet he had a light side too, and after ten months, even if I didn't see him often, he had still become an integral part of my life.

"When I hear your voice, it's like medicine," he'd said during one of our many phone calls. But now, apparently, the medicine was no longer necessary, and it was time to think about my mental health, not his.

And, since the rabbit appropriately advised a short trip for my health, I decided to go to Pamukkale, an ancient Roman healing resort in southwestern Turkey where hot springs gushed from the ground and spilled over the hillside, leaving a white calcium crust in their wake. The ancient Romans had traveled there, seeking cures for their various ail-ments. Now it was my turn.

A few days later I arrived by night bus. It was 6 AM and still dark, but a pink haze was creeping up around the building edges. A man named Moham-med picked me up. Tall and energetic, he owned the Koray Hotel, where

I had booked a room. He also organized tours of Pamukkale, which he assured me he could get me on, even though I hadn't asked to go.

I slept until nine and then got up for the tour. Other than Mohammed, it was an all-female foray consisting of me; Taiko, a college-age student from Tokyo; Renee, a tanned, heavyset woman from California; and our young guide, Ozii, who had sun-streaked hair, a perfect, compact figure, and a jaw that jutted just slightly too far forward.

Mohammed steered the van through the winding streets of Pamukkale and along the bottom of the white hills that rose above the town. They looked as if they were coated with marshmallow topping. Our first destination wasn't the calcium-crusted hillside, but the red spring of Karahayit, a village a couple of miles away. Here, the iron-rich water formed a small natural pool that stained the ground red. A row of sleepy inns stood behind us, and in the distance were dry hills dotted with cypress and pine.

Ozii kicked off her sandals and waded into the pool. The water was burning hot and I high-stepped through it after her, heading to the far edge, where a stout woman in a headscarf was slapping clay onto her legs.

"For veins," she told Ozii in Turkish.

Vein therapy? Count me in. This was a healing journey. I hiked up my pant legs and started scooping clay onto my thighs.

The woman shouted at me, something like, *"Ovmak! Ovmak!"*

"She says rub it in," Ozii translated.

After I'd rubbed and rinsed, I waded over to a fountain formed from stones piled above the source of the spring. The iron-rich water that burst out was hot and tasted like a red mineral tea.

"Good for woman's problems," Ozii said.

"Excellent," I said, filling up my travel mug to go.

Our next stop was the Necropolis of Hierapolis. Hierapolis was an ancient city built on the long plateau above Pamukkale's white hillside. The city's vast number of tombs and sarcophagi proved that a tremendous number of people had died here, which didn't say much about its power as a healing resort. It did confirm that the sick and elderly had flocked here, though, seeking solace for their pain. It was in disarray now; monuments had fallen and stone lids were tipped askew, as if a giant had picked them up and tossed them around in his hands.

"Grave robbers and earthquakes," Ozii said.

Afterward, we stopped at the Temple of Apollo, the patron deity of Hierapolis. The grounds had been fenced off by Italian archeologists, but someone had forgotten to latch the gate. Ozii fiddled with it and ushered us through.

"I hope we don't get arrested," Renee said.

"No problem," Ozii smiled. "My father is the police."

We walked over old foundations and down a few worn stone steps.

"So where is it?" I asked. "Pluto's poisonous cave."

Also known as the Plutonium, this cave, believed to be the dwelling place of Pluto, was the dark side of Pamukkale. Tucked away within the temple complex, it harbored a deadly spring that released poisonous vapors.

"Here," Ozii said.

She turned right at the bottom of the steps toward a corner of the temple, where a small, weathered arch was blocked off by cement blocks. One block had been left out, creating a gap in the stones. I put my ear to the hole and could hear the water burbling up, evil and noxious. Holding my breath, I peered in. It was so black, I could feel it. I don't know what compelled me, but I thrust my arm into the hole as far as it would go.

"Two German tourists died here," Ozii said, "before the entrance was closed off."

I pulled out my arm.

"How stupid can you get?" Renee said.

But I could understand it. If the cave weren't blocked off, I'd be tempted to wade into it, too. Deadly as this grotto was, it was a sacred site, the genesis of Pamukkale's reputation as a magical place. Priests, trained to hold their breath, would make ritual forays into the cave along with an assortment of small animals, which would keel over impressively beside the holy men as they walked. These merciless displays of invincibility were the evidence that proved Hierapolis was a place of the gods. I felt like spray-painting "Pluto lives here" over the cinder blocks.

Our last stop was Cleopatra's Pool, also known as the Sacred Pool, one of the area's biggest draws. Fed by thermal effervescent water known for its curative properties, it has hosted bathers since before Christ. (St. Paul was murdered just a few hundred feet away.)

A day resort, complete with souvenir shops, deck chairs, and cafés, had risen up around the ancient swimming pool. The pool itself was a translucent turquoise green. The bottom was littered with toppled columns that had lain there untouched since they'd fallen in after an earthquake. And though some of the columns were coated in algae, the thought of Cleopatra swimming here propelled me on. No man left Cleopatra; she was the ultimate femme fatale. When I questioned Ozii about the pool's claim to fame, however, she admitted that there was absolutely no documented evidence that the Egyptian queen had actually swum here.

"But she was in the area at the time," she said brightly, "so it's possible."

"The beauty of myths," I said, "is that they're hard to prove wrong."

The next day Mohammed called me in the morning and told me he had a trip going to the ruins of Aphrodisias, a ninety-minute drive away.

"Okay," I said sleepily. *When your boyfriend has left you, you might as well pray to the goddess of love,* I reasoned.

"Transportation only," Mohammed said. "Twenty-five dollars."

"Twenty."

"All right."

When I got to the minivan, Ozii was there too.

"I thought it was transportation only."

She motioned to an elderly Chinese couple already in the van. "I'm their private guide."

Better them than me. I liked Ozii, but it wasn't facts and figures I was after today. It was something more elusive, so elusive I wasn't even sure what it was.

Even in the morning it was a long, hot drive. When we finally arrived, the entrance appeared like a little oasis in a parched yellow landscape, with toilets, a café, and a museum. Farther on were the remains of the city, which thrived from the first century BC until the sixth century AD. The creamy, pale ruins were interspersed with sage-green trees, tall and thin as swaying minarets. The sky was a brilliant blue.

I set off walking clockwise around the circular trail. I was aiming for the temple but ended up instead first at the agora—the ancient marketplace—and then at the Baths of Hadrian. It was hard to tell from the map in my guidebook exactly where I was. Though the city had been deserted after an earthquake, almond and pomegranate trees still flourished in what once were people's gardens, giving the impression that a trace of life still flowed through the city's veins.

When I finally found the temple, it was unmistakable. Large, rectangular, and graceful, it was paid for by a devoted fan, Gaius Julius Zoilos, a freed slave of Augustus, the first Roman emperor. According to a plaque in the temple, Zoilos had been a native of Aphrodisias when he'd been enslaved, possibly by pirates, and then sold to Augustus. Slavery in the emperor's house had worked out well for him. Somehow, though the plaque didn't go into detail, he'd been freed and returned home a wealthy man, building the temple, perhaps, in gratitude.

I went in through a side entrance—at least, I took it to be an entrance, as there were steps leading up. Fluted columns still stood along the temple's perimeter, many broken off at different heights, like snapped feathers. The head of the temple was compressed, like a squished-in snout, a half circle without the grace or organic flow of the rest of the temple.

I sat on a stone ledge against the snout and tried to imagine where the source of the power would have been. Where would the devotees have worshipped? An old well sat in the center of the temple, two-thirds up, toward the front. That was it, I decided. I walked over and peered into the well. A grate covered it now, and through the grate there was nothing but dirt. I fluttered my fingers through the covering as far as they'd go. There wasn't much down there, but I still wanted to pay homage. What could I offer Aphrodite? I decided to give her half the cheese sandwich I'd stolen from the breakfast buffet. It didn't seem like much, but I was starving and this lent my humble offering importance.

I ripped it in two and dropped half down the well, where it landed with a dull smack. It didn't seem very personal, this offering. I dug through my bag to see what else I could come up with and pulled out a Toronto subway token. At least Aphrodite would know where I was from, I decided, and dropped it in after the sandwich.

Not sure what else to do, I retreated to the ledge and ate the rest of the sandwich, as if Aphrodite and I were sharing a meal. I tried to imagine the temple when it was a living, vital space. My guidebook made a tantalizing mention of orgies taking place here before the Christians took over and transformed the temple into a church. It was the Christians who'd redesigned the place. They'd built the snout, which, in religious terms, was an apse.

I tried to picture the orgies. Would they have taken place all over the temple floors? Were they wild and out of control? Or were they a careful choreographed dance, involving selected participants only? I tried to channel some feeling of energy, some spiritual power left in Aphrodite's wake, but it was hard to do without knowing the ancient rituals.

I paced to the back of the temple and then explored the front snout. A hollow space, like a cave or a storage room, was formed between the outer and inner wall of stone. I looked through a little window, but there didn't seem to be anything mystical waiting there, just dead, musty air.

Two figures approached, Ozii and the Chinese woman. They'd lost her husband somewhere, no doubt in the shade.

"Do you know about the well?" Ozii asked. "When it was full of water, people would look inside it to see their future."

"I knew it was the place of power!" I said. "I was drawn to this very well. I didn't know about looking for my future, though. I'll have to look at it again."

Ozii and the Chinese woman went off toward the stadium while I returned to the well. I stared as hard as I could into it, but all I could make out through the dark hole was a dirt floor and half a sandwich. I kept looking. There had to be something there. I needed the well to tell me something. I'd been at a loss since Gabriel had left me. I supposed, by moving to Budapest, he'd simply decided to make a new start. It was a coward's way to end things, though, leaving me with no closure. That's what I was after—some closure. Surely, the temple of love could provide me with that.

Maybe I wasn't looking hard enough. I'd read somewhere that signs were everywhere; you just need to be open to them. I kept staring into the well under the fierce Turkish sun until my vision blurred. Maybe the future would emerge through this mist. Or did the well need to be full in order to work?

I straightened up and looked around. Possibly, just possibly, this was too easy. Maybe my quest entailed more than staring into a well.

And, of course, I'd probably used the wrong entrance. I left the temple and started walking around the outside.

Ozii and her charge were tramping up a path.

"Did you see the stadium?" she asked.

I looked down the road. "It's too far. I think I'll skip it."

"You have to see it," she said. "It is one of the biggest stadiums of Hellenistic times."

I groaned. I was here on a mission, and a stadium seemed irrelevant. Still, I'd come a long way to visit Aphrodisias, and I'd likely never be back. I could just hear people saying, "And you missed the stadium! The very best thing of all."

"Maybe I'll go," I said. "But first I have to go back to the temple to try to see my future. Where's the main entrance?"

Ozii pointed ahead of us to an impressive gateway with Corinthian pillars and a carved frieze above the door. It was some distance away, so I hadn't realized it was part of the same temple at all. I made my way over, went reverently through, and then returned to the well.

As I stood there, looking down, I suddenly felt a rush through my body. It was almost sexual, or maybe it was spiritual ecstasy.

"Whoaa, Aphrodite!" I said.

I suddenly realized how little I knew about this cult. "Goddess of love" sounded so benign and pure, but, of course, there was also an element of lust and sexual abandonment to it. Was there a dark side as well? The dark, poisonous vapors of Pluto's Cave came to mind.

Feeling that there was little more I could do, I exited again. The stadium was shimmering in the heat, like a mirage, so I headed that way.

There was no one inside, just rows and rows of empty stone seats. I could almost hear the cheers and jeers of ancient Romans as I threaded my way down through the stands to the stadium floor. Off to one side was an arched tunnel. Maybe that's where the gladiators came out? Or the lions? Or the Christians? I wished my guidebook had more to offer on the subject. I'd recently seen a TV show about gladiatrices, female fighters who fought to the death in the ring. Did any gladiatrix ever emerge from this tunnel? I went over and stared into the round passageway. It was dark, but at the far end a small star of sunshine was visible, so I knew you had to be able to get through.

Feeling as if I were trespassing, I stepped inside. Dusky gray air enveloped me and my breath became short. Were there snakes in Turkey? Stepping carefully, I made my way to the back of the passage. A small arch led out, but it was about five feet up. I climbed up over a pile of carved stones and, heaving myself up, emerged out the other side.

Then I saw it. My sign.

It was a big, heart-shaped rock sitting in the dirt as if it had been planted there. My pulse quickened. Of course it was a sign. Why else would it be sitting here, at the end of my quest? Obviously it was a good sign, too—what could be ominous about a heart? It didn't tell me anything about Gabriel, exactly, but signs aren't literal. I ran my fingers over the white rock. It wasn't a carved heart; it looked natural, slightly jagged. Near it was a snail shell, a perfect little labyrinth faded as creamy as a marble. What was a snail shell doing here, nearly sixty miles from the coast? Obviously, it was part of the sign. It didn't make sense at the moment, but signs could be cryptic. I snapped a photo and left.

It wasn't until late that night, back in my hotel room, that the meaning of the heart and the snail shell hit me. *Oh, hell,* I thought, *I have a heart of stone and an empty shell of a life. What kind of future is that?*

The next day, still worried about the sign, I caught a minibus back to the red spring at Karahayit. Good for woman's problems, Ozii had said, and with a heart of stone and an empty shell of a life, I'd say I had woman's problems indeed. After soaking my feet and drinking two cups of the thermal water, I went in search of a bathroom.

I walked down the road lined with motels without seeing a single person. A small outdoor café looked open but there were no signs of life. The toilets were around the side of the building, so I went in and locked the door. I sat down and looked straight ahead. The gray metal lock on the door was in the shape of a heart. Was it part of the sign? Could you get a spiritual sign from a toilet? It seemed a bit of a stretch, but I was desperate.

Back in Pamukkale, I returned to Cleopatra's Pool and lay in a deck chair at the rear of the complex. I couldn't help obsessing over my heart of stone and my shell of a life. Is that why Gabriel had left? Had he sensed this about me?

The crowds were dwindling and the shadows were growing long. Realizing I should go too, before it got dark, I lifted my water bottle, tilting my head back to take a sip. My hand paused in midair. The pine boughs from the tree in front of me formed a huge, perfect heart in the sky. A cerulean blue heart surrounded by lacy evergreen boughs. Where were all these hearts coming from? What did they mean?

Whatever this one meant, exactly, it was an improvement over a toilet lock. I was starting to think Aphrodite was lobbing message after message at me, shaking her head, as I was obviously too thick to understand what they meant. Doubtless the ancient Romans were better at interpreting signs, but I bet not even an ancient Roman wanted to receive a message more than I. Part of me knew it was crazy, that pagan gods did not fly out of the sky delivering personal notes, but another part of me knew there are times when you need to reach out. That being alone sometimes isn't so much about solitude as about tapping into a larger whole.

The next morning I left for Ephesus—the largest ruins in Turkey. After a three-hour bus ride I arrived in Seljuk, the nearest town. By the time I checked into a hotel, it was too late to go to Ephesus, so I walked through town to the museum. It was a small building, pleasant and cool, like walking through ruins except in the shade. In the very first room was a statue of Aphrodite. She was missing her head, but that's not why I stopped. She was holding an enormous shell in her arms.

Something clicked. While in Greek mythology the goddess was known as Aphrodite, her Roman name was Venus. Who doesn't know Botticelli's painting *The Birth of Venus*, reproduced on postcards around the world? The shell was her symbol—she'd risen from the foam of the sea. I flashed back to the small, perfect snail shell I'd found beside the heart-shaped stone in Aphrodisias. Now I was sure it had been an actual sign—she'd left her calling card to prove it.

And whatever the message meant exactly, it no longer seemed to matter. Somehow in this strange, dry land I'd managed to suspend my tendency toward skepticism and disbelief, finding solace when I needed it the most. And while I still had no answers about my relationship, by making this solo journey, this pilgrimage to the goddess of love, I'd come to feel not only a connection with Aphrodite, her city, its inhabitants, and their ability to believe, but not nearly so alone anymore.

Where Clouds Are Born

Amy Novesky

This is not a story about adventure. Or traveling alone to some forlorn destination halfway around the world. It's just me and my unborn son, flying to an island in the middle of the Pacific Ocean. It's about taking one last trip before one becomes two.

   I'm seven months pregnant with my first child, leaving the husband at home, and flying alone to Kauai. I've traveled alone before, and I make it to Kauai at least once a year, but this trip is different. It's the last time

I will ever truly be alone in a place I love. It's a farewell to my life as a single girl. Life is about to change forever in ways I can't even imagine, least of which is my ability to sit, totally unencumbered, on a white-sand beach; to read a book cover to cover in one sitting; to have the luxury of thought; to do absolutely nothing if that's what feels right; to come and go as I please. I please.

But this trip almost doesn't happen at all. I'm not sure I can get on the plane. Somewhere along the way I've become terrified of flying, and it's only gotten worse now that I am pregnant and abuzz with all those hormones and newborn maternal instincts. What if the plane goes down and I never get to meet my son? Maybe I should just stay home. Despite my fears, I know better. I know it's more dangerous to drive a car—something I do, recklessly and with pleasure, every day. And I know that I don't want to live this way—if not for myself, then for my son. I don't want him to fear the world. And so, while this trip is a last in many ways, it is also a first: It's the first time I am teaching my child how to live. Get on the plane. Go.

The flight from San Francisco to Lihue is just about long enough for me, fear or no fear. I'm as restless as a toddler. Five hours after leaving the curve of California coastline behind, and hovering above a Georgia O'Keeffe–like blue sky dotted with white clouds, I spot the green belly of an island on the horizon. Land is always a welcome sight when flying over nothing but ocean for thousands of miles, and even more so when you are carrying the love of your life. My fears dissipate, for now, when the plane lands on the familiar strip of tarmac—a red-earth field in the middle of the ocean—and I remember why I came.

I crave Kauai. I crave this lush and lovely air. I crave bare skin and walking barefoot in the sand. I crave the scent of plumeria and wearing leis of cool pikake. I crave the ocean. I crave solitude and sleep and a sense of well-being. I crave pink guava juice, strong coffee, and raw, lava-like honey. And, let's face it, taro chips from the little mom-and-pop shop in Hanapepe and strong mai tais I can't drink from beachfront bars. I crave this life, which for two weeks of the year is the perfect life.

The old Land Cruiser—the only family member that lives here year-round—greets me at the airport curb. A pink-throated shell strung on black leather cord hangs from the rearview mirror, and a sticker on its chrome bumper boasts: I'LL STILL BE HERE WHEN YOU'RE GONE. I hoist my belly into the hibiscus-print front seat, coax the ignition, roll down the windows, and head south on the two-lane highway.

The tall fields of sugarcane are long gone from the town named after them, and there's lots more traffic on the highway than ever before, but not a lot has changed since I began traveling here twenty years ago as a teen with my parents and two sisters. We've sat on the same beach all these years. My bag of bikinis and an old pair of running shoes, still sandy from the last run, await me at our home away from home. Once the clothes are thrown into drawers, the fridge filled with food, and the windows pulled wide open to the bright blue sea, it's as if I never left.

My daily beach ritual goes something like this: I wake early to the *cock-a-doodle-doo* of feral roosters and the cooing of morning doves—a particular coo that says *Kauai* to me. (It's easy to wake before the sun rises when your body is naturally three hours ahead. It lasts about a day or two, before the body catches on and wants to sleep in past seven.) Early morning there is no one about. The beach is empty and the world feels dewy and unspoiled. I walk up the road to the cliffs and watch the sun rise out of the ocean and color the surrounding clouds. This is my temple, my altar. When I've given my litany of thanks, I head back, the rising sun warm. At home, I make a pot of coffee and take my eggshell-blue mug down to the beach, barefoot in the sand still cool from evening, and I sit. I sit and I write. I'm never without book and pen. Early morning is my favorite time of day here. I wish the whole day could be 7 AM.

A few hours later, I'm back on the sand, the sun still low in the sky and playing peekaboo with the palm trees overhead. Black bikini and white sarong, my uniform. Sunglasses that get bigger by the year. A sun-bleached cloth chair and clean white towel. My bamboo-handled beach bag with the essentials: book, water, lip gloss. I stare at the sea and the sky for hours. I notice the tides change. I study the horizon. I watch the births of clouds. This must be where clouds are born. It's like seeing rare animals in their natural habitat. A caravan of elephants traveling, tail to tail, east across the ocean. I imagine them cresting the green hills above our house in the Marin headlands, above our pug dog, George, as he sleeps on his pillows on the couch.

And while I sit in the sand doing these very important things, I think about thinking about my life. Before every trip to Kauai, I make a list of all the things I will do. There's always that belief that, because I will have nothing but time to think, I will discover all the answers this trip. I will figure out what to do with my life. I will find my missing inspiration. I will write a story. I will uncover the perfect ending to another. I will run every day and drink eight glasses of water. I will lose that five extra pounds and gain a nice, even tan. I am never more ambitious than when I travel. And then I'm here, and it's just so nice to not think or do anything.

I just about still fit into my favorite bikini. While I never considered covering up with a one-piece, I'm a little bit shy about being so out there. What if someone says something? But I'm proud of this belly. I've waited all my life for this belly. And when else can you feel good about having a big belly? Lying on the sand is not as comfortable when you're carrying twenty-five extra pounds up front. But oh, that sun feels good. I imagine my womb glowing, warming Baby. Instead of gazing at round clouds, I watch him swim beneath my skin, his movements rippling across my stomach. This must be where the term "navel-gazing" comes from.

Counting his kicks, I drift in and out of sleep. I imagine the birth, the moment my son is born. How they will put him on my chest and I will cry. I wonder what he will look like and who he will become. I daydream he's an Olympic gold-medal swimmer, excelling in the elegant backstroke. I ponder baby names. I consider Cloud, saying the word aloud, and again, to see how it fits on my tongue. I skim a Hawaiian-language dictionary. I look up the words: sea, sky, blue, green. There are some lovely possibilities: Kai (sea); Makaio (gift from God); Nohea (lovely). It's fun to consider a Hawaiian-inspired name, but in the end these names don't feel like ours to take. And I'm pretty sure I know what his name will be.

This baby is my first. He's due in July, a week before my thirty-fifth birthday. I'm secretly hoping he arrives on the nineteenth, which is also the birthday of my maternal grandfather, Theodore. At seven months, I feel great. I'm big, but not too big. I still feel like me, just a bit rounder. I love being pregnant. It is undeniably wondrous. And I love being pregnant here. I'd always hoped to be. I want Kauai—the air, the water, the flowers, the fruit—to be a part of the baby boy growing inside me. I want to bring him here (again) as soon as I can and introduce him to the sea and the sky.

I always imagined having this little long-haired, sun-kissed girl—an idealized version of me, I guess. I didn't see the ocean until I was six years old, but I'm a beach girl at heart. I've rarely lived farther than a few miles from the ocean since the first time I saw it—sparkling, blindingly bright, and vast—out the back of my family's green station wagon the day we arrived in California. I lived in the water. My hair became an impossible shade of blond; my skin, freckled brown. I wore OPs and Vans. I had subscriptions to *Surfer* magazine and *Vogue*. I was ten years old.

On Valentine's Day we had the sonogram, and we learned what I already instinctively knew. There it was in 3-D, a pointer pointing to his magnificent boyness, and the letters BOY printed at the top of the image. And a new image began to form in my mind. A little long-haired, sun-kissed boy. There he goes now, towheaded and naked, toddling across the green grass beneath the palm trees. If there's one hope I have for my son, other than that he is healthy and happy, thoughtful and good, it is that he will be at home on the beach, comfortable in the water. And that he will always wear sunscreen. I think my husband would agree. He grew up in rural Illinois, surrounded by an ocean of corn and yearning to be near the real thing. He dreamed of the ocean. Drove a school bus west, till he hit the coast, and never left.

On the same day as the sonogram, my parents were in Kauai. A local surfer took my father far out in the ocean, where the reef drops off and the water is an even deeper blue. With his naked ear just beneath the water, he listened to the lullabies of whales. Seeing our son for the first time, floating in his own little ocean, was the perfect valentine. His spine like a delicate feather. His fists tight as sea anemones. His face familiar, like my father's. And from that deep, warmly lit place, we could hear his beating heart, a hummingbird, a wild horse. We celebrated by eating noodles and mooncakes at a baby-pink Chinese restaurant in San Francisco, not far from the hospital. It's a brand-new year.

When the sun gets too hot and bright for my pale (and sun-damaged) skin and the beach crowds up, I head in, just when most people are starting their day.

The local farmers market is held every Monday at noon in a community-center parking lot in town. At five to noon, there's already a crowd swelling behind a rope, as if queuing up for a race. This is one of the only times I feel anxious while in Hawaii. At the top of the hour, the rope is dropped and they're off! I resist the rush of aggro haole locals and type-A tourists, all looking to get the pick of the crop. The funny thing is, there always seems to be enough of everything for everyone. Moving slowly due to the crowd, the heat of the high sun, and my condition, I peruse the booths, the neat piles of blushing fruit, the shiny happy vegetables. Armfuls of leis and buckets of flowers: Heart-shaped anthurium with their phallic pink stamens, birds of paradise, red and pink ginger flower—bouquets for $5—make me smile. The goodness of all this homegrown produce is almost enough to make me want to move here and live this way every day, something I half-seriously consider every time I am here. Oh, to live in a place where wearing flowers is the norm.

But right now, it's time to fill my market bag and go. I'm red faced and dripping beneath a droopy white hat and an oversize Indian tunic. I'm cursing my fair-skinned ancestry when I hear someone whisper "beautiful" in passing. When I turn to see the speaker, I find the lithe and sun-browned yoga teacher I took classes from the last time I was here. She's already gone. And this is one of the things I love about Hawaii: It gives so generously and doesn't ask for anything in return. I leave the market with much more than I expected: a pineapple, a papaya, five mangos, two bouquets of bananas, and a handful of gardenias for less than ten dollars.

Midday, when the sun is high in the sky, the ocean is a brilliant gem of a blue. To be outside at this time is murder for my skin, so I sequester myself indoors for a few hours, lunching, napping, reading the local island paper. My favorite section, besides the police blotter, is the weather report. It is a study in how many different ways there are to describe the same daily forecast: sunshine and the possibility of rain. Sunny with a chance of a shower. A mixture of clouds and sunshine. Clouds and sunshine with a shower possible. Times of clouds and sun with a shower. Sun, rain, sun, rain. It is, after all, one of the wettest spots on the planet. But this is not California rain. This is warm, quick, and heavy, lovely rain.

When the sun drops, I go for a swim. The water feels a little cold at first, and there's always that initial breathtaking instant when you go under. But then it is delicious. I stand shoulder deep, my feet in the soft sand. It's ebbtide, that sublime moment between high and low tide when the ocean feels its fullest and roundest as it's pulled between its two loves: the earth and the moon. It rocks me back and forth in its arms. How wonderful it is to be weightless, to be floating in this giant womb. I let the water buoy me up, arms and legs stretched out like a four-point star, belly to the sky, ears just below water, and it's like listening to the universe. The sparkling star—like sound of sand. That soft bass hum of moving matter. This is what it must sound like in utero. And then I hear a voice and I realize it is my own.

.

While I'm thrilled to be having a baby, I'm in no rush to give birth. I know I still have two and a half months to go, and my feelings might change the bigger I get, but for now I want him to stay inside for as long as he likes. I love having him all to myself, being connected in a way we never will be again. He might be the only child I carry, and I don't want the moment to pass too quickly. But it will. Granting my wish, he'll miss his due date by a week. My water will break, a slow trickle, early morning the day before my birthday. Amniotic fluid, I'll discover, does indeed smell sweet, like the sugar water hummingbirds covet.

Two days later, I'll be drowning on an operating table. The anesthesia will rise past my lungs, and it will feel like I am breathing water. None of the books mentioned this. I won't be able to speak, to tell them I can't breathe, but my husband will see the wild panic in my eyes. *This isn't good,* I'll think. Meanwhile they will begin cutting me open and my husband and I will make that decision we thought we'd never have to make: Something is going wrong, and he will go with the baby. Minutes later, while I fight to breathe, our baby boy will be lifted high into the air—a single, perfect cloud in my sky—and take his first big, beautiful breath. My husband will bring him to my cheek—the only thing I will be able to feel, besides my heaving heart.

Evening, the bright colors of the day subdue to muted blues, greens, roses. Everything soft again. Fresh from a shower, how nice it is to slip into a pretty white dress, skin tanned and warm. A pink hibiscus behind the ear. Tonight I'm taking myself (us) out to dinner at a sushi restaurant just down the beach overlooking the water. It's still early—the sun has yet to set and many are still on the beach—and I have the restaurant nearly to myself. The hostess wishes me a happy Mother's Day and tells me I'm having a boy. My first Mother's Day. I order avocado and cucumber rolls, mineral water, green tea ice cream.

I've learned how to take a meal by myself. I've grown to be less self-conscious, especially here. Yes, I am a lone woman. But I am not lonesome (although I do bring that Hawaiian dictionary to skim until my food arrives, just in case). And I'm not really alone. There's something quite communal about carrying a child. Your belly becomes you. It's all about the belly. A maternal synecdoche. A belly puts people at ease. It invites attention of a different kind. Instead of men, it's women who approach me, touch me, share intimate details, and this time it's welcome.

Perhaps this is the secret to traveling alone as a woman. You can wear that bikini. You can wear a sexy dress—as, for once in your life, you have cleavage. You can even dine alone. Those cute guys—the ones who, even a few months ago, would have shamelessly held your gaze—lower their eyes when you pass. Of course, it's nice to feel like a woman still (did I mention the cleavage?), but when your belly precedes you, there's a freedom in for once not feeling like just—to use another synecdoche—a set of boobs. I'm a mother now. And this mama's spoken for.

It's my last day and I've done absolutely nothing this trip. I didn't drive all the way to heavenly Hanalei. I didn't sit in my favorite open-air, Billie Holiday–playing café in Kapa'a. Didn't visit the exquisite blue jade flower, hug the trees that turn worries into fruit and fruit into beads, or burn my thoughts at the Hindu temple. No shave ice or antiques in Waimea for me. Didn't even make it down the deeply rutted dirt roads beneath green mountains to swim at Kipu or my favorite, Mahaulepu.

I have the beach all to myself. I'm ready to lie there for hours like a monk seal. I've just smoothed out the sand beneath my bottom and have blissfully closed my eyes. Soon I'm dreaming of pudgy-legged clouds crawling across the sky. Happy, nappy-bottomed babies. And suddenly there are babies everywhere. Someone has chosen this spot, just a few feet away from me, to set up camp for her fussing brood. Then another mother stops with her own toddlers in tow. I give them the stinkeye, but it goes unnoticed. The two are busy discussing the difficulties of removing sand from little bottoms. Babies are whining, babies are crying. The sand around me is littered with stuff—bright-colored beach toys and sticky bottles of sunscreen, sippy cups and swim diapers. And just like that, it's all over: my last bit of prebaby solitude, my quiet, childless life. It is, quite literally, a rude awakening.

Naively, I know, I hope to still be me—this girl on the beach—when I am a mother. I hope to travel, if not lightly, then as efficiently and neatly as possible. To wear spit-up and spilled milk with grace. I hope to be the mama in the bikini (okay, maybe *tank*ini), the mother who barters a few hours of quiet beach time, reads books on anything other than parenting, converses about ideas in addition to sand-removal remedies (baby powder works like a charm, I will soon learn). I hope to be the mother whom you—gentle, once-fellow solo traveler—don't cluck your tongue at. For if motherhood is anything like traveling, then I vow to be a good traveler. In the least, I will try to keep my voice down and my cute child from kicking sand on your towel. Could it be that every well-intentioned mother-to-be hopes these things?

It is time to go. There's always that moment when you cross over from being present away from home, to looking forward to just being home.

Mentally you're already gone. You begin undoing everything you did when you arrived: throwing out uneaten food, folding your clothes, pulling tousled sheets off the bed, tossing the old gardenias. You make a to-do list of all the things you'll think about when you get home: *Make room for nursery in office. Buy and assemble crib. Paint vintage dresser? Wash and neatly fold baby clothes* (clothes you can't imagine someone—your son—wearing soon). *Pack hospital bag. Read new Zadie Smith book* (I won't, and one year later it will still be untouched, in the same spot). *Send revised story ending to editor.*

I know coming here will never be the same. I am going to miss it all terribly. I'm going to miss solitude and sleep and a sense of well-being. I'm going to miss this beach ritual. I'm going to miss me, here. But I've had many mornings. So much time to think and write and be. It's time to go, and I'm ready. I have someplace even better to be.

The sun is still low, and rosy-bellied clouds hang heavily overhead. I place my suitcase by the door and walk down to the ocean one last time. This is my goodbye ritual. There's no one on the beach, but my family's presence is everywhere. Three sisters running and jumping into the ocean. My father boogie boarding on "his" reef. My mother searching for her turtles. A ring found in the sand. A wedding. A honeymoon. The palm tree under which my husband and I kissed during a sudden storm. A baby born. And there, in the usual spot, is me sitting in the sand. And this time I'm holding my son in my arms, and I'm watching him watch the clouds.

My Little Prince

Edith Pearlman

Tokyo in December seemed more than usually dense, vast, and gimcrack. The citizens followed their unenviable routine. They were compressed into small apartments every evening, released every morning to tumble underground for an hour's ride on a packed subway car, and then solemnly discharged to ascend into a high-rise office for ten hours of dry work. Was it any wonder that at night the bars were full? Or that on every subway car, all the riders, sitting *and* standing, were sound asleep? Perhaps they were dreaming of other lives on other planets.

My son and daughter-in-law and infant grandson certainly felt bliss-ful in their tiny apartment with a view of the Edogawa. My Japanese rela-tives, bearing gifts, were delighted to visit me there. But I craved a brief vacation from this vacation so crowded with people and things.

So I resolved to go to Hakone, an area between the Izu Peninsula and Mount Fuji, a place of forests and mountains and watery splendors: a lake, rivers, waterfalls, steaming springs. Hakone is the essential Japan, I'd been told. I took a train, and then a tram, and then a funicular, and then a series of swaying gondolas. The final gondola descended to the shore of Lake Ashi. And at last I rode a taxi to my inn, a low calm place whose thermal bath looked out on pines, mist, and untroubled birds.

After a bath in the company of other naked, middle-aged nymphs, and a small cup of rice wine, I set out for an exploration. I walked down a narrow road and turned its corner, ready to feast my eyes on essential Japan.

Instead, I found myself staring at a piece of Provence: a cobbled square, a series of shops, and a patisserie. What had been in that rice wine? The place was, I noticed as I approached it, not a mirage, yet nonetheless faux. The houses were one brick deep. The shops were only facades. Amidst it all was a single real building, which announced its purpose in three languages: to recapitulate and memorialize the life of the aviator Antoine de Saint-Exupéry, author of *The Little Prince*.

Saint-Exupéry, bard of flight, lover of Saharan solitude, unilingual, monomaniacal, and very tall, had no connection with Japan. He served on the other side in World War II (and disappeared while on a reconnaissance mission). The Far East does not appear in his writings—the nomads of the desert were his inspiration. As a schoolboy poet he tried his hand at villanelles and sonnets, but not haiku. As an adult memoirist he wrote about Africa and Europe. Yet *The Little Prince,* translated into eighty languages and still a bestseller in France, does very well in Japan.

I entered the museum. I followed its winding corridors, gazing at collections of clothing and tools, at painstakingly assembled reproductions of rooms and cockpits. Here—a photograph of the extremely young count in his infant clothing. There—an early letter; in doodles in the margins, one can see the beginnings of the author's enchanting drawings, four decades later, for *The Little Prince.* His boyhood room, behind glass. The reconstruction of the control room of Aéropostale in North Africa, where he spent the happiest three years of his life delivering the African mail in an open-cockpit biplane. A reconstruction of that plane, suspended by wires from the ceiling—how did anyone brave the skies in such a toy? How did anyone survive its crash? Saint-Exupéry survived many crashes, and he wrote about them with zest.

There are photographs everywhere. Photographs of Madame de Saint-Exupéry, his mother. Photographs of Madame de Saint-Exupéry, his wife. The wife, Consuelo, looks beautiful and fragile—and was, as I know from Stacy Schiff's biography of Saint-Ex, imperious and unfaithful. She wore floor-length minks whatever the weather; she threw crockery at her husband. More photographs of the members of Saint-Ex's reconnaissance unit, the 2/33. He flew with the 2/33 from 1939 until the fall of France, and then from 1943 until July 31, 1944, the date of his disappearance into thin air. (The remains of his downed plane were discovered off the coast of Marseille sixty years later.) A full-length photograph of the pilot in baggy street clothing, showing the smile and the famous gaze.

"Oh, he was wonderful to look at!" said the actress Fay Wray. "Big, tall, great black eyes that themselves looked like radiant stars."

Another reconstructed location—this a dreary hotel suite, one of the many New York rooms in which he wrote, and rewrote, and rewrote again *The Little Prince*—a book for children, though he had no children; a book that takes place in the stratosphere, though, in self-imposed exile, he had no opportunity to fly; a book of melancholy despite its sunny illustrations.

The three final rooms of the museum are devoted to *The Little Prince*—facsimiles of the original drawings and manuscript; copies of the book in all its languages, and a holographic representation of the little prince himself, glowing in a dark room, seemingly three-dimensional yet impossible to touch.

In the book shop—I was the only customer, as I had been the only patron of the museum—I bought three copies of *The Little Prince:* in Japanese, French, and English.

Kids recognize as one of their own the small monarch of Asteroid B-612 whose beloved companion is a proud and difficult rose. Not able to understand or satisfy the rose, the prince leaves his asteroid. He makes a speedy survey of adults in six visits to neighboring asteroids, each populated by a single peculiar figure, including a lamplighter, a geographer, and a drunkard. He lands finally on Earth, in the Sahara, where he meets the downed aviator who serves as the book's narrator but who never appears in the drawings. From a wise fox the prince learns lessons about love and responsibility and longing. From a snake he learns how to speak in riddles. The prince teaches the aviator that "one sees clearly only with the heart." Then, in eerie prophecy, the prince disappears into thin air.

"To know is not to prove nor to explain. It is to accede to vision," says Saint-Exupéry in *Flight to Arras.* The Japanese sensibility—consisting, in the words of the scholar Donald Keene, of Suggestion (meanings even in ordinary conversation are only hinted at); Irregularity (symmetry is avoided); Simplicity (ornament is also spurned); and Perishability (the revered cherry blossom blooms for only a few days)—may be particularly well adapted to accede to the suggestion, irregularity, simplicity, and aching perishability of *The Little Prince.* And people in this island country, stuffed into its cities, alone among each other, may yearn for the airy isolation of the little prince on his asteroid.

For some or all of these reasons—and for others that have eluded this Westerner—the prince and his creator have captured the hearts of the Japanese, so much so that one citizen spent his yen creating a bit of Provence in Hakone. The museum is not mentioned in guidebooks, though. Perhaps it fell from an asteroid the day I visited Hakone. Perhaps—while I was making my solitary way back to inn and bath and rice wine—it vanished upward, out of human sight. One sees clearly only with the heart.

Later, in my room, by a rather dim light, I read:

"It's a little lonely in the desert . . . " said the prince.
"It's also lonely with people," said the snake.

Hai, I agreed. *Oui,* I added. Yes. Words are the most reliable company.

This Nigeria Will Eat You Up

Faith Adiele

Raymond calls Monday evening to report that the university students have been rioting since Sunday. After looting the commissary of chickens, they set fire to the vice chancellor's car. Rumor has it that the Mobile Police are en route. There have been several incidents of local police joining the protesters, so the government is deploying northern Muslims who don't speak Igbo. The VC has declared a state of emergency; the campus gates are closed to all but foreign and graduate students.

"Come quickly," Raymond advises, before the Nigerian telephone and telegraph service collapses with exhaustion. "While it's still quiet."

Twenty-five years after my father's return home to Nigeria, I arrive for the first time. I am optimistic though armed with little: a research fellowship, a few names, a binder of letters he wrote to my mother and me back in America when I was a child. I tell myself—and anyone who asks—that *no,* I have not come to find him. I've come, on my own, in search of what it is to be Nigerian. I'm hungry for heritage, yes. Siblings, perhaps. But a father, no. At twenty-six, I say, it's too late for one of those.

Ironically, schooling, the very thing that propelled my father out of colonial Africa for more than a decade, is what calls me back. I plan to enroll at the University of Nigeria, the institution he helped build. The brother of a friend gets me within sixty kilometers, delivering me to the home of his senior brother. The senior brother, a businessman with inky skin who spits a rapid battery of words, peers hard at me, as if from a distance. The junior brother explains my plan to spend the year in Nigeria, learning, as he puts it, "how to be Nigerian."

I smile, trying to look easy to care for.

The senior brother raises his hand and shouts, "Raymond!"

The young man who lumbers in blocks the space where the ceiling light would be, if the electricity actually worked. His face, framed by a tight fade, is nonetheless gentle.

The senior brother explains that Raymond is a student at the university and can show me how to make the sixty-kilometer trek. "She can't live on campus," he says, leaning toward his junior brother and lowering his voice. "She'll stay here."

On Monday they take me on a dry run from Enugu, the provincial capital where they live, to Nsukka, the village closest to the university. For some reason, the University of Nigeria is in the countryside, several kilometers outside Nsukka village. They point out the bus and taxi parks. After a sixty-kilometer bus ride from town to the village, I will have to catch a taxi to campus. There is no direct route.

As the guard waves us through the front gate, Raymond explains the high cement walls surrounding the campus: "to protect the university cars from thieves." I'm a bit surprised to enter Eden: lush, manicured shrubs against red soil, pastel stucco buildings with open corridors, a cream and raspberry–colored bookstore with a sloped roof like a smashed petit four. Clusters of students in dress shirts and slacks, shoes polished within an inch of their lives, loiter on the paved lanes, staring.

Raymond heads for the Men's Hostel, and I enter the Graduate College. After the brilliant sun, the dim room is blinding. Hovering just inside the entrance, I finally make out the outline of a woman filing her nails behind a desk. At my approach she points the nail file at a man seated behind a larger desk. The man, wearing the ubiquitous gray safari suit and thick black plastic spectacles of the Nigerian bureaucrat, has wiry hair, a wide Igbo face, my father's mouth. I peer at his name placard, followed by the title: ASSISTANT TO THE SECRETARY OF THE GRADUATE COLLEGE.

When he glances up, I greet him and introduce myself.

"You're four months late!" he bellows. "Don't expect to be admitted to the University!"

"But, sir," I stammer, trying to mold my words into the courtly, measured tones of Nigerian English, "the acceptance came so late, and I had much to prepare! The visa. My plane ticket—"

The Assistant to the Secretary waves his arms as if directing traffic. "Ah-ah! I don't care *whose* father is *who!* There's nothing like special services at the University of Nigeria!"

I stop in midsentence, my mouth an open O. Who's talking about my father? He is a binder of fading letters, a map to the past. What does he have to do with this? I plump with indignation. I've come to Nigeria quite on my own, to try my hand at becoming Nigerian, at Nigerian education. My breast heaves in the heat. I glare at the Assistant to the Secretary of the Graduate College. Besides, I may be new to the country, but from what I've heard, the University of Nigeria—in fact, the entire country of Nigeria—is all about special services. Doesn't everyone decry—and then exploit—Nigeria's infamous nepotism?

The Assistant to the Secretary displays a row of gold caps, obviously pleased that he's made an impression. He allows himself a small smile, a patch of shade for me to rest in. "Anyway, you're a Nigerian now," he says. "You'll learn to suffer like the rest of us!" He returns to his paperwork.

I droop before his desk, suddenly aware of the hum of a gas generator coming from an inner office. The sound vibrates the room, smelling faintly of petrol. It must be true, then: There is indeed no electricity on the nation's campuses. Which VIP gets to use a generator in his sanctum—the actual *Secretary* of the Graduate College?

I realize I have no contingency plan, no ace up my sleeve. All I have is time. I fold my arms.

After a full ten minutes, the Assistant to the Secretary glances up from the stack of cheap manila folders, eyes flashing surprise. That I am still there? Still silent? I am new to this Nigeria; I have not yet learned to shout.

He stands and strides out of the room.

Two doorways down, he pauses. "Well? Come *on*—if you are going to register!"

I scurry after him, trying not to smile, imagining that what I've won is actually worth something.

When the Assistant to the Secretary of the Graduate College begins a new tirade—"Your demands were unreasonable. There's nothing like accommodation for you!"—I am better prepared for the performance, the strategy of false anger. Panting, I think back. "Unreasonable demands" must refer to a telegram I sent inquiring about housing, back before I knew about the shortage. "That's fine," I parry. "I intend to stay in the capital with friends."

Again he allows himself to relax. Tweaking my cheek, he laughs. "Stubborn girl."

We charge through a series of darkened rooms peopled with safari-suited, middle-aged men at empty desks, women in gauzy blouses and skirts, who lift blinking, sleepy heads off folded arms. The countless mimeographed forms he snatches up en route wilt before he can hand them to me. The sleepy staff welcomes me by name, and I wonder just how many have perused my application.

As we depart, I hear the topic shift, the whispers trail, the speculation about my father begin: *Eh? Our Commissioner own? You don't mean it! Is this one really the daughter—o?*

272

It takes weeks to complete registering. On Raymond's advice, I learn to lay an elaborate groundwork of "dash"—small-small gifts like a bunch of mini-bananas or a paper cone of fresh, roasted groundnuts that aren't readily identifiable as bribes—among the countless frontline personnel. Thank you, surly guy in the pale blue safari suit for relaying that message to your boss. Thank you, woman with lye burns on her cheeks from skin bleaching for not destroying my files. Thank you, assorted bespectacled clerks on the strength of the possibility that you might be in a position to help or harm me in the future.

The few faculty members and administrators not out moonlighting are only mildly interested in my quest to register and acquire a research advisor. Why, they ask, roaring with laughter, would somebody want to come to Nigeria to study? Everybody with sense is running abroad!

"And why bother to study women?" the chairman of the social science department asks, leafing through my proposal on female religious leaders.

I gnaw my lip and keep quiet. Life in Nigeria is all about conserving energy.

Invariably there is the hiccup of recognition at my last name and the tentative stammer, "Any relation to our Honorable Commissioner?" At my yes, shock erupts into embraces and shouts of joy, arms flung around my stiff American body: *Our daughter! My sister! Welcome home!*

For a few weeks, these hugs, these shouts of *"Nno! Nno!"* are enough to sustain me, to convince me that despite the dire prospects for my research, I am getting what I came to Nigeria for. Eventually, however, their joy subsides into vague mistrust. As weeks pass, I read the questions clouding their eyes. *Why is she trudging around, trying to register herself? Why is she even bothering to study at all? Surely a degree can be arranged. . . .*

I shake my head, not so much optimistic at this point as stubborn, just as the Assistant to the Secretary of the Graduate College has said. *Stubborn girl.*

Here is not like the civilized countries, someone is always reminding me. *This Nigeria will eat you up if you don't have big men or the extended family to help you!*

My declarations that I want to do things for myself meet with half-believing smirks. *There must be a problem in the family,* I imagine they gossip as soon as I slog out into the heat. *Perhaps the daughter is not the daughter, the father not the father.*

Finally the chairman of the social science department assigns me an advisor and tells me to go away and leave him in peace. The advisor also tells me to go away and leave him in peace, but not before buying a textbook on the marriage patterns of European missionaries—odd advice, until I realize that the book was written by him. Two weeks later *he* goes away, accepting a long-standing invitation from a German university amidst the envy of his hungry colleagues.

One Sunday afternoon a few months after the advisor's disappearance, Raymond announces, "There are going to be student protests tomorrow." Home for the weekend, he looms over the ironing board, pressing the week's clothes quickly, before the Nigerian Electrical Power Authority cuts: one pair of khakis, a pair of navy trousers, five dress shirts. "You should stay home."

"Protests—why?"

"They're saying that *Ebony* magazine in your America published a list of the world's richest men." He squeezes a rag milky with starch and rapidly peppers a sleeve with it. "This dictator calling himself president was listed as the richest general in the world. The government has now banned the magazine."

"So we can't tell if the story is true or not," I point out.

After only a few months in this nation of jailed journalists, I've smelled the rumors rotting in the streets like sewage. Every few months a major scandal breaks, gripping the country in a fever of outraged speculation, then dies, proven close to false. Zik, the father of independence, is dead, his body held hostage by the military. Ojukwu, the rebel leader during the civil war, is engaged to a beauty queen thirty years his junior. Okoroji, the expatriate footballer, was poisoned on the field by Nigerians resentful of his defection to Belgium.

"Perhaps the ban itself is a rumor."

"It's true enough." Raymond worries his newly manicured fade.

"I have to get my letter," I whine. My tourist visa about to expire, I need certification from the university to get a student one.

Raymond buttons his shirts, even the tiny top button, wrapping the starched collars around his index finger. Squinting with concentration, he matches the frayed sleeve ends and shirttails, folding each shirt like new.

275

"What should I do?" I ask, watching him layer them into a vinyl Adidas sports bag. "I don't have much time before my visa runs out."

He shrugs, used to inconvenience. "Wait for my call." He shoulders the bag and ducks through the doorjamb. "I'll let you know if it's safe to come to campus."

When he calls, Raymond reports that the Mobile Police arrived in the middle of the night and started firing tear gas into the student hostels. Little missiles trailing white smoke arced through the sky, and a smell like rotten eggs mixed with pepper descended upon the campus, covering everything with a humid yellow pall. The standoff is my opportunity.

The bus ride from the capital is uneventful, but half a mile from the university, the taxi driver refuses to go on. "Students, dey seize cars," he declares, speeding off in a cloud of leaky petrol. I walk the rest of the way.

A guard with a heavy black machine gun and Northern tribal markings like an irritated panther blocks the gate. I wave my international student ID in front of him. He clutches it before his nose as if smelling it. His narrowed eyes are impossibly red—from drink, I worry. He continues sniffing my ID, and it occurs to me that he probably doesn't read English.

"American," I say, thumping my chest. Now would be the time for those so-called special services. I'm mildly amazed I'm doing all this, that I actually want a letter extending my status as a student whose advisor has run off to Europe and whose university is under military occupation.

The guard slings his machine gun over his shoulder and opens the gate.

I creep inside. Campus is eerily quiet, the students presumably in the hostels, sleeping off the last two days. Classroom after classroom stands empty. I skirt circles of tarmac blackened from burning tires, piles of shattered glass. The yellow air, redolent with sulfur, adds to the dreamlike quality of the landscape.

For the first time in all my months of visits, the actual Secretary of the Graduate College of the University of Nigeria himself appears. The door to an inner office flies open, and out he strides, all smiles and quick laughter.

"Faith, my dear!" the Secretary of the Graduate College says, clasping my hand in both of his. "You made the dangerous journey." He shakes his head and chuckles. "You are truly your father's daughter!" He waves me through the dim anteroom into his airy office. "Come in, come in. I understand you have plans to travel to Senegal, a fascinating place. Are you a fan of Senghor?"

I study the Secretary of the Graduate College, my first happy bureaucrat. He's younger than his assistant, impeccably groomed, with a stylish flare to the cut of his safari suit and a watch that gleams not with metal, but with gold. Settling into a wide chair, he eyes me over a stack of grimy mimeographed copies.

"So, how is your research going? Tell me what you have learned."

Stunned that someone actually wants to know, I have to think. What was my research? I mutter a word or two about attending charismatic prayer meetings.

277

"Good, good." He nods. "You are very resourceful." The Secretary of the Graduate College brings his manicured fingers together and leans back. "How can we help you to achieve your aims? What can I do?"

Blinded by the light of his attention, I stammer about the immigration letter.

"Is that all? No problem!" With a snap of those fingers, he tells me to return in exactly two weeks to pick it up. The snap transforms into a V. "You know," he says, "you shouldn't be having to get a visa. You're a Nigerian now!" He flashes a row of perfect teeth. "Think about getting a Nigerian passport. That way we can see you often."

I allow myself a smile, hopeful for the first time in months.

Exactly two weeks later, I wake early, girding myself for the journey to campus: first the trudge down the hill on dusty, unpaved roads, children trailing along behind as if I were the Pied Piper, shouting, *"Onyeacha!"* ("White!") and *"China!"* Then the wait along the busy road choked with diesel exhaust, trying to flag down a rusty, weaving taxi with room for one more. The open stares and laughing comments of passersby and the other passengers as I explain my destination across town to the driver who pretends not to understand. I crowd into the backseat with two office girls who stare straight ahead and refuse to shift over, earning myself the privilege of being the one to hold the door, a sheet of pounded metal, shut with a length of wire.

At the bus park, two hundred people wait for a sixty-seat government bus that is already three hours late. I decide to walk to the long-distance taxi park to take a shared taxi, which is much faster—and much less safe.

There is one nearly full taxi waiting to go, its occupants four brooding fraternity boys. My greatest fear used to be breaking down on the road late in the day—everyone is so afraid of armed robbers that no one ever stops at night—but Raymond has equally frightening stories about these frat boys in their tight haircuts and snowy shirtsleeves.

I stagger back in the shine of eight eyes, testosterone billowing out the open car window, and resolve to wait for the next taxi. The driver, eager to leave and pick up a return fare, curses me out before the entire park.

This time, I curse him back, then ask to have the driver of the next taxi pointed out. This one teases me gently as I make a big show of checking the tires and jotting down the license plate number before getting in the front passenger seat. *"Nne,"* he jeers, *little mother.* "Wetin you be tinkin? I no go for to rob you this day—o!"

After thirty minutes, the taxi fills, a tangle of limbs and parcels and struggling chickens, and we depart. Slowly, slowly, my grip on the length of wire holding the car door shut loosens, the blood returns to my knuckles. We speed through lush emerald farmland, the road littered with broken-down buses and taxis, their stranded occupants waving desperately at passing overcrowded vehicles. An overturned truck lies on its side, two-foot-long yams and potatoes scattered across the macadam. Workers who'd no doubt been riding atop the cargo stand dazed and barefoot. A pet monkey perches atop the shoulder of one, its black face ringed in a ruff of white fur.

Two-thirds of the way to Nsukka, the engine erupts in a cloud of black smoke. The taxi chokes and shudders to a halt. Laughing, the passengers disentangle and climb out to join the driver in looking under the hood at the web of rusty wire and soldered bottle caps. A barrage of Igbo is exchanged. After twenty minutes of poking the surface with sticks and bathing it with handfuls of water and fanning it with handkerchiefs, they all agree that the taxi is in fact dead.

It's finally happened. The inevitable outcome of this commute I make in actual terror and shame—terror that this very thing will happen, shame that after all this time I, who have traveled halfway around the world alone with nothing more than a backpack and foolish confidence, can't manage Nigeria. I can't mimic the tough indifference of the other female students I see making the journey in sunglasses and high heels. The twice-weekly ordeal hasn't, as my host instructed, toughened me up. After months of study, I'm still not Nigerian. I take deep breaths, checking the sun's position in the sky, and the others finally seem to notice that they're stuck in the middle of nowhere with a foreigner clearly on the verge of tears. The road stretches empty for miles. All eyes regard me uneasily.

Twenty minutes later, a shiny BMW pulls up ahead. One of our group picks up his satchel and bids us farewell. Another passenger begs the young man with the satchel to ask his friends to take him along. "I'm a businessman," he pleads. "Please—o. I'm late for an appointment."

"No, sorry—o," the young man refuses. He stops and points at me: "You can come."

Up ahead in the BMW, the men twist around to stare. As he motions me toward the car, they give him the thumbs-up.

"Thanks, but no."

"Hey, there's nothing to be afraid of. We're all students."

I smile. "Who said anything about being afraid?"

He smirks, tries another tactic. "That's a big man driving the car. Very rich." He leans in, dropping his voice. "No one here speaks English. You'll be stuck. It's foolish to be afraid."

I turn away.

Out the corner of my eye, I see him shrug and run to the car. The businessman trails behind, cracked briefcase in hand, still begging. The student brushes him aside and climbs into the backseat. The men look back one last time, and then the car spins ahead, covering the businessman in red dust.

Just when I've reconciled myself to the idea of dying on the road between Enugu and Nsukka, a government bus stops, and we're lucky enough to get standing room. Four hours after leaving the house, I reach the university.

The office of the Secretary of the Graduate College is closed.

"Please, is *oga* coming back?" I ask the pale-blue-safari-suited clerk who sits fiddling behind a bare desk.

"*Oga* no dey" he states noncommittally, blinking behind his spectacles.

Fighting the urge to shout (*Yes, thank you, I can see that the Big Man isn't here!*), I instead call one of the market women patrolling outside and invest in some "dash" through the open window. The clerk and I peel finger-size bananas together, suddenly friends, and I learn that *oga* is out of town for a few days and no, has not yet done my letter. I ask him to tell *oga* that I will return in one week.

281

He nods and gulps the last banana. When I ask to use the staff bathroom before the ride back, he claims there is no water.

This time I don't wait a week. Three days later I'm back on campus. And after having been chased off by the students, the Mobile Police are too, this time shooting bullets, not tear gas. One student was reportedly hit in the thigh as he ran for cover, and after carrying him to the bare-shelved clinic, the protesters rolled another government car before the back gate and set it ablaze.

I arrive to an empty, barricaded campus. Again the Secretary of the Graduate College himself welcomes me warmly. "My dear," he says, propping open the door to his humming, air-conditioned office, "come in, come in!" He wears a safari suit of metallic-looking sharkskin.

The Secretary of the Graduate College nods to the safari-blue clerk. "Go and get banana and groundnut."

His gaze then shifts to a woman fiddling in the dark behind an ancient manual typewriter. "You there, do an immigration letter for the Commissioner's daughter!"

"Ah," he says, sinking into his chair and forming a steeple with his hands. "So you are back." The steeple parts, and both hands saw the air, buffed nails gleaming dully. "You've certainly inherited your father's stubbornness. You know, he was practically the only politician who wouldn't take bribes!" He says it as if it is something to be ashamed of.

Still shaking his head, he asks about my advisor.

I blink. "You don't know? He's gone to Germany."

"*What?*" the Secretary of the Graduate College shouts. "Surely you don't mean it!"

I nod, and he wipes the back of his hand against the palm of the other to show disgust. "You've had too many troubles, and now this hungry, runaway advisor. *Shah!*" He advises me to persevere on my own.

I am indeed persevering, but with what?

The clerk delivers a bag of banana and groundnut. "Take, take," the Secretary of the Graduate College says, shelling the nuts one-handed, the gold of his watch glinting as his wrist rotates.

University officials pop in and out, carrying small bits of paper requiring his approval. Once inside, they try to outdo each other, making puns on the latest news stories, sharing humorous tales of Nigeria's latest embarrassment. One man has heard about a Nigeria Airways plane taken hostage by a European government for nonpayment of fees. Another recounts a tale in which a schoolgirl traveling home for the holidays gives birth, and yet the baby is missing when the train pulls into the station. *Ah, this Nigeria,* is the invariable refrain, accompanied by roars of laughter and a gentle shake of the head.

After the last guest leaves, the clerk brings in the letter, all four sentences of it, which the Secretary of the Graduate College reads aloud for my approval. "Yes? It's okay?"

"Perfect! Thank you, sir." Eager to beat the sun, I pop up from my chair and smooth my skirt. "I am most appreciative."

"Ah, you're a sweet girl," he says, holding out the letter. As I bend to slip the paper into my schoolbag, he leans forward and bites my neck.

The teeth of the Secretary of the Graduate College cling to my neck. Like Nigeria's infamous utilities, my mind sputters and cuts off, leaving me in darkness. Somehow the back-up generator of my body kicks in. The torso straightens. The arms heft my bag. The legs keep walking toward the door. My body steps out of the Graduate College of the University of Nigeria.

Due to the riots, the bus back to town is unusually empty without students. I worry the two grooved half-crescents of tooth marks that the Secretary of the Graduate College of the University of Nigeria has left on my neck. If not for them, I could not believe that what just happened really did happen. Even though I was there. I finger the proof and replay the scene: the letter, the bending, the bite. My silence. And then I have a Nigerian thought, involuntary and indignant: *Even if I look like I'm alone, doesn't the man know who my father is? What in the world makes him think that he, a lowly secretary, can bite the neck of the daughter of the former Commissioner of Education for East-Central Nigeria?*

In a few weeks I will finally meet my father in the dim stairwell of my host's apartment building. We will stand in silence, staring curiously at each other, half smiling, shy. I will wonder what to do with this man I said I didn't want, until I notice his hands, holding out a gift for me, trembling ever so slightly.

I settle back into the bus seat I have all to myself. As my finger traces the fading crescents, I smile. It won't scar. This Nigeria didn't eat me up.

The Getaway

Marion Winik

When I had only two children and they were small, I spent a few days in a cabin in the woods at a retreat for artists and writers. I remember standing in the grocery store in Georgia, befuddled. What did I eat? I had no idea. It was not Hot Pockets or sliced orange cheese. Eventually, I put in my cart a bag of rice, a bottle of Tabasco, one can each of beans and mustard greens, chosen for their endearing Southern brand names and labels. Oh, coffee. And a bottle of wine, and a peach.

A mother can forget what she likes. She can even forget what she is like. Wherever you go, there you are, say the Buddhists—but so are they. The fruit of your loins, in their Fruit of the Looms. Buy them, clean them, fold them, fix them, hunt them, buy some more. Eventually, you run out of memory, like a computer running too many applications. Before you were the finder of socks, the maker of sandwiches, the driver of carpools, the kisser of boo-boos, the full-service factotum of family life, you filled whole days with something. What was it? Who were you? There is only one way to find out.

Though it is difficult to abandon those who count on you for their very undergarments, if you play your cards right, distant obligations arise. Business trip. Personal duty. Obligatory invitation. Really, you must go. If only to pry yourself loose from your pathetic martyrdom and see what is left.

Goodbye! Back soon! Just microwave them for two minutes on high!

To gaze at the ocean. To meditate on a mountaintop. To steam in lavender and eucalyptus. To this list must be added what I have found to be an equally restorative experience of spiritual solitude: to sit in the airport terminal. For while there are few things more stressful than being in this environment with a horde of children, when you travel alone, the place is transformed. In its airy, comfortable reaches, wholly devoted to sitting, reading, and snacking, you are resurrected as an individual.

One person, one seat, one ticket, one will. No argument.

Whatever automatic reaction people have to you when you appear in public with your family—pity or amusement, aesthetic appreciation or concern—it is nowhere in evidence, nor is the presumption that because you are with children, such reactions may be displayed with impunity. No, instead of conducting your private life on a public stage with generally humiliating results, you will be untroubled as if wrapped in a cocoon, reading *The New York Times* and drinking Starbucks coffee. How could aromatherapy in Big Sur be better than this?

And you never know, perhaps they will announce a delay. When traveling with children, your powerlessness over such things is a problem, a violation of natural law that must be explained and re-explained even to teenagers. When solo, powerlessness is the dharma. The fact is, you will have to sit there, accomplishing nothing, for many hours. Try to adjust. You have packed three books, and even now someone has discarded a copy of *The New Yorker* containing a fifteen-thousand-word article by Janet Malcolm or Diane Middlebrook. This may be your only chance in your adult life to get through this article.

After a while, you might stop looking up every time a small voice utters, "Mommy." Or maybe you won't. Either way, you will soon remember what you like to eat.

You might think a hotel room a more luxurious experience of solitude than a terminal gate, and it has its points, but it lacks the invigorating friction of a public setting. It is the presence of strangers, combined with the act of transit, that resets your sense of self. See: You are a woman in black jeans sitting in a chair reading a fifteen-thousand-word magazine article. A compact, self-contained organism.

If someone speaks to you, they do so politely, and if they look at you, they do so covertly, because that's all that's allowed. Your boundaries, under continual assault by the condition of motherhood, start to firm up. You are mutating into that least maternal and most impermeable of beings: a stranger.

My first experience of the pleasurably heightened self-consciousness of solo travel occurred years before my pathetic martyrdom, when I took a trip alone at eighteen. I flew to New Mexico for a yoga retreat in Taos, first staying overnight in Albuquerque in a Holiday Inn, then catching a bus the next day to the mountains. I had a sense of who I was during that wheezy journey I wrote about excitedly in my journal. *Girlness is separated from airness by red flannel shirtness*, I began. (Sorry, it was 1975 and as I said, I was eighteen.) I filled pages with the bubbly chronicle of my experiences purchasing a bright-green Navajo blanket the day before. I leaned against the yellowed window glass of the bus, that blanket in my lap, as small, dusty Southwestern towns went by outside, populated by ethnic groups I had never seen before.

No one knew a thing about me. I could tell them my name was Kitty, or that I was an orphan. I could tell them nothing, and let them wonder. Look at me: a traveling spiritual seeker in a Navajo blanket, off to transcend the illusion of self for good. After so much adolescent self-loathing, I almost had a crush on myself.

In maturity, autoromantic opportunities are rare; also endangered are the crushes on strangers that were such a standard feature of younger travels. Not that I can't still fall in love with someone on the basis of a ten-minute conversation. I can, but now my life is overpopulated. At this point, most people I meet remind me so much of someone I already know that it just confuses me. And in any case, if I talk I won't be able to read my book. Or make my lists, for the other urge that comes over me shortly after liberating myself from my schedules and responsibilities is the compulsion to make lists of things to do when I return. Even on car trips I do this, scribbling messy columns of verb phrases in a notebook open on the passenger seat. It is hard to write in the car, but I always remember a slightly dotty, doe-eyed poet I used to know named Sandra Lynn who said she wrote her poems while driving. If Sandra Lynn can do it, so can I.

Lists of things to do are poems of a kind. The free verse of a vast and efficient future, in which cars are inspected, birthday presents wrapped, videos returned, boxes of books packed up and sent off to young nephews. *What a beautiful life I'm going to have when I get home.* And yet, despite the bright promise of the lists, and the refreshed quality of my identity, I have never once managed a smooth homecoming. Two seconds into re-entry, the traveling me has vanished, my self-possession left behind at baggage claim.

I walk in the door and all the things I am responsible for seem to fly toward me, neglected and furious. Everything is wrong, and crooked, and left out on the counter. My husband, who has done everything a person possibly could, is annoyed in advance, knowing I will be a bitch. "So how was it?" he asks.

"Oh, god, it was great," I say. Already, in the other room, they are shouting, "Mom!"

"They never stopped the whole time you were gone," my husband says wearily. "So what did you do?"

"Nothing," I say, dropping my suitcase and moving swiftly toward a jar of peanut butter with the lid off, also shouting my name. "Nothing."

About the Contributors

Faith Adiele's travel memoir, *Meeting Faith: The Forest Journals of a Black Buddhist Nun* (W. W. Norton), won the PEN/Beyond Margins Award for Biography/Memoir in 2004. That same year, "My Journey Home," a documentary based on her writings and travels, aired on PBS. Her writings on travel and culture have appeared in such publications as *A Woman Alone: Travel Tales from Around the Globe* (Seal Press), *The Best Women's Travel Writing 2006* (Travelers' Tales), *Ploughshares*, *A Woman's Asia* (Travelers'

Tales), *Transition, The Best Women's Travel Writing 2005* (Travelers' Tales), *Essence, Her Fork in the Road: Women Celebrate Food and Travel* (Travelers' Tales), and *Ms.* magazine. *Coming of Age Around the World: A Multicultural Anthology,* which she coedited for The New Press, is forthcoming in 2007. Adiele makes her home in Pittsburgh, Pennsylvania, where she is professor of creative writing at the University of Pittsburgh. She is currently at work on *Twins: Growing Up Nigerian/Nordic/American,* a work of memoir and cultural history.

Amy C. Balfour practiced law in Richmond, Virginia, for several years before moving to Los Angeles to pursue screenwriting. Her parents, after recovering from their initial horror, now support all her crazy endeavors as long as she maintains proper health insurance. When she's not traveling, Amy works as a writer's assistant for the television drama *Law & Order.* Her essays have appeared in the *Los Angeles Times,* the *South Florida Sun-Sentinel,* and the Travelers' Tales anthology *The Thong Also Rises.*

Julianne Balmain is the author of *Night+Day San Francisco* (Pulse Guides), *Abroad: A Travel Organizer and Journal* (Chronicle Books), and many other books, including a series of mystery novels set in the culinary landscape of California's Napa Valley, written under the pen name Nadia Gordon and published by Chronicle Books. An insatiable traveler, she inevitably returns to her home in the San Francisco Bay Area. To find out more about her books, visit www.juliannebalmain.com.

Alexia Brue is a New York City–based writer and author of *Cathedrals of the Flesh: My Search for the Perfect Bath* (Bloomsbury, 2003). Brue has written about travel, home design, and health for *The New York Times Magazine*, *Vogue*, *Organic Style*, *Luxury Spa Finder*, *Spa*, *Modern Bride*, *Lexus* magazine, British Airways' *High Life*, and a variety of British and American newspapers. She serves as the home design editor for *Luxury Spa Finder* magazine. For her British Airways *High Life* column, "Stateside Broadside," she was short-listed for Britain's APA Journalist of the Year Award in 2003. She was the featured expert on the Travel Channel's "Top Ten Most Amazing Baths" and has appeared on a variety of radio and television shows, including *All Things Considered* and *The Leonard Lopate Show*. To read more, visit Brue's website: www.perfectbath.com.

Alice Carey's memoir, *I'll Know It When I See It*, was initially published by Clarkson Potter in 2002. The paperback edition was published by Seal Press in 2005. She divides her time between New York City and County Cork, Ireland.

Freelance writer **Kate Chynoweth**'s books include *The Risks of Sunbathing Topless* (Seal Press), a collection of women's travel essays inspired by the tragicomedy of her on-the-road assignments. Needless to say, she had many stories to draw on for this anthology. Her work appears in magazines such as *Real Simple* and *Sunset*, and she is the author of other books including *The Bridesmaid Guide: Etiquette, Parties, and Being Fabulous* (Chronicle Books). She lives in Pittsburgh, Pennsylvania.

Alison Culliford was born and brought up in the West of England and educated at Oxford. She has spent most of her adult life working as a journalist and trying to leave England, finally succeeding in 2001, when she moved to Paris. She is the author of two books about the French capital. She dreams of one day returning to Labrador and learning to drive huskies.

Eileen Favorite's poetry and prose have appeared in many literary magazines, and her essays and poems have aired on WBEZ, Chicago Public Radio. She received an Illinois Arts Council Fellowship for poetry in 2005 and for prose in 2001. Her first novel, *The Heroines,* is forthcoming from Scribner. She teaches at the School of the Art Institute of Chicago.

Stephanie Elizondo Griest has mingled with the Russian Mafiya, polished Chinese propaganda, belly danced with Cuban rumba queens, and rallied with Zapatistas. These adventures are the subject of her award-winning memoirs: *Around the Bloc: My Life in Moscow, Beijing, and Havana* (Villard/Random House, 2004) and *Mexican Enough: A Story About Borders* (Atria/Simon & Schuster, 2008). She is also the author of *100 Places Every Woman Should Go* (Travelers' Tales, 2007) and has written for *The New York Times, The Washington Post,* and *Latina* magazine. Stephanie once spent a year driving forty-five thousand miles across the United States, documenting its history for a website for kids, and is the founder of the Youth Free Expression Network. From 2005 to 2006, she was a Hodder Fellow at Princeton University and is currently a Senior Fellow at the World Policy Institute. Visit her website at www.aroundthebloc.com.

Gail Hudson's most recent book is *Harvest for Hope,* coauthored with Dr. Jane Goodall and published in November 2005 (www.harvestforhope .com). Previous books include *I Wanna Be Sedated: 30 Writers on Parenting Teenagers* (www.iwannabesedatedbook.com), which she coedited with Faith Conlon for Seal Press and was published in April 2005. Her features and personal essays about adventure travel, natural health, and parenting have appeared in numerous publications, including *Self, Utne, Natural Health, Parents, Body + Soul,* and *Good Housekeeping.* Gail teaches classes and workshops on personal narrative and memoir writing. She is also a writing coach for numerous authors. She lives with her husband and two children in the Seattle area.

Jennifer Bingham Hull is the author of *Beyond One: Growing a Family and Getting a Life,* winner of *ForeWord* magazine's Book of the Year Award. Her work has appeared in numerous publications, including *The Wall Street Journal, Time, The Atlantic Monthly, Working Mother, Parenting,* and the anthology *Life As We Know It: A Collection of Personal Essays from Salon .com.* Previously a foreign correspondent, she now lives in South Florida with her husband and two children. These days she doesn't have to search for rebels. They occupy her house. Contact her at www.jenniferhull.com.

Katie Krueger first caught the solo travel bug in England in 2000. Since then, she has traveled alone in Europe, India, Sri Lanka, West Africa, and the United States. She studied French and Wolof in Senegal during 2003–2004 as a Rotary Foundation Ambassadorial Scholar. She lives and writes in Madison, Wisconsin.

Lucy McCauley's travel essays have appeared in such publications as *The Atlantic Monthly*, the *Los Angeles Times, Harvard Review, Science & Spirit*, and Salon.com. She is series editor of Travelers' Tales' *Best Women's Travel Writing*, and editor of three other Travelers' Tales anthologies—*Spain* (1995), *Women in the Wild* (1998), and *A Woman's Path* (2000), all of which have been reissued in the last few years.

Holly Morris is the author of *Adventure Divas: Searching the Globe for Women Who Are Changing the World*, which was named a *New York Times* "Editors' Choice." She is the editor of *A Different Angle: Fly Fishing Stories by Women* and *Uncommon Waters: Women Write About Fishing*. Her writing appears in *Outside* magazine, *The New York Times*, and numerous anthologies and publications. Morris is the executive producer/writer/host of the primetime PBS documentary series *Adventure Divas*. She has also been a correspondent for the television series *Globe Trekkers, Treks in a Wild World, National Geographic Today*, and *Outdoor Investigations*. She can be reached at www.adventuredivas.com.

Amy Novesky is a children's book editor and writer. She is the author of *Elephant Prince,* a picture book about Ganesh inspired by her travels in India. A book about Georgia O'Keeffe in Hawaii and another about Billie Holiday will both be published by Harcourt. Amy lives with her husband, photographer N. D. Koster, their son, Quinn, and their dog, George, just north of San Francisco.

Edith Pearlman's fiction has appeared in *Best American Short Stories,* the *O. Henry Prize Collection, Best Short Stories from the South,* and *The Pushcart Prize Collection.* She is the author of three story collections: *Vaquita* (University of Pittsburgh Press), *Love Among the Greats* (Eastern Washington University Press), and *How to Fall* (Sarabande Books).

Carol Perehudoff is a freelance travel writer based in Toronto. As well as writing a regular column on solo travel for the *Toronto Star,* her articles have appeared in *enRoute* magazine, the *Chicago Tribune,* the *New York Post,* the *San Francisco Chronicle,* the *St. Louis Post Dispatch, The Times-Picayune,* the *New Hampshire Union Leader, The Chronicle Herald,* the *Vancouver Sun,* the *St. Petersburg Times, Student Traveler* magazine, *Transitions Abroad,* Toronto's weekly *NOW* magazine, and *Connecting: Solo Travel News.* Her work is featured in the 2004 anthology *A Woman's Europe,* published by Travelers' Tales. She is a member of SATW (Society of American Travel Writers), NATJA (North American Travel Journalists Association), and TMAC (Travel Media Association of Canada). She is a recipient of two 2005 NATJA travel writing awards, a first prize in the Cruise category and a second prize in the Leisure category.

Michele Peterson was born in Flin Flon, a mining town north of the 54th parallel where her grandfather operated a trapline on the shores of Hudson's Bay. Although she didn't inherit his outdoor expertise, an overactive imagination and abundant curiosity have taken her around the world. She lives in Toronto and works for Canada's largest environmental justice organization. Her writing has appeared in publications such as *The Toronto Star*, *Dreamscapes*, *Homemakers*, the *Boston Herald*, the *Vancouver Sun*, *The Globe and Mail*, and many more. Watch for her in bestselling anthologies such as *Sand in My Bra* (Travelers' Tales), *A Woman's Asia* (Travelers' Tales), and *The Risks of Sunbathing Topless* (Seal Press).

Susan Richardson is a Wales-based writer and tutor of writing. Her travel writing has been published in a wide range of magazines and anthologies, including *Transitions Abroad*, *International Living*, and *Even the Rain Is Different* (Honno, 2005), while her first collection of poetry, *Creatures of the Intertidal Zone*, is forthcoming from Cinnamon Press. She was recently awarded a Churchill Memorial Travel Fellowship to journey through Iceland, Greenland, and Newfoundland in the footsteps of Gudrid, the tenth-century female Viking. For more information about Susan's work, please visit www.susanrichardsonwriter.co.uk.

Aarti Sawhney teaches English at a public high school for new immigrants in New York. A native of New Haven, Connecticut, she is equally at home in Brooklyn, San Francisco, Seville, and New Delhi. Someday, she hopes to spend time in Bombay and pursue a career in screenwriting for Bollywood.

Barbara Sjoholm is most recently the author of *Incognito Street: How Travel Made Me a Writer* (Seal Press). Before changing her name in 2001, she published a number of books of fiction, mystery, and nonfiction as Barbara Wilson. Her memoir *Blue Windows: A Christian Science Childhood* (Picador, 1997) was nominated for a PEN USA Award in Creative Nonfiction, and won a Lambda Award for best lesbian autobiography. *The Pirate Queen: In Search of Grace O'Malley and Other Legendary Women of the Sea* (Seal Press, 2004) was also a finalist for the PEN USA Award. Her essays have appeared in *The New York Times, Slate, Smithsonian, Harvard Review,* and *The American Scholar.* She lives in Port Townsend, Washington.

After returning from Buenos Aires in June 2005, **Lara Triback** found herself headed for Portland, Oregon, epicenter of Argentine tango in the United States. During her first seven months in a new city, she worked at two major tango festivals, helped organize a weekly tango event, began working as a professional Middle Eastern percussionist, and put her master's in education to use by developing a rhythm and movement–based music curriculum that she teaches to young children. She continues to seek ecstasy in the realms of world music and dance.

Marion Winik is the author of *Telling, First Comes Love, The Lunch-Box Chronicles, Rules for the Unruly,* and *Above Us Only Sky.* A commentator on NPR's *All Things Considered* since 1991, her essays and articles have appeared in *O, Salon, More, Travel + Leisure,* and many other publications. She lives in Glen Rock, Pennsylvania, with her husband and children.

About the Editors

Faith Conlon was editor and publisher of Seal Press for twenty years. She is currently a freelance editor and writer. Her books include *I Wanna Be Sedated: 30 Writers on Parenting Teenagers*, coedited with Gail Hudson; *A Woman Alone: Travel Tales from Around the Globe*, coedited with Ingrid Emerick and Christina Henry de Tessan; and *Gifts of the Wild: A Woman's Book of Adventure*, coedited with Ingrid Emerick and Jennie Goode. She lives in Seattle, Washington, with her husband and son.

Ingrid Emerick is coeditor of *Gifts of the Wild: A Woman's Book of Adventure* and *A Woman Alone: Travel Tales from Around the Globe.* Her own writing has appeared in *A Woman Alone* and on HipMama.com. She teaches editing and publishing for the University of Washington Certificate Program. She is a freelance editor and cofounder of the recently launched Girl Friday Productions, a book development company. She also leads writing workshops, the next one on New Zealand's South Island with Adventure Divas. She lives with her husband and two children in Seattle, Washington.

Christina Henry de Tessan is currently senior editor of Pulse Guides' *Night+Day* series, a collection of city travel guides. She is also the originator of Chronicle Books' *City Walks* decks and author of *City Walks Paris, City Walks San Francisco,* and *City Walks Chicago.* She has also had two anthologies published with Seal Press: She is editor of *Expat: Women's True Tales of Life Abroad* and coeditor of *A Woman Alone: Travel Tales from Around the Globe.* She currently lives in Portland, Oregon, with her husband and two sons.

Selected Titles from Seal Press

For more than thirty years, Seal Press has published groundbreaking books. By women. For women. Visit our website at www.sealpress.com.

Zaatar Days, Henna Nights by Maliha Masood. $15.95, 1-58005-192-8. One woman finds spiritual rejuvenation on a journey from Cairo to Istanbul, with countless unforgettable detours on the way.

Stalking the Wild Dik-Dik by Marie Javins. $15.95, 1-58005-164-2. Funny, ironic, and resilient, Marie Javins captures the unpredictable essence of Africa and the experiences of a woman traveling alone.

Incognito Street by Barbara Sjoholm. $15.95, 1-58005-172-3. From the founder of Seal Press comes this eloquent coming-of-age travel narrative about her beginnings as a writer.

Greece: A Love Story edited by Camille Cusumano. $15.95, 1-58005-197-9. A rich tapestry of the classic, idyllic, and sun-drenched Greece is gracefully depicted in this collection of women writing about the country they love, and why they fell for it.

The Risks of Sunbathing Topless edited by Kate Chynoweth. $15.95, 1-58005-141-5. The best of women's travel misadventures, missteps, and misjudgments.

Single State of the Union edited by Diane Mapes. $14.95, 1-58005-202-3. A witty and revealing collection not only of what it means to be single, but independent as well.

No Touch Monkey! by Ayun Halliday. $14.95, 1-58005-097-2. A self-admittedly bumbling tourist, Halliday shares—with razor-sharp wit and to hilarious effect—the travel stories most are too self-conscious to tell.